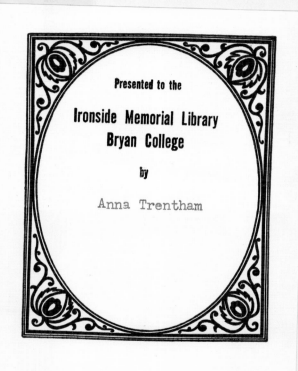

PENNIES AND MILLIONS

DOROTHY M. ARMBRUSTER

PENNIES AND MILLIONS

A Woman's Guide to Saving and Investing Money

DOUBLEDAY & COMPANY, INC.
GARDEN CITY, NEW YORK
1962

Library of Congress Catalog Card Number 62–7597

Printed in the United States of America

IN LOVING MEMORY
OF MY PARENTS,
CHRISTIAN AND HELEN SERGEL ARMBRUSTER

Foreword

Two years ago I wrote a brief account of my career as a banker and had it privately printed to give to my family and a few close friends at Christmas. One of these friends suggested that an expanded and detailed story of my experiences would be interesting and of practical value to a great many women in handling their financial affairs. And so I have written this book in the hope that it will help women—and the men in their families too—in solving the money problems that become increasingly difficult as our society and our economy grow and become more complex.

All of the stories in this book are true. I have used fictitious names in most cases and have altered certain details to avoid identifying living persons, but otherwise all the stories and the people are actual.

Inevitably, a discussion of money involves matters that are subject to change: costs, taxes, and the laws that regulate financial transactions. This book does not attempt to be a legal guide or a tax manual; but where questions of law and taxation arise, I have referred the reader to the proper sources for detailed and up-to-date information.

This book gives me an opportunity to acknowledge the debts of gratitude I owe to so many people who have enriched my life: to my colleagues at the bank, who gave me the opportunity to be of service to others; to the wonderful women from all walks of life who found their way to my desk in the bank and gave me their confidence and friendship; to every member of my unfailingly devoted and understanding family who gave both a purpose and a reward to my efforts; and to my three secretaries, Dorothy P. Eckhardt, Dorothy Gainer, and Roberta Hunter, whose faith and loyalty and daily assistance made possible such success as I have had in business.

I owe a special debt to my friend Ralph Reinhold, who conceived the idea of this book and persuaded me to write it; without his vision and his useful advice, it would not have come into being.

I am also grateful to Donald Elder, who so painstakingly and with genuine interest helped me to organize the book.

To Dr. Lowell R. Ditzen, pastor of The Reformed Church of Bronxville, of which I am a member, I am indebted not merely for commending my book in his introduction but also for helping me always, through his example and his teaching, to maintain personal security through Faith.

DOROTHY M. ARMBRUSTER

Bronxville, New York
June 15, 1961

CONTENTS

INTRODUCTION

I cherish for you the pleasure that lies before you in these pages written by Dorothy Armbruster.

You will meet a delightful person. But long before you have put this book down, you will have been acquainted with *a remarkably satisfying friend.*

Dorothy Armbruster's biography is unique. Daughter of a clergyman, brought up in a beautiful Christian home, she will make you feel the strong faith that motivates her character and her acts. But you will be drawn in admiration to a person who is as practical as a safety pin. Few women have equaled her unusual career in American banking. There is but one mold that has created a woman so warmly human and personally involved in the lives of those whose spirits have touched hers, no matter whether they had pennies or millions.

I have known a number of people who have sought Dorothy Armbruster's financial advice and who have been boundless in their appreciation of her business acumen and thoroughness in the management of all details. But, inevitably, she is valued above all as a "personal counselor, confidante, and friend."

That will be your experience in the pages that lie ahead.

Down-to-earth practicalities will be given you. Charming anecdotes, from one who has had unusual opportunity to be close to some of the most interesting families in our American life, are found in the ensuing pages.

You'll like what Dorothy Armbruster has to give you in the way of solid counsel. But, most of all, you'll be warmly happy in the fact that you have found a real and most helpful friend, who will be as personal as your checkbook.

LOWELL R. DITZEN

The Reformed Church
Bronxville, New York
June 15, 1961

PENNIES AND MILLIONS

CHAPTER ONE

GOING TO THE BANK

How circumscribed is woman's destiny.
—Goethe

A woman approaches the door of the bank, pauses, then enters slowly. Looking about, she does not know quite what to do. She only knows that she is in trouble, and her trouble concerns money. Her husband died suddenly; he was in his forties, a fairly successful small businessman, and he always handled their business affairs. They had a checking account together, in which he deposited money from time to time so that she could write checks for household and personal expenses; now she does not know if she can still do this or how much money is in the account. He always balanced the checkbook. Her house is her own, but some sort of payments have to be made on it to the building and loan association. He carried life insurance—of that much she is certain—but she doesn't know where the papers are. She has three young children to think of, and she doesn't know what to do next. Ask one of her husband's business associates in the firm? Some are friends, true enough, but she does not know what, if any, interest they have in her husband's affairs. One of them has asked her to sign something—he and her husband were business partners—but she doesn't understand the paper; it is still in her bag. Her husband's lawyer—he was the firm's lawyer, really; she knew him only casually—did not know of any will. The business would have to be appraised, her husband's interest determined.

As she looks about her, a uniformed guard comes up to her and asks if he can help her. She explains that she wants to find out about her husband's bank account, that he died recently. Which window should she go to? They all look alike, although some are labeled "Foreign" and "Collections" and other things that have nothing to do with her. There is an open area, where several men with their secretaries sit at desks. The guard suggests she speak to one of them, Mr. Brown. She doesn't know him, and suddenly she feels her affairs are too personal to talk about to a stranger. The guard says, "Why don't you talk to Miss Smith? She's in charge of the ladies' department." And he takes her to a young woman who rises to welcome her.

In a few minutes the woman leaves the bank with a somewhat lighter heart. She has learned a great deal. There are two accounts in the bank, one in her own name, the other in the names of her husband and herself or survivor. There is a balance in her account and she may write checks against it; and she has been told the simple steps by which the other account may be cleared of tax claims by the state and transferred into an estate account. She has also found out that her husband had a safe-deposit box, which doubtless contains all the papers that relate to his affairs—except a will. Miss Smith knew what to do about that, too; after making a phone call, she told her visitor that the will is in the hands of a lawyer known to the bank—it doesn't happen to be his firm's lawyer—and that the terms of the will are also known to the bank, since it has been named as an executor, with her, of her husband's estate. It is not large, but there is no need to worry at the moment.

She realizes suddenly that she has told Miss Smith about her husband's heart attack and the baby's operation, and she doesn't mind at all. She has got a great deal off her mind, and while her trouble isn't over she knows what to do about it. When the insurance money comes, she'll take it to Miss Smith to talk about investing it, and so on.

This woman might have been one of hundreds who came to me when I was in charge of the ladies' department at The Fifth Avenue Bank and, later, The Bank of New York. She might be you. In this particular case she was lucky: her husband had been farsighted enough to provide for her in the event of his death. More typical were the women whose husbands had neither taught them how to take care of money nor designated anyone to do it for them. And then there were the unmarried women in business or professions who came to the bank to learn how to make the most of their limited resources and earnings and to provide for their future security.

Most of my life as a banker—forty-one years in all—was spent in helping women with their particular financial problems. When I started as a girl of sixteen, my only experience with banking had been a small savings account which my father had opened for me when I was a child.

One June morning in 1917 my father read in the *Christian Intelligencer* that banks were hiring women to replace the men who were called to service when the United States entered the First World War. I had just finished high school and a six-month business course, and I planned to enter college in the fall: I wanted eventually to become a missionary in China. But the summer was ahead and my father thought I should occupy my time profitably. Besides, we were a large family, and poor, and it was important that each of us contribute what he could. My mother was not enthusiastic about the idea of my working, partly because she needed me to help her, partly no doubt because of the wrench she felt at her first-born's leaving home. But she agreed, and my father and I left our home in Sherwood Park, Yonkers, to go to New York City—via the trolley that ran through a virtual wilderness to the New York Botanical Gardens, where we could take the Third Avenue Elevated to the city.

Father talked to me seriously all the way to town. He and my mother had saved hard so that I could go to college; after graduation he expected me to help my younger brothers and sister through school. The war was going to change American life, and women would have opportunities to make money that they had never had before.

When we reached Forty-second Street we got off the El and

started west, stopping at each bank as we came to it. Father waited outside for me while I went in alone; he thought I would make a better impression if I seemed to be independent. So, wearing the new blue silk dress my mother had made for me and trying to look as old and experienced as possible, I went in. I was only five feet two, so I wore the highest heels I could find and piled my hair on top of my head to increase my height.

At each bank the personnel director gave me a form to fill out, then asked me why I had come to that bank. "Because the *Christian Intelligencer* said that banks were hiring women now," I said. By three in the afternoon it seemed that I had received this information somewhat in advance of the banks, because no one had shown any great interest in me. My father was tired and discouraged and we were about to give up when I looked across Fifth Avenue and saw a handsome brownstone building with high, arched windows and a plaque that said "The Fifth Avenue Bank of New York." There was a liveried attendant at the door, which was still open.

"Let me try one more," I said, and went in. A floor man greeted me, and when I told him that I wanted to apply for a job he escorted me into the cashier's office as deferentially as if I were a wealthy depositor and introduced me to Mr. Foley, who asked me to excuse him while he signed his mail. I looked around the handsome paneled room and at the ornate chandeliers.

"So you are thinking of entering the banking world," Mr. Foley said. He was a heavy-set Irishman who combined an impressive bulk with a certain elegance: he wore a stiff wing collar and a wide black tie with a stickpin, and gold-rimmed pince-nez glasses attached by a ribbon.

Somehow I felt that Mr. Foley would settle for nothing less than the whole truth, so I explained that I wanted to work only during the summer, until I went to college. I filled out a form, and when Mr. Foley had read it he said there was a place in the transit department that a young lady might fill: it required typing but not shorthand and paid $40 a month; in addition, I would get a hot lunch. If I passed the doctor's examination, I could have it. He did not even mention checking my references.

I was overcome but not too shy to tell him that other banks paid $45 and, besides, I had typing *and* shorthand.

"Young lady," he bellowed, "do not boast to me of your accomplishments; you should thank the good Lord and your parents for them. Do you want the job or don't you?"

I later found that Mr. Foley's dignity and friendliness were occasionally punctuated by severity and by lapses into informal language that shocked me—and also that he had a warmth and an impetuous generosity not usually associated with bankers.

"Yes," I said meekly. He called the doctor and made an appointment. I was to go there at once, and if I passed the examination I was to report for work at eight-thirty the next morning.

I hurried outside, where my father was waiting for me.

"I can have the job if I pass the doctor's examination," I told him, and he became more excited than I was. We took the Madison Avenue trolley, and on the way uptown I told him of the interview in detail. When I finished, he said, "Tell me again what he said, dear," and I went over the story again word for word, while he listened in a state of mingled happiness and shock. When I finished, he asked to hear it again, and I repeated every word, feeling a deep pleasure and contentment because I knew he was proud of me. At such times his customary formal manner vanished and we were very close to each other.

The doctor was waiting for me and hurried me into his consultation room. He asked me a good many questions and then told me to strip for the examination.

I was dumfounded. "I can't possibly," I said. "I have never undressed before anyone in my life."

He looked at me pityingly. "Child, child," he said, "where on earth do *you* come from?"

"Why, Yonkers, New York," I answered before I realized that the question was rhetorical.

He handed me a bed sheet. "Hurry, now," he said, a little annoyed. "I have other patients waiting."

The examination was brief. I only remember that he said, "I don't know why they sent you to me. You're the healthiest human being I ever saw. Yes, by all means go to the bank in the morning. I'll tell Foley about you."

Father and I were silent most of the way home. Perhaps he felt a little sad at my growing up and entering a completely unknown world. As for myself, I realized with apprehension that from now on I was actually going to work every day on Fifth Avenue in New York, which before had always seemed a little unreal to me. I thought of the prairies and mountains and cornfields of my childhood and became frightened. That night was one of the few in my life when I could not sleep.

I left home very early the next morning, since everyone at the bank—officers as well as clerks—had to be at his desk before eight-thirty. I took the trolley and El into the city and walked up Fifth Avenue to the bank, passing the Temple Emanu-El, which stood at that time at Forty-third Street, and hearing the birds singing in the belfry, a greeting I learned to listen for every morning and evening.

My first job was in the transit department, through which all checks drawn on banks outside New York were routed for collection. On a large rack, there was a slot for each of our correspondent banks in big cities, and the checks sent to us by the tellers, and charged to us, were sorted out there. Every day we had to write letters listing the checks. At the end of the day the checks listed in these letters had to add up to the account with which our department had been charged.

That afternoon after the bank closed we found that we were $1,000 short and set about finding the error. At nine-thirty we still had not found it, and the department manager called Mr. Foley, who came down to the bank. He sent the clerks home and stayed himself to trace the error.

All evening I had worried for fear I was responsible for the mistake; now, in addition, I had to face the anxiety of my family. They expected me home between five and six and it was now nearly midnight. We had no phone; there was no way for me to call them. When I got off the trolley, my father was standing there, his face rigid and white. I am sure he was angry, but he never said a word as

I explained what had happened. At home dinner stood on the table untouched and the whole family looked sick with worry. If I had not come back within the hour, they would have called the police.

The next morning the cleaning woman at the bank found the missing check stuck behind a desk—not, thank heaven, mine. Now that the first day's fright was over, I loved the work. Mr. Foley only laughed when I told him of my parents' anxiety, and he seemed to approve of my work.

One by one the boys in the cage were called by the draft; we said good-by to them and more women took their places in the bank. When fall came, the influenza epidemic postponed the opening of the colleges until spring, and I worked on, happy in my job but looking forward to going to college; in the spring I told my immediate superior that I would be leaving.

The next day Mr. Frissell, chairman of the board of directors, sent for me and asked me to reconsider my decision. He was a gentle, dignified man, fatherly in his manner toward me.

"I understand your father is a minister and there are four children in your family," he said. "You are the eldest. It's very necessary that the boys go to college—more important than for you. Wouldn't you like to stay on here so that you can help your family?"

"But I have to go to college," I said. "I want to become a missionary in China." It had never occurred to me to question that deep-rooted ambition.

"You can do more missionary work on Fifth Avenue than in China," he said. "You've done very well here. Mr. Foley says you'll undoubtedly be made head of the department if you stay. That will mean $10 more a month salary. As for an education—if you really want one—I have the feeling that you'll acquire it."

He asked me to think it over and consult my parents, and I left the bank that day facing the first decision of my life. Father said at once that I must go to college; he believed profoundly in education. Mother said the choice was up to me, but I could see that she leaned toward Mr. Frissell's suggestion—not that she believed less ardently in education than Father; but mothers are never resigned to sending their daughters to school or to China. Both of them told me to pray over it, and I did. After three days of reflection and meditation, I went to Mr. Frissell and told him I would stay.

He told me it was the better choice; and in this, as in so many other things, he proved to be right. And he was right, too, in saying that I could acquire an education. No one has ever had a better opportunity to educate himself not only in business but in the arts and humanities than I did in my position at the bank.

⚜ ⚜ ⚜

Although I was born at the turn of the century, long after the United States was settled, I come of pioneer parents. I was born in the wilderness, in the San Luis Valley of Colorado, where my father was minister to three mission churches scattered over a wild area sparsely inhabited by Mexican-, Russian-, and German-American farmers. My parents had lived there in isolation for more than two years, ever since my father had gone east to marry my mother and bring her back to share the lonely life of a frontier pastor.

My father was born in 1872 in Kniebis, Germany, close to the Black Forest. He emigrated to this country when he was fourteen, going to live with an aunt in Syracuse, New York, where he was apprenticed to a tailor. He had no liking for the trade but hoped to earn enough to help his family. His real longing was for education, travel, and a home of his own. Shortly after he came here, he was deeply moved by a sermon he heard at the Baptist Church, and soon after he knew he had a vocation. He worked impatiently for three years until he could enter the German Baptist Academy in Rochester to prepare himself for the Rochester Theological Seminary.

While he was still a student there he met my mother, Helen Sergel, in her home town, South Wales, New York, where he went to speak at a revival meeting. After he was ordained in 1898, he tried to persuade her to marry him and go with him to Denver to his first church. My mother, however, was teaching eight grades in a country school and had set her heart on becoming a school superintendent. And so they decided to wait. But three months later, after receiving from him a letter that described the loneliness of his new life in the West, she sent him out of her savings, which totaled $198, a railroad ticket to come back east to marry her. They were married in June 1898 and returned to Denver to live in my father's two small furnished rooms.

Soon after, my father received a call to the three mission churches. My mother, already far from the comfort and security of her New York State farm home, could hardly have liked the idea of moving further into the wilderness, but she urged Father to accept it and spent the rest of her savings on furniture, including a piano so that she could continue to study music. She obtained a teacher's license and was given a one-room country school near their new home. During the week she taught the children of farmers and settlers, and on weekends she accompanied Father on his circuit. In order to hold services on Sunday in each church, he had to leave home Saturday afternoon by horse and buggy, traveling difficult roads in barely inhabited mountainous country, fording streams and often encountering wild animals.

It was hardly the life my mother was reared for, yet she never betrayed the terrible homesickness she felt those first two years. She and Father were devoted to each other and equally dedicated to the way of life they had chosen, and they fulfilled their rigorous duties with a quiet confidence, which they seemed to have instilled in me from early childhood. Mother was a tiny, fragile person—she weighed only ninety-eight pounds—beautiful, with chestnut hair and big, lively eyes; yet, like my father, she had great force and was capable of quick, unpremeditated actions that somehow turned out to be right. One warm day a bat flew in the open window of the schoolroom and got entangled in the long golden hair of a little girl, daughter of a prominent farmer. With the entire classroom in a panic, Mother calmly picked up the scissors and cut the girl's hair off; then she took the frightened child home, expecting to be rebuked for cutting off her hair. To her relief, she was not.

She had a rare grace and the gift of winning her pupils' trust so that she could discipline them effortlessly; and, of course, these qualities were a great bulwark to my father's work as a minister.

The third week of December 1900, in bitter cold weather, Father went out alone to his churches, leaving my mother in the care of the little daughter of a Russian neighbor who lived five miles away. On Christmas Eve my mother was sure I would be born that night as the coyotes howled and the wind whistled down the peaks; at dawn she sent the little girl for the midwife. I was born on Christmas morning, and when Father came home that night he and Mother sat poring over Webster's Dictionary looking for a suitable name, finally deciding on "Dorothy"—which means "gift of God." My arrival marked the end of the homesickness from which Mother had suffered in the adobe house in that lonely parish.

When I was three years old, we moved to Omaha, where my brothers John and Raymond were born, and then to Fremont, Nebraska, where I started going to school, and from where I have memories of the midwestern landscape, sweet-smelling meadows of clover, and vast fields of corn stretching to the horizon. I can remember my early terror when I was lost in one of them. Here, too, I learned of the neighborliness of small-town life; our parishioners, mostly farmers, were generous, and the stores of food they provided—meat, winter vegetables, preserves—did a great deal to ease the burden of a minister's family whose cash budget was almost nonexistent.

While we were in Fremont, a serious epidemic of smallpox broke out. As there were few doctors and nurses, Father and Mother left us in the care of neighbors and went about caring for the sick without a thought for the possibility that they might catch the disease or transmit it to us. Both of them looked on such trials as their simple duty and trusted the Lord to see them through. I recall some years later when I was in school and many of the children had mumps. My brothers and I never missed a day's attendance. When I got a slight case of mumps, my mother combed my hair low on my neck so the swelling would not show and, since I did not feel sick, I kept on going to school. My parents felt that a minister's children should set an example in punctuality and regularity. I am a little shocked to think of this now; a modern parent would never have permitted it. But Mother was moved not by a willful determination or any lack of concern for us or the other children but simply by a strong faith and a complete innocence of infectious diseases.

Mother was happy when Father got a call to a church in Cowlesville, New York; it meant she would be closer to her family. We lived in nearby Folsomdale until Father went to a church in Buffalo and then to the Pilgrim Baptist Church in Jersey City. Each move brought us closer to New York, where Father wanted us to live, to have every educational advantage; and in 1911 he went to the Eagle Avenue Baptist Church in the Bronx, which wanted a young and energetic German-speaking minister, well enough grounded in doctrine to satisfy the older members of the congregation, yet modern enough in his viewpoint to hold the interest of the younger ones. Here I became a member of the church and was baptized by my father and decided to follow my parents' example in serving the church by becoming a missionary.

There were four children now, myself, John, Raymond, and my younger sister Marion, and we were all in school. I attended high school, studying Latin and German. Two of my German teachers I remember well—Professor Altschul and his daughter, both of whom later became my clients at The Fifth Avenue Bank. She nearly flunked me in German, and I feared my father's wrath, but she let me pass, assuring me I'd learn to do better. Years later I took pleasure in telling her the same when she came to me in the bank in a woeful state of ignorance about her financial affairs.

The outbreak of the First World War was a disaster to our family and our church long before the United States entered it. The congregation was largely German-American and the older members were fine people, like those we had known in Fremont, but merchants rather than farmers. Even though they had been good American citizens for years, they became entirely German again, while the younger ones felt a greater loyalty to the United States. The church was deluged by propaganda from both sides, and soon no one dared even mention the Allies.

For my father it was a tormenting situation; he had a deep love for his native land but an absolute loyalty to his chosen one. Early in the war he believed that America should remain completely neutral, and he refused to preach in German any more, as he had always done at the morning service. The church was divided, and those who took his view—the younger members—were not numerous enough to support him, so he was forced to leave.

It was not an easy decision for him to make, and the years that followed were hard. By the end of the war, he seemed to have aged a decade; his face was lined and his expression sad. He never achieved very much of what he had worked for so selflessly; he was compelled to renounce his loyalty to his native country and to leave his own denomination for a community church under the Reformed Church and to adopt a different religious doctrine. Aside from the home and family he had longed for, few of his youthful ambitions were ever fulfilled.

Again Mother obtained a teaching license. She took summer classes for children who had failed the previous term and needed preparation for the next one. This time I could help her: I taught the first three grades, while she took charge of the five upper grades. We received fifteen cents a day for each pupil; it was hard work, but we managed to make enough that summer to stay out of debt until my father found a pastorate.

This came about as if by a miracle. Some time before, my parents had befriended a woman who was in trouble: her husband had left her, and it was through my father's efforts that the couple and their children were brought back together happily. When she heard that a church in Yonkers wanted a pastor for a growing congregation composed of several denominations, she recommended my father and he was accepted.

Although it is now in a solidly built-up suburban district, the Mile Square Reformed Church at that time stood isolated in a field of daisies some distance from the trolley line that ran from the end of the subway line to Yonkers. There were hardly any houses nearby, and no place for the pastor to live, so Father rented the top floor of a two-family frame house in Sherwood Park, a mile and a half away from the church. It had no electricity; our only heat came from coal stoves and we used gaslight. Twice a day on Sunday, in all weathers, we walked to and from the church for the four services, along mostly unpaved streets. Although Father made $1,500 a year now—he had received only $300 at his first church—and our family situation had improved, we still had to work hard. The boys delivered for the grocer and butcher after school, and I helped Mother in the house, while Father had to look after the needs of a growing congregation.

It was here that we lived when I first went to work in the bank; and we liked the community so well that we never moved far away from it.

The time came when I had to make the decision to stay on at the bank, to help my family and make a career of my own in a field where women had not yet advanced very far. It meant giving up my deep desire to become a missionary and foregoing a woman's most important role—that of having a home and rearing children. But I have never regretted my choice. My parents gave me a great responsibility, but they also gave me the love, the faith, and the confidence that made it possible for me to carry it out. I have achieved many of my parents' hopes for their children, and I have been able to help many women in the task of building security for themselves and their families.

CHAPTER TWO

FIRST STEPS IN THE BANK

The distance is nothing; it is only the first step that costs.
—Mme. Du Deffand

When I told Mr. Frissell that I would stay on at the bank, he assured me it was a wise decision, and a short time later, as he had foreseen, I was made head of the transit department. In June, after I had been there a year, I took my first vacation—one week—and visited my mother's brother, Uncle Herman, in South Wales, New York. He took me to his bank in Buffalo, where he had considerable business, and introduced me to the president—rather proudly, I remember, as I was still one of very few women in banking. The president took me on a tour of his bank and explained to me how they had completely reorganized their transit department, clearing all out-of-town checks through the Federal Reserve Bank. When I returned to work, I told Mr. Foley about it and he arranged for me to spend two days in the Federal Reserve Bank of New York to study the clearing operation. As a result, our own transit department was reorganized on the model of the Federal Reserve's.

The years 1917 to 1923, with the war and the business boom that followed it, brought great changes in the bank. The volume of checks that came through my department increased unbelievably, but because of our new system we could handle them much more quickly and we had more time to give to the Liberty Loan campaigns. In 1920 the Woman Suffrage Amendment was passed; already women were taking a greater part in business and public affairs. My department was now entirely staffed by women, and the time was coming when the bank would have to expand its services to women depositors.

My own life was busy and happy. The financial help I was able to give my parents was a real boon, and life had become better for us. Father and Mother insisted that I handle my own money from the start, and I worked out a budget that enabled me to give 10 per cent of my earnings to charity and put 10 per cent into a savings account for future investment. My first investment was one share of stock in The Fifth Avenue Bank; my second, some years later, one share of U. S. Steel, then called "the barometer of business."

In 1921 my mother was expecting another baby. We were pleased and excited, but at the same time I had misgivings for my parents. The family was already large, the boys were growing up, Mother was frail, and Father had aged terribly during the war years. One Sunday night in March, as we were walking the long mile and a half home after the last church service, Mother said, "I wouldn't be surprised if Christian"—she had already named him—"arrived before morning." At five-thirty the next day Father awakened me and told me to run for the doctor. I dashed to the Mount Vernon railway station, where there was a telephone, but it was closed; so I went on until I found a drugstore open at the top of the hill and made the call. By the time I got home, the doctor was there, and Christian was born soon after. That morning I was late to work for the first time, a matter which stirred my father's disapproval more than my employers'.

I had begun a three-year course in banking and investment at the New York chapter of the American Institute of Banking, and in June 1923 I was graduated with a diploma; in the class of thirty-two, there were only two women. I felt like a fully qualified banker; but, actually, my experience had only begun.

One night in September, after the rest of the department had gone home, Mr. Foley told me that Mr. Frissell wanted to talk to me in the morning about a matter the officers considered very important. It would mean a temporary change of position for me. "It will be a challenge to you and a chance to get ahead. I wanted to tell you this much myself." I was glad later that he had warned me, because the "opportunity" that Mr. Frissell offered me the next day seemed singularly unpromising at the beginning.

Mr. Frissell told me in his usual gentle way that the bank was not satisfied with the way women's accounts were being handled. The bank had as many women depositors as men, some of them quite wealthy, and special services had always been provided for them: the Ladies' Drawing Room of the bank was famous. But the bank felt that women did not take advantage of all its services. They hesitated to approach a man with their financial problems; they might more readily confide in a woman counselor. My task would be to sit at the desk in the ladies' department, between their teller and the writing room, and to discover their problems and answer their questions. I would have no specific duties and no authority; I was assigned only to investigate the possibility of extending the bank's services to women. First I would spend several days in each of the various departments of the bank, acquainting myself with all their functions. I would have access to all the bank's officers, and they had been asked to help me in every way. I would not know the answers to everything I might be asked, but I was to find out what women wanted to know. At the end of each day I was to report to Mr. Foley what had happened.

A position with duties and without authority may be challenging, but it can also be a little frightening. I rather dreaded leaving my well-defined functions in the transit department to sit at a bare desk facing a corridor. But after spending a few days in the loan, investment, collections, trust, and foreign departments, I took my place just outside the ladies' reception room.

This was the "Gold Room," one of the handsomest rooms in New York. It stood at the end of a corridor in the half of the bank that was devoted entirely to women. The walls were brocaded gold silk damask, with ivory woodwork and pillars decorated with gold leaf; the floors were teakwood with oriental rugs, and there were elegant writing desks of white mahogany inlaid with rosewood and satinwood. On the mantel over the fireplace was a Tiffany clock, and above it was a painting, "The Temple of Love," done especially for that room. On a table lay the latest fashion magazines and newspapers. There was free telephone service, and a maid was there to attend the ladies.

Since the bank was founded in 1875 to cater to the family needs of the "carriage trade"—the well-to-do people who lived in the residential neighborhood—it had become a fashionable meeting place for women. The room was so much a Fifth Avenue tradition that it was incorporated in the ladies' wing of the new building of The Bank of New York, erected in 1958.

My desk, of mahogany, stood just outside this room, and the ladies had to pass me to go to the teller's window. In the reception room, Annabel, the maid, greeted them by name and took care of them in a rather possessive manner. She had welcomed me graciously enough, but I sensed a certain reserve: I was intruding on her domain. These were *her* ladies and she was used to serving them. A Negro from Virginia, Annabel had worked for First Families for years and had definite ideas of social status. Mine was ambiguous, but the ladies knew Annabel well, and she was much in demand among them when they needed extra help at large social functions in their own homes.

For three days the ladies swept past me holding their heads high, to speak to Annabel and to chat with the teller. I might as well not have been there. This was all I had to tell Mr. Foley each night after work.

"Well, for goodness' sake, what are you going to do about it?" he demanded on Friday night. "Haven't you any ideas?"

By this time I was getting used to Mr. Foley's occasional overemphasis. "I think if I had a lamp to light the desk," I said, "they'd at least know I was there. And a vase with one rose in it. It looks so bare." He nodded. "They can see I have nothing to do. Why should they pay any attention to me?"

"Very well. Get a lamp and a vase on your way to work Monday," he said, and left the rest to me.

I bought a Chinese lamp of jade on a teakwood base, a statuette of a woman in a contemplative attitude—of prayer, I hoped—and a French vase, in which I put a rose, a variety new that year and called, with the optimism of the era, "Better Times." Mr. Foley approved.

I sat at my desk apprehensively, pondering what might happen if I failed to attract any inquiries that day and watching an attractive and well-dressed woman who stood in the reception room gazing out the window, then around the room, obviously uncertain and preoccupied. Finally her eye came to rest on the rose and she walked over to my desk.

"What a beautiful rose. 'Better Times,' isn't it?" she said. "I think one rose looks better than a dozen, don't you?"

"Yes," I said, wondering what more I could say without being too forward. To offer help might seem officious; I decided it was better merely to be agreeable.

"Are you new here? I haven't seen you before." She was in early middle age, stylishly dressed, and she spoke beautifully; but, despite her poise, she was clearly in trouble. "I wonder if I could ask you—I hate to seem stupid . . . . I'm Mrs. Todman. My husband and I have had an account here for years, but I've never used it. I've never made a deposit or drawn a check, and I've never seen a statement, so I don't know what the balance is. I don't even know whose name it's in, his or mine or both. Could you tell me?"

I asked her to sit down while I looked it up. I found that it was an alternate checking account; that is, either her signature or her husband's was honored on checks, and they had equal access to the funds. The balance was between $5,000 and $6,000.

"I could sign a check, then," she said; "but would my husband know about it?"

"Yes, he would," I told her.

"Then I'll have to tell you why I'm asking," she went on, nearly in tears. "Perhaps you can advise me."

Her husband was a businessman who made a very good salary. They had been married for twenty-three years—they had no children—and had always been very close, but in the past few months she had observed a change in him and felt that he no longer loved her. Recently she'd learned that he had been seeing a good deal of his new secretary. What should she do?

This was not exactly what I had expected to be asked or was prepared to answer. I saw other ladies passing my desk, glancing curiously at Mrs. Todman, who was now in tears. I could not let my first client go unanswered, and I had to have something to tell Mr. Foley. And she seemed so distressed. So, with all the brashness of youth and innocence, I said exactly what I thought as gently as I could.

I am dumfounded now when I think of what I told her—I could not do it today—but all I knew then of marriage was that my parents loved each other and I did not see how it was possible to live with anyone you didn't love.

"I am sure he loves you still," I said, "but maybe he has just lost his head. Why don't you take a trip? Have you any family you can visit?" A sister in California, she said; but she hadn't seen her for years. "Why don't you visit her?" I said. "Go to Grand Central and get a ticket; then buy a new suit and wear it and look your best when you tell your husband. Tell him that you don't know when you'll be back but if he wants to ask his secretary to the house while you're gone, it's all right; that it's his happiness that matters; and that right now you think you're only causing him to be unhappy. Tell him you've drawn $3,000 from the bank to pay for the trip."

She thanked me and told me she would do it and left me feeling a little bewildered. What happened afterward amazed me even more. A week later her husband followed her to California, and they returned together to New York and remained devoted to each other until he died seventeen years later. I used to visit them in their log cabin in the Adirondacks, and Mrs. Todman enjoyed telling the story of how a young and inexperienced bank clerk had saved her marriage while explaining her bank account to her.

At the end of that day, however, all I had to tell Mr. Foley was that what women seemed to need was advice for the lovelorn. He took this in silence, as if it were part of a banker's daily duty, then said, "Did you advise her to withdraw the money? Was it *her* money?" But he did not seem displeased.

The next day at ten o'clock a woman in deep mourning came down the aisle and seated herself at a small desk across from mine.

Her veil was of black crepe lined with white, and as she lifted it I could see through her thick glasses that her eyes were red and swollen. She opened her bag, took out a check, and sat looking at it for a while. Then she spoke to me and asked the date. I told her, and she came across and sat down at my desk.

"You must be in very deep trouble," I said. "Can I help you?"

"I don't know what to do with this check," she said. "My husband has just died, and I don't know anything about his affairs." Then she went on to tell me that her only son had died two months before of tuberculosis, which he had contracted while serving in the Army. She had two daughters, one married four times, hopelessly extravagant, knowing nothing of the value of money; the other mentally ill, attended in her own home by night and day nurses and a couple to keep house.

She was Mrs. Lewis. She was alone now, and she realized that her affairs were in disorder, but she did not know where to begin. The check she held, for $79,000, was the payment from the sale of their home, on which there was a mortgage of $52,000. Besides that, she had $25,000 from her husband's life insurance. Her lawyer had told her that her debts amounted to $65,000. She had never written a check or paid a bill in her life.

We talked for two hours, going over her checkbook and putting it in order and discussing a plan for her future security. She was not in so bad a financial situation as had first appeared: she had an income of $15,000 a year from a trust fund left by an aunt. When she rose to say good-by, she seemed relieved.

"This is the grandest bank," she said. "My husband swore by it. You are so wise. It must be wonderful to know all you know."

She could have no idea, I thought, of how little I knew of money or of such grief as she had suffered. I felt utterly inadequate, but I knew I had to help her somehow.

I reported this interview to Mr. Foley and added that Mrs. Lewis had asked me to lunch but that I had declined.

"Never do that again," he said. "Always accept every social engagement. That's how you will get to know more people and bring in more business."

Mrs. Lewis and I became fast friends and remained so until her death. She had an important influence on my life.

⚜ ⚜ ⚜

Although I didn't realize it at the time, with Mrs. Todman and Mrs. Lewis my career had really begun.

Of course, it was the money in the bank, not my advice, that made Mrs. Todman's trip possible. She had one of the commonest kinds of account, the alternate, sometimes miscalled the "joint account," which is another matter entirely.

The simplest and best kind is the individual account: only your own signature is valid on checks. To open one, you have only to go to the bank with your money or its equivalent, such as a check, and fill out a card, which an officer of the bank will give you, with such information as is needed—your name, address, occupation, and husband's name and occupation and by whom you were introduced. Then you sign your name exactly as you intend to sign it on your checks (and remember always to remove your gloves when you sign). This is important. This signature is your identification, the one with which your bank will compare the signatures on your checks; it will be a necessary part of all your future dealings with the bank. A married woman should use her Christian name, without any titles or additions. Once this signature is on record, do not change it; do not alter the form of your name or embellish it in any way. It is your protection. It cannot be exactly duplicated except by the most skillful forgery, and bank employees are trained to detect these.

The bank will probably require a minimum balance of $500 or $1,000: it varies in different banks (in New York and other large cities it is almost uniformly $1,000). Many people are reluctant to keep a minimum balance in a checking account; they regard it as idle money. In a savings account it might earn them $25 to $35 a year; invested, it might earn them more. Actually your minimum balance is not idle; it is working for you in a very effective way. In the first place, the interest it earns just covers the cost to the bank, in time and bookkeeping, of servicing your account, cashing and clearing checks. And if you make a mistake in balancing your checkbook and have less money in your account than you think, the bank will not return the check for lack of funds; with a minimum balance your checks do not "bounce." The balance is your money subject to your order.

But, mainly, this first simple step in banking establishes your credit. In the eyes of the bank and, as you will find out, of the community, you are a person of substance. If you want to open a charge account, you can give the bank as a reference: if your account is in order, the bank will inform the inquirer that you have an account with a four-figure balance and add that it is managed in a businesslike manner and that you have been known to the bank for as long as you have been a depositor. Without the minimum balance it would do you no good to give the bank as a credit reference.

With a regular checking account, you are now a depositor of the bank and your affairs are its concern. You now have access to all the departments of the bank—collections, foreign, credit, investment, safe-deposit vaults—and any help and advice you need. Because you are a small depositor, do not think the bank is not concerned with you: you may be rich some day. Once you are known to the bank as a responsible depositor, your credit standing in the community is good. At a time when so many things are bought on credit, this is a great service.

And what is only a convenient service now may be a matter of vital importance some day. I remember the case of a young man who, on his way back from San Francisco, stopped in Reno and lost a good deal of money gambling. He wrote a check on our bank and tried to cash it; the Reno bank called us by telephone to verify his credit. We knew that his account did not warrant so large a check, but we also knew the boy's parents, who had been depositors for many years. We asked for a few moments to look into the matter and called the boy's parents who told us at once that they would guarantee the check—and so we were able to tell the Reno bank to cash it. The boy was in debt for some time after this, but because he and his parents were known to our credit officers he escaped serious trouble.

It works the other way too. If you are contemplating a business venture with someone of whose credit you are uncertain, you can ask the credit manager of your bank what his status is. If it is questionable, the bank can warn you, without violating any confidences.

All your dealings with the bank are confidential; it will give out no information without your approval. I once infringed this rule, to my great discomfort. Two sisters, women in their fifties, one a widow and the other a spinster, frequently came to the bank, and I knew them well. They seemed to be inseparable and handled their affairs in exactly the same way. If one bought a certain stock, so did the other; if one cashed a $100 check, her sister did too. One day one of them came in alone and asked me for the balances of her account and her sister's. Although I knew the rule well, I didn't hesitate in this case to give both balances. One account, I was surprised to see, had about $40,000 more in it than the other.

Two weeks later the president called me in and asked me to whom I would give out the balance of an account. Only to the depositor, I said. But I quickly added that I had once broken that rule and I told him about the two ladies.

"That's why I sent for you," he said. "You shouldn't have done it, although I probably would have done the same thing."

He told me that the maiden lady was quite upset. Years before, her father had given her a gift of $40,000 because she had not married and had taken care of her mother during a long illness. The other sister was never to have known, but now the secret was out, the women had quarreled, and I was to blame. It turned out well, though: the unmarried sister said she had always felt unhappy about the money and transferred $20,000 from her account to her sister's. So we all remained friends.

If you do not have the money to establish a regular checking account, there are special checking accounts which require no minimum balance; instead, you pay a monthly service charge and/or a small fee for each check, plus fees for additional services. Your account will be well serviced, but you will find that it has no value as a credit reference, and the chances are that your annual total of fees or service charges will be as much as the interest on the required minimum balance.

Husbands and wives often share alternate accounts, like Mrs. Todman's; that is, either the husband's or the wife's signature is valid on checks, and in the event of the death of either party the account passes to the survivor. Both signatures must go on record at the bank and both parties must keep their checkbooks in conformity, letting each other know of every deposit and every check written.

The advantage of this kind of account was obvious in the case of Mrs. Todman—although she would have been much better off with her own account. And the disadvantages of alternate accounts are worth noting.

In the first place, the account may not pass immediately to the survivor in case of the death of one party. Theoretically the bank cannot release the account at the death of one party until the state has been put on notice and has released it. In some states it is simply a matter of getting a tax waiver, which will enable the survivor to continue to use the account—not difficult, but something that ought to be foreseen, since it may tie up the account when you need it most. So if you open an alternate account, be sure to ask your banker what conditions are imposed on it by the state you live in.

Then it is necessary for husband and wife to compare checkbooks frequently; otherwise they might be in trouble. Mrs. A. may think her husband has made a deposit and may buy that new dress; but Mr. A. may have been held up at the office at lunch time and unable to get to the bank. The result will be reproaches that will strain tempers.

Or Mrs. A. may want to buy something without Mr. A.'s knowing it—maybe a surprise for him, maybe something for the children that he's not entirely enthusiastic about. He will find out.

Most married couples have alternate accounts because they trust each other, they share their worldly goods, and it is a symbol of their unity. But every woman, no matter how devoted to her husband, has perfectly legitimate personal uses for money that she ought not to have to account for to anyone—and so has her husband. If they trust each other, the best way to demonstrate it is to trust each other with individual bank accounts to avoid the strains on family life that result from either forgetting to enter a check or record a deposit or committing harmless extravagances. A housewife can keep a tidier budget if she knows that her balance isn't going to be upset by her husband's new outboard motor or an unexpected business trip; and those family responsibilities which the husband may have assumed—the payments on the car or house, the educational funds for the children—will be more neatly discharged if they are not threatened by his wife's emergency expenses, which may or may not reach the joint checkbook without tears or recriminations.

I have always counseled husbands and wives to keep separate, individual checking accounts. If it is advisable for them to have access to each other's accounts in case of emergency, then each may give the other power of attorney. This is a written statement that a particular person is the agent of another person with the powers stated in the document. It may be a full power of attorney or it may be limited to the authority to make deposits in or withdrawals from the bank account. The bank has a form for this on hand; you have only to execute it before a notary and provide the bank with the signature of your agent.

A joint checking account requires the signatures of both parties on every check and will not pass to the survivor in the event of death unless a special provision has been made. This type of account keeps both parties informed of every expenditure, but it is of no use to a wife whose husband is out of town or vice versa. It is useful mainly in trust accounts or in small businesses where two partners agree to authorize every expenditure jointly.

Once you have a checking account, form the habit of keeping it in good order. First learn how to write a check properly: fill in the date, the name of the payee, the figure for the amount. Then, on the line below, write out the amount in words, always beginning at the far left of the line so that no one can add "One hundred" or

"One thousand" to the amount. This line is known as the "filling"; if there is a disparity between the figures at the right of the check and the amount written on the filling, the bank will pay the amount shown on the filling. And remember to sign the check; a surprising number of people forget this.

Now enter the amount of the check on the stub or counterfoil, subtract it from the balance, and carry forward the new balance. Number each check for your own convenience. Enter the date, to whom paid, and what for—"To: Dr. Jones; For: Junior's tonsils" . . . . "Theater tickets" . . . "Repayment of loan to X." Your canceled check is positive proof that you have paid a debt; but your checkbook record is also valuable as a handy reference, a memorandum to yourself. It shows where the money goes, it is the history of your financial life, it is of great help in budgeting your income, and it is useful when you prepare your income tax figures.

Each month you will receive from the bank a statement of your account and the canceled checks which have been paid. This should agree with your own checkbook unless there are outstanding checks. Outstanding checks are those which you have written but which have not yet reached the bank for payment: your checkbook provides you with the only record of these until they are paid. Taking these into consideration, you reconcile your checkbook with the bank's statement. If there is a difference between what the bank says you have and what your checkbook says you have, go over your checkbook. You may have forgotten to enter a check, or made an error in subtraction, or neglected to record a deposit. If you cannot find the mistake, do not assume that it is your fault. Banks can make mistakes too—even electronic machines can. The bank can find the error and correct it.

Taking care of your checkbook protects you against the possible misuse of your account. I remember one lady who kept a very neat checkbook; yet, at the end of the month, there was a difference of $100 between the bank's statement and her checkbook. At the end of two months, there was a $200 difference; and after six months there was $600. I went over her checkbook; the canceled checks matched her stubs exactly, but the statement showed a $100 withdrawal. I suggested that the following month she come into the bank to pick up her statement and canceled checks instead of having them sent to her and said that we would go over the matter again. We found a canceled check for $100 that was not accounted for in her checkbook, and this led her to discover that her secretary, who had learned to duplicate her signature perfectly, had been drawing $100 a month from the account and then removing the canceled check from the statement when it came in the mail.

If you lose one of your own checks bearing your signature, or if someone else loses it before he has a chance to cash it, you can notify the bank and ask it to stop payment; when the check appears at the bank, the bank will return it unpaid. If you have a valid reason for changing your mind about a check you have written, you can have payment stopped. One of our depositors came to me one day quite ruffled and annoyed. She had stopped in a linen store near the bank, attracted by notices of its perpetual closing-out sale, and had been persuaded against her better judgment to buy a great deal of linen she did not really want. When she offered a check in payment, the store refused to hand over the linen until the check was cleared. Bristling, she hastened to the bank and asked me what she should do. I suggested stopping payment, which she did. A few minutes later the proprietor appeared with the check; he was too late.

If you do not keep your checkbook in order, you risk overdrawing your account because you don't know how much is in it. If you keep a minimum balance, that will usually cover the payment of the check. Even if you overdraw that sum, the bank may pay the overdraft because it does not like to return its depositors' checks and because it reflects on the bank's credit as well as the depositor's. So if the bank knows you and realizes that the overdraft is the result of your error, it will pay the check and notify you. But depositors who overdraw habitually are soon asked to close their accounts.

The few minutes you spend each month reconciling your checkbook with the bank statement are well worth while. If you accept the bank's statement without question, you risk the errors it may make; in addition, you are overlooking a handy way of keeping your budget and tax records in order.

⚜ ⚜ ⚜

Most people's first experience in saving money is with a piggy bank, and it's a very good start. In fact, many banks now give little banks away free in one form or another to encourage children—and unthrifty adults—to accumulate coins to open a savings account. (Most can be opened with $1.00.) And nearly all of us can remember our first savings account—the one we opened ourselves with money earned doing chores or saved from our allowance, or the one our parents opened for us.

It is the best possible way to be thrifty—and also the safest. It involves no risk and it earns interest, ranging from 2½ to 4 per cent, depending on what kind of bank you use. It is the very first step in banking and the best way to save for a specific purpose. A regular deposit that is hardly missed from your salary or allowance becomes a sum to conjure with—"Ready money is like Aladdin's lamp," Byron said—and there is nothing more gratifying than finding that you have money that has been saved painlessly from force of habit and that now enables you to buy something you've always wanted or to make a promising investment. Try to save 10 per cent of your income; if you can't manage that, save 5; but save regularly.

I had one depositor who was a great believer in savings accounts, although she was a little untidy with her checking account. Each month it was overdrawn a few dollars below the minimum balance. This balance is meant to be taken literally; if it is not maintained, the depositor incurs a small service charge. Mrs. Johnson often stopped at my desk to ask me a question: What was a good savings bank? (At that time our bank did not have a savings department.) Why did Federal Savings and Loan Associations pay higher interest than savings banks?

She was a pretty, well-dressed woman of about thirty-five; she often wore an expensive mink coat and much jewelry. One day when she stopped to ask me to help her locate an error in her checkbook I had an opportunity to inquire why her minimum balance was a few dollars short each month. We went over her checkbook, and she kept it quite well; there was only a minor mistake in arithmetic, but that didn't account for the monthly deficiency. She was a little shy about telling me at first, but then she smiled and admitted that she wasn't always perfectly candid with her husband about money matters and that she never asked him for extra money to keep her checking account straight.

Then she opened her handbag and brought out twenty-six savings bank passbooks. Ten of them were in one bank, under various designations, such as Special Account No. 1, No. 2, and so on. She explained her system to me. Her husband was a successful and well-known commercial artist who made about $40,000 a year—and spent it all. He was a free lance, and the kind of business entertaining that other men do on their expense accounts he paid for out of his own pocket—and he entertained well. At the end of the year he was always broke.

Each month he gave her $2,000 for household expenses and she put this in her checking account so that her monthly overdrafts were always covered. The rest of his income he spent, and she had learned not to count on him for emergencies or special needs. She made a small income as a book illustrator, and this she put into savings accounts, adding to them what she could spare from her household allowance. Each account had a specific purpose: one was for her older son's prep school, one for the younger's, another for the older boy's college education, one for a new piano, another for a new car, and so on. Everything she wanted to save for had its special account, and she kept each one separate and inviolate, putting aside a certain amount each month in each of the twenty-six funds. What happened, invariably, was that she did not manage to make all twenty-six deposits by the end of the month, and so, to make up the sums required, she drew on her checking account. That is why her balance was always falling below the minimum requirement.

At first glance this looked to me like an unnecessarily complicated and rather scatterbrained way of banking; yet Mrs. Johnson was an extremely intelligent and very practical woman. As she went over her passbooks to show me what she was doing, I began to have a real admiration for her. All I could do was to suggest mildly that she might watch her minimum balance to save the service charge; aside from that, she was doing very well.

She had perfectly understood her husband's spending habits and her own saving habits. She knew that the only way to make a savings account reach the goal she had set was to make regular deposits and to let nothing stop her. At one point, it is true, the piano fund had to be plundered in the interest of the boys' school accounts. But the oldest boy's college fund already amounted to $5,000, and he would not be ready for college for eight years; in the meantime she thought she would invest it. She discussed it with me and we selected some stocks—and her oldest son got through college in style. He is now a junior officer in a bank and doing well.

As some of her other accounts reached their goals, and she found she had no immediate need for the money, she invested them too, against the time when her generous but improvident husband would no longer be earning money. But she never lost the habit of keeping separate accounts for special purposes; it was her way of keeping a budget, and a very good one. Although her handbag was untidy, her financial affairs were not.

I can't remember now if she ever did learn to watch her minimum balance; her investments became much more absorbing.

If you haven't the need—or the time—for twenty-six savings accounts, two or three are not a bad idea. But one is absolutely essential: it is the basis of all your future security, as well as of your future pleasure. You can save for emergencies—illness, an unexpected trip, family troubles. You can save for future investments. If you already have some stocks, it is a good idea to keep a savings account for further investment, so that if an unusually good opportunity comes up you can take advantage of it without disturbing sound investments that you want to keep. And if you are like Mrs. Johnson and require the systematic subdivision of your savings in order to keep them intact for your purposes, then do as she did.

And do not make withdrawals from your savings account for current expenses; that is what a checking account is for.

You may be thrifty by nature, but that is not enough. Don't tuck your savings away around the house; put them in the bank. Among my clients were two sisters, the Misses Adams, well-to-do women who lived in a hotel in the West Forties. One of them, a college professor, had assembled a valuable library of which she was very proud. When she died she left it, along with the rest of her estate, to her sister, who asked my advice about it. I went to have dinner with her at the hotel and she told me she planned to sell the books, even though they would probably not bring much money. I began to look at them purely out of curiosity. When I opened one, some currency fell out; I looked at another and found more bills. All evening long we went through the books, until we had examined every one. Altogether we found $9,875 in cash. The sale of the library brought about $4,000.

Miss Adams was luckier than another of our depositors, who came in to talk about buying common stocks. She had decided to buy ten shares of General Electric, which would cost her $600. "You place the order," she said, "and I'll go home and get the money. I always keep it in the sugar bowl at the top of the china closet. There must be more than $600 there now."

I decided not to place the order until the money was in the bank. You can guess the rest of this story: the money was gone. Painters, plumbers, all kinds of service people went in and out of the house.

It sounds too trite to be true, but ask yourself how many times you've tucked money under the paper in a dresser drawer or put it in a book or some place thieves would never think of looking. That is usually where they look; their minds work very much like everyone else's. And even if thieves do not get it, don't trust your own memory; if you hide money in an obscure place, you can easily forget what you did with it.

Most of the women who came to me with money to invest had accumulated it in savings accounts. If it is more convenient, you can have a savings account in the commercial bank where you keep your checking account. Or you can put it in a mutual savings bank, perhaps at a slightly higher rate of interest. This kind of bank is owned by the depositors; its only capital is their savings, and its investments are limited by law to fairly secure bonds and mortgages and a few of the highest grade stocks. When its earnings increase, the depositors receive an increased rate of interest. All such accounts are insured up to $10,000 by the Federal Deposit Insurance Corporation, which guarantees you against loss in case the bank fails. Federal Savings and Loan Associations pay a good rate on savings: almost all their investments are in real estate and mortgages. These are not readily convertible, but they enable the associations to pay a better interest rate. Interest rates also vary from bank to bank and in different types of accounts.

Keep your passbook in a safe place. You cannot withdraw money without it, and if you lose it the bank must go through a good deal of red tape before it can release the money and you may have to wait several months. If you have savings accounts that you do not use very often, it's a good idea to keep the passbooks in a safe-deposit box.

If you withdraw a large sum of money from a savings account, don't transfer it from one bank to another in cash. Ask for the bank's check, drawn for the amount you are withdrawing from your savings account and made payable to your order.

One of our depositors once brought to me the money she had withdrawn from several savings accounts to deposit in her checking account. I watched her in surprise as she counted out twenty $1,000 bills, and I verified the count at her request. I took them to the teller, who recounted them and found only nineteen. We looked high and low for the missing bill but did not find it; finally we credited her with $19,000 and promised to look everywhere for the missing $1,000. By this time I was trembling: it was my responsibility. I foresaw the loss of my job and disgrace and passed a miserable two hours until the woman called up and said she had found the bill in her coat pocket. After counting the money, she had picked up some blotters from the desk and the bill had mysteriously clung to them. This is one of dozens of cases where carrying cash nearly had disastrous results—this time for me.

There are various titles to savings accounts, just as there are various kinds of checking accounts—single, alternate, or joint, or accounts held in trust for a beneficiary. As in the case of checking accounts, I think the individual account is preferable, and for the same reasons. It also simplifies your tax problem. The interest on savings accounts is taxable and must be reported on your income tax return. If you have an alternate or joint account, this question arises: Which party shall report the tax? Keep your accounts separate and avoid complications.

Like any other good habit, savings accounts can be too much of a good thing. Many of the women I counseled had put away large sums of money in them to no purpose; they merely didn't know what else to do with the money. If you have a sufficient income to meet your needs and a safe margin for possible emergencies—say $5,000—and still have savings for which you have no immediate use, then invest them. As we'll see in a subsequent chapter, savings can be put to work to make more money for you.

⚜ ⚜ ⚜

Mrs. Vanderpool was a retired opera singer who had made a good deal of money during her active career and had managed it wisely. She lived on the income from an annuity she had bought when she was young and from certain conservative securities, mostly bonds and preferred stock. Occasionally she came to my desk to consult me about her holdings, although she had no real problems. Her bonds were properly kept in a safe-deposit box and she took regular care of the coupons by which she collected the interest. She also had a well-conducted checking account with a good balance. Altogether she seemed well situated. She had been a widow for many years and she lived in a small, pleasant Greenwich Village apartment and took most of her meals in nearby restaurants.

One day she came to see me with a handsome and well-dressed man whom she introduced as Mr. Clendening. "He has just persuaded me to marry him," she said, "so I hope you will be seeing him often." We talked awhile, and then she asked me if she ought to make any change in her banking arrangements. Should she make her checking account alternate with him or give him a power of attorney? Should she make him a deputy of her safe-deposit box?

Knowing that her affairs were in good order, I told her so and said I saw no need for any changes. This is not the answer I would invariably have given to that question, but something about Mr. Clendening made me suspicious. He was charming but a little too smooth, and he was showing an excessive interest in Mrs. Vanderpool's affairs. A counselor is always being asked advice that might be sought from a family friend, a minister, or sometimes even a clairvoyant. In banking one cannot rely on intuition, but a measure of discretion is needed. And it is very hard to tell a middle-aged woman in love that her fiancé doesn't look trustworthy.

"I'm getting older and I've been alone a long time," she said. "It will be so nice to have someone to look after my affairs."

I assured her that I felt that they were well looked after.

Mr. Clendening must have detected my misgivings, for he said amiably, "I can tell you don't approve of my handling her affairs, and we hoped you would. Well, since she tells me she always follows your advice, I'll just have to try that much harder to convince you."

I smiled and said good-by to them.

Several months passed and I heard nothing more from Mrs. Vanderpool. Then she came to see me alone, looking ill and downcast. "I should have listened to you," she told me. "I married him, and I didn't change the title of my account—I didn't want you to know—but I did make him deputy of my safe-deposit box, and he cleaned me out except for a few registered stocks that he could not use. I have nothing left now but those and my annuity."

It seemed that she had met Mr. Clendening at a restaurant where she had often had dinner; he had joined her at her table frequently, and they had become engaged. She had really known nothing about him. He had been kind, and the first few months of her marriage had been happy. He had taken a great interest in her affairs and his motives and judgments had seemed sound. They had opened a brokerage account in both their names and he had handled it—all except the registered stocks: she had remembered that I had told her never to endorse them to anyone else until she was ready to sell.

Then she had fallen ill with pneumonia. He had taken good care of her; every night he had given her a hot lemonade and her medicine. The last time she had not awakened for two days. By that time he had gone, her jewelry had been taken, other jewelry had been charged to her accounts in stores, and the bonds had been removed from the safe-deposit box. They had been sold through the brokerage account, in which only a small cash balance remained. Through them Mr. Clendening had been traced to Chicago and St. Louis; the case was in the hands of the police. Mrs. Vanderpool was utterly defeated and, moreover, ashamed; she had acted against her better judgment. Now she had no one to confide in but me; she could not face her friends.

All her banking arrangements and precautions for security had been impeccable. She had made only one mistake: she had given Mr. Clendening access to her safe-deposit box.

A safe-deposit box, like a savings or checking account, can have various forms of title, and this is of the utmost importance. You rent the box from the safe-deposit company—a separate corporation owned by the bank—under a signed rental contract, and the title of the box, *not its contents*, belongs to the owner. If it is in your name only, then only you can open it. You will be given two keys at the time (the only two keys in existence; the bank does not have any others), and these two keys should never be kept in the same place. If both are lost, the only way you can get to your box is to have it *sawed* open by an authorized locksmith in the presence of a representative of the safe-deposit corporation and yourself, and this is costly.

If the title is alternate with someone else, then you each have a key and either of you has independent access at any time. If the title is joint with someone else, then each party has a key and both must be present whenever the box is opened.

If you want your husband or anyone else to have access to your box, you can appoint him deputy: you sign a sworn statement authorizing the deputy to have full access to your box and all its contents, with power to surrender the box. A power of deputy ceases with your death.

This is what Mrs. Vanderpool did. Although the contents of the box belonged only to her, Mr. Clendening had access to them and could get away with anything that was negotiable.

In the case of alternate or joint titles, complications may arise at the death of one of the parties. One of my clients, Mrs. Wilson, had a safe-deposit box jointly with her daughter for what she thought were very good reasons. She was experienced in financial affairs, a shrewd investor, and meticulous about all her banking arrangements. She handled her daughter's affairs as well as her own, since she thought that her daughter did not know much about them and was generously inclined toward giving handouts to friends. Mrs. Wilson made the bank the executor of her estate. I thought the estate would be in good order, yet after her death it proved to be one of the most embarrassing and complicated estates we ever handled.

When a safe-deposit-box holder dies, the bank, on receiving notice, seals the box, and no one may open it again except in the presence of a member of the state tax authority, an officer of the safe-deposit corporation, and a representative of the estate. The contents are listed and considered the property of the deceased until ownership is proven.

When Mrs. Wilson died, we found that she had safe-deposit boxes all over the state of New York, and I had to be present at the opening of each one, since the bank was executor. All of them were held jointly with her daughter, who was her heir. As we opened the boxes, wads of currency—$100, $500, $1,000 bills—fell out of them. The state maintained that all of this currency was the property of the deceased and would be taxed in full. Mrs. Wilson's daughter claimed that the money was equally hers—her mother had used *her* money in accumulating it. The struggle between the state's claims and the daughter's was long, disagreeable, and expensive, and the daughter lost much because of it. After this, I was more convinced than ever that the safest and most efficient way to have a safe-deposit box is in your name alone. If it is absolutely necessary to name a deputy in an emergency, then be sure it is someone you can trust.

A safe-deposit box is essential even if you do not own securities. It is the only safe place to keep valuable personal possessions, such as jewelry, and your important legal papers—birth and marriage certificates, life insurance papers, deeds to property. Two things should not be kept in it: your will and cash. Your will should be kept where it is safe but where your executor or your attorney can find it; it would require a court order to get it out of your safe-deposit box after your death.

Money hoarded in a safe-deposit box is completely idle: it earns no interest for you and it has been withdrawn from circulation. One of my early clients, Mrs. Louis Greer, wife of a prominent society figure and corporation executive, had been hoarding not only cash but also gold pieces for years before I knew her. She had been an actress, and not too good a one, when Mr. Greer's eye had fallen upon her as she had ridden in a carriage past the Harvard Club, and he had persuaded her to marry him. She was a great beauty and had the poise of a woman born to the highest society, although her origins remain mysterious to this day. One of her ambitions had been to be a society figure, and when I met her she was generally accepted as one. Another of her ambitions had been to be very rich in her own right. Each time her husband had returned from a directors' meeting of his company, he had given her the $20 gold piece he had received as his honorarium. She had saved every one and put them all in her safe-deposit box. One morning, to my great surprise, she told me of her hoard and asked what she could do with it. I advised her to invest it, and we went down together into the vault. She had the largest safe-deposit box we had, the size of a steamer trunk, and it was filled, like a pirate's chest, with gold pieces. It took two men to move it, and I spent nearly a whole day counting the money. It came to almost $40,000, and some years later, after Mrs. Greer had invested and reinvested it, it had increased to a quarter of a million dollars.

Legal papers, even if they do not represent financial assets, should be safeguarded: you may need them. One of my depositors came to see me about arrangements for a trip abroad with her daughter. I reminded her that they would need their birth certificates to obtain passports. Did she have them?

"Of course; they are in a safe place," she said. "I remember putting them away. They're either in my desk drawer or else in the trunk in the attic. I know because I put them with my marriage certificate and John's discharge from the Army and the deed to the house. They're all together," she said proudly, as one who had outwitted fate.

The only trouble was that she did not remember *where*. This precipitated a panicky search that lasted four weeks and caused bitter family quarrels. Finally her husband's secretary found the papers in a lower drawer of his office desk.

You can save yourself a good deal of trouble by keeping valuables in the proper place; then you do not have to remember what you did with them.

A chronic problem at the bank was looking for U. S. Government Series E bonds, which many of our depositors bought. Mrs. Ethredge had saved for years to buy a house; every dollar she could spare had gone into savings bonds. She finally found the house she wanted and arranged the terms; the deal was to be closed at the bank, but she could not find the bonds. We looked in her safe-deposit box, though she assured me that she had never kept them there. She had not always bought them at the bank or at any one place; she had bought them when she had had the money and wherever it had been convenient. So there was no single record of the serial numbers. She had usually kept them in a shoe box in her closet because she liked to count them and watch her savings grow. Could we stop payment? Could we have them replaced? I was very worried; we would be able to do nothing.

Finally she remembered where she had last put them. She'd been in the closet counting them when she'd heard a neighbor calling at the door and had quickly put them away. She had a large muff with a pocket in one side; that was where she had stuffed them. She looked relieved. But—she had sent all her furs to storage. We immediately called the storage company, which located the muff and found the bonds. I had them delivered directly to the bank. Mrs. Ethredge nearly died of anxiety before she'd even lived in the house for which she had saved so long.

Safe-deposit boxes are of various sizes, but one that will serve most people's needs costs only $6.00 to $8.00 a year, a very modest sum for the security it gives and the worry it spares you. If you want to count your bonds, you can go to the bank and count them to your heart's content in the safety of a private room.

⚜ ⚜ ⚜

It was Mrs. Todman, with her marital problem, who broke the ice. After she consulted me, the women depositors came in a steady stream; and once the bank's regular clients discovered that I did indeed have some business sitting at a desk outside the ladies' drawing room, they came to me with questions and they sent their friends. My tasks were to persuade them to use more of the bank's services, of which the three basic ones I have described are only a small part, and to learn what their particular problems were. I found that I seldom had to ask; they were quite eager to confide in someone.

As they unbent, so did Annabel, the maid, who had first regarded me as an interloper. She not merely warmed up but also virtually adopted me; she called me her "baby," and our understanding became so cordial that some of the ladies seemed to disapprove. Annabel knew all their little eccentricities and warned me about them; she helped me get to know them and urged them to ask me questions. She was used to humoring the more difficult clients and I learned a great deal from her.

I learned even more from the astounding things they asked me. Some of their questions were merely naïve, but some of their confidences were so personal that I wondered why I, sitting in a bank, should be listening to them—stories of unfaithful husbands, ungrateful children, scapegrace brothers, scoundrel sons-in-law. On the other hand, they told me often of years of happy marriage, of their pride in children and grandchildren, of their devotion to their faith, of their wish to leave money to a church, a school, an orphanage. Whatever it was, I came to realize how close to their hearts lay the matter of money—how even a trivial financial gain could mean the difference between happiness and sorrow, how a substantial one could mean the difference between a ruined life and a successful one. This was not merely a materialistic attitude. True, I know women to whom the mere idea of making money was an obsession—and they were never happy. But I also knew many who worked hard and cared for their money wisely and were happy because they used it to enrich their lives or gave it to their children or their friends.

Whatever the women's needs or aims, the means were very much the same and always began with the most elementary steps in banking, which seemed, since I had worked in the bank, so simple that I could hardly believe that grown women would ask to have them explained. One woman told me she had run out of checks; did that mean she had no more money in the bank? Another could not believe her account was overdrawn because she still had checks in her checkbook. Almost all of them needed help in balancing their checkbooks. How, if they had had money in their families for generations, could they be so unaware of how it was handled?

Some of our clients were the great-granddaughters of the prosperous businessmen of early New York; they had money in their own names and their fortunes passed to their daughters—but none of them had ever had much to say about how the money was handled. Their fathers, husbands, or sons took care of that. Mr. Frissell, one of the founders of the bank, knew that the women of the neighborhood had a good deal of money, and he made a point of giving women special services—the "Gold Room," the free telephone, the fashionable décor. But he also knew that they understood very little about the uses of a bank: going there was for many of them a social pastime rather than a serious business matter. And he suspected that women did not like to confide their financial affairs or reveal their ignorance of them to men.

Why should they? I thought. Their husbands had always regarded money as a man's affair and had seldom discussed it with women. And as for bankers—they were cold, hard men, the very image, I suspected, of many of those husbands.

I used to observe the distrust with which women approached me. Some of them had the idea that the bank somehow controlled their money in such a way that they couldn't do as they pleased with it; others seemed to think of the bank as a benevolent institution that handed over money on demand. Sometimes the bank's willingness to offer services aroused their suspicions; there must be a catch in it somewhere, they felt.

This was forty years ago, and since then millions of women have learned to earn and save and invest their own money. Yet the traditional attitude persists: many women still feel that money matters, outside the household budget, are beyond them. Recently a young woman, daughter of a depositor whose affairs I handled for years, asked me to have lunch with her and help her straighten out her checkbook. She is an attractive person in her early thirties, well educated, and a talented writer. She is also used to having money, and so is her husband—but she would not reveal the state of her checkbook to him. When I went over it, I found that her trouble was not lack of money or faulty arithmetic; she simply had no idea of what banking was all about and did not understand what she was doing. Money was a mysterious realm beyond her comprehension.

This is nonsense, of course. I found that our women clients, once they had talked over money matters freely with a counselor, quickly learned how to handle their own accounts. Men proverbially respect the budget-stretching ability of their wives in household matters, but many of them would not think of letting them share in making investments or buying property. This same ability applied to higher finance pays off well: many women are much better earners, spenders, and investors than the average man.

Still, the bank is the place where they must learn. The first thing to understand is that the bank is a business and its purpose is to make money for its owners by taking care of your money for you. While you are not using your money, the bank is lending it out to businessmen to make more money. In return for the use of your money, you receive interest and many services. Sometimes specific services will cost you specific fees—such as the charges for a special checking account. These services and fees are explained to you when you open an account and there is nothing mysterious about them.

Banks are regulated by law and their accounts are audited by federal or state examiners to prevent loss to depositors through the incompetence or dishonesty of bank employees. What is not regulated by law is established by common practice. Banks are in competition for your account; it is to their advantage to give you the best service, the highest rate of interest possible, at the least cost to you.

Our bank was the pioneer in establishing a special women's department; now nearly all large banks have followed its example. Smaller banks, too, even if they do not have a special department, are aware of the particular needs of women and are equipped to serve them. Even if your bank does not offer all the services you may someday require, it is the place where all your financial transactions begin and where you can learn everything you ought to know.

CHAPTER THREE

YOUR BANK WILL LEND YOU MONEY IF . . . THE CREDIT DEPARTMENT

If confidence is a plant of slow growth, credit is one which matures much more slowly.
—Disraeli

There is hardly anyone, no matter how fortunate or prosperous, who does not need at some time in his life to borrow money. Sometimes it is literally a matter of life and death; at other times it may be only a convenient way of getting through a temporary difficulty with a minimum of trouble and cost. In either case, the bank and your credit standing are of vital importance. And since it is impossible to foretell when you may need this credit standing, you should never allow it to be impaired through carelessness, neglect, or extravagance. Your credit is first based upon your bank account: if you conduct it well, avoid overdrafts, make regular deposits, pay bills on time to keep your credit good in your community, then you have already gone a long way toward establishing your name and character, on which your credit depends. In an emergency you will find it much easier to get financial help than you would if you had managed your bank account in a random or irresponsible manner.

One of my depositors was Mrs. Meyer, who seemed a singularly happy and well-favored person. She was the wife of a successful clothing manufacturer. They were devoted to each other, and he gave her a generous allowance; they lived well, in a beautiful Park Avenue apartment, traveled often, and gave a good deal to charity. Each month she came into the bank, smiling and buoyant, to deposit her allowance or to make a small investment with some surplus funds. One could hardly imagine that Mrs. Meyer would ever have to borrow money for an emergency.

But her husband died quite suddenly of a heart attack. His affairs were in good order; his will had been drawn leaving everything he had to her. The day after his death she called me, since we had become personal friends, and I went to see her. She told me that since she would not be able to touch her husband's bank account until the estate account was opened, she would need some money for living expenses and might need to borrow some. I told her it could easily be arranged if she would come to the bank.

When she came in she told me she would like to have $10,000 for three months and we quickly arranged a collateral loan. She had $15,000 worth of bonds in her safe-deposit box, and she brought them to me as security (collateral at that time had to be 30 per cent more than the loan). Then she had only to sign a note, which read as follows:

> New York, April 15, 193–
>
> $10,000
>
> For value received, and with the following as collateral, in three months after date I promise to pay to the order of The Fifth Avenue Bank of New York Ten Thousand Dollars at 4½% interest.
>
> Elizabeth Meyer

The bonds were listed in detail.

This note and the bonds were held by the loan department of the bank, which watched the market value of the securities to be sure that the loan was amply covered. (Sometimes, if the market drops sharply, securities placed as collateral for a loan will decline in value, and the bank must always be sure that it has enough security. This did not happen in Mrs. Meyer's case; if it had, Mrs. Meyer would have given the bank additional collateral.) She did not have to sell the bonds or lose any interest on them, and she knew they were in a safe place. In three months she would either repay the note (if the funds from her husband's estate were available), pay off part of it and renew the balance, or extend it in its entirety. As it turned out, she repaid it and regained possession of her bonds. The cost to her was $112.50 (one quarter of the annual 4½ per cent interest).

Mrs. Meyer had no children, and her own relatives were all dead. She took a great interest in my family, became a close friend of my mother's, and was devoted to my brothers, whom she took to the circus each year, planning special parties and treats for them. But she did not have much to fill her life, and so she decided to carry on her husband's business just as he had run it. She became president of the company, leaving his trusted associates in the positions they had held under him. Her chief concern in life was to see that the business prospered and that its products lived up to the distinguished reputation he had established for his trade-mark.

One day she came to the bank as president of the company to ask for a loan to meet current operating expenses. She did not want —or need—to put her personal funds into the business; she insisted that it be self-supporting.

She knew it was easy enough to get a personal loan on collateral, but she was not sure that the company could have one. But when she showed us a statement of the company's liabilities and assets, which indicated a sound financial condition, it was a routine matter to give her the loan she wanted; the bank had seen such statements before and knew the company's situation. Making such loans as these to businessmen is one of a commercial bank's chief functions. Its main concern is to make sure—since it is lending its depositors' money—that the loan is safely placed.

A little later, even when times were hard and money was more difficult to borrow, Mrs. Meyer had no trouble in obtaining loans for emergencies—at current interest rates, slightly higher because of general business conditions. At such times, when many other firms were going bankrupt, the bank carried the Meyer company through because of its excellent credit reputation.

But finally Mrs. Meyer had to sell out her business, although it nearly broke her heart to do it. It was prosperous enough, and she did not need the money, but times had changed. The rest of the management wanted to adopt policies that were at odds with her husband's as she knew them; mass production replaced careful individual styling of clothes; the workers organized. Mrs. Meyer could not cope with this new situation, and she would not permit her products to be downgraded. So she sold out her controlling interest in the company, stipulating that her husband's name and trade-mark could never be used again. After she had retired, the heart was gone out of her; she had nothing to devote herself to, and she literally wasted away.

She was only one of thousands of such people. I saw many of them during my banking career—proud artisans and merchants who saw their old high standards destroyed in the rise of mass machine production, their businesses turned over to the manufacture and sale of cheap goods instead of the fine hand-crafted products on which they had built their names and fortunes.

⚜ ⚜ ⚜

A bank extends credit not only to persons of property and businessmen but also to any depositors whose means and character warrant it.

Mrs. Hilton was a young widow employed as a telephone operator. She had to go to the hospital for a rather serious operation. Her medical costs would be more than her health insurance would cover, she did not know quite what the surgeon's fee and additional expenses would be, and she wanted to have ready money at hand if she needed it. She had $2,000 in a savings bank; it was June 1, and she did not want to withdraw the money before July 1 (when the quarterly interest would be added to it) and lose the interest. So she came to me and asked if she might borrow the money for two months to see her through her convalescence. She brought her savings account passbook with a signed draft; this would be the security for the loan. The bank, without question, gave her the loan at a low rate and put $2,000 into her checking account. When she was well and back at work, she repaid the loan. It cost her $8.30. She would have lost $15 in interest if she had withdrawn the savings before July 1, and while she was in the hospital she had the comfort of knowing that she had plenty of ready money at hand and that, if all went well, she would have some balance left in her savings account after she had repaid the loan.

Sometimes one has to have money quickly to take advantage of a good opportunity. Miss McGregor was a free-lance writer whose income varied from month to month, so that she never knew exactly what it would be, but averaged out well over the year. Her checking account always had a respectable balance and was occasionally replenished by a large deposit when she sold a story or article. One day she came to me and told me that she had inherited a small house on the Hudson River from her aunt. She loved the house and had always hoped to own it, but, now that she did, it was not much good to her. Her work required her to be in New York three or four days a week for appointments and editorial conferences. She could not afford to keep the house and an apartment in town, too, and the house was too inaccessible to reach without a car. She had heard that a bank would give her a loan to buy a car. The interest rates were rather high, but if her credit was good and she gave the bank a chattel mortgage on the car, it could be done.

First I asked her if the house was mortgaged. It was, she said, for $2,000; it was valued at $15,000. Since she already had a mortgage on it, she didn't think she could get another. I told her that she might increase the mortgage to two thirds of the value of the house if she needed to. But I suggested that she increase it by $3,000. This would cover the cost of a car, some repairs to the house, and moving. She could have this mortgage at a lower rate of interest than that of an automobile loan, and I suggested that she go to the bank that held the first mortgage.

She was a little surprised. Our bank, then, didn't want to give her a loan on an automobile? I assured her that we would gladly—

her credit was good, she sold regularly to large magazines, and she had always managed her affairs well. But it wasn't the best kind of loan for her.

In the first place, the mortgage would cost her less in interest and would run for a longer period. She would not have it on her mind as she would an automobile loan; she would not always be worried about missing a monthly payment. Being a writer, she needed the peace and quiet of that country house, with as little extraneous worry as possible.

After I had explained why she would do better with the mortgage, she went to the local bank on the Hudson, which was very glad to lend her the money at 6 per cent. (Savings banks are required to invest to a large extent in mortgages.) After she had settled down in her house, she wrote more and sold more; the account which she kept with us grew, and I was very satisfied to have sent her to another bank for the loan. Some time later she came to me for advice on her first investments, very pleased with the course of her career.

Of course, banks are quite willing to give automobile loans, but they must charge a higher rate of interest because they run a greater risk. So they investigate the borrower's credit status carefully. Most people actually do buy their cars on such loans, either from banks or from finance companies, which charge a much higher rate of interest. If you must buy your car that way and your credit standing with your regular bank is good, you will do better to go to the bank than to a finance company.

⚜ ⚜ ⚜

One evening at a dinner party I met a woman—also a writer—who told me that she was working on a book but had gone stale on it. She could not make it move, she was in low spirits and poor health, and she longed to take a vacation trip, but, of course, like most free-lance writers, she could not afford it. I asked her if she owned any property or had a paid-up insurance policy she might borrow on. No, she shook her head sadly.

"But you have a nice diamond ring," I observed. "You could borrow on that."

"That was left me by my mother," she said. "I wouldn't ever part with it." Still, she was hesitating.

"If you love it enough, you'll get it back," I said. "But just now maybe the vacation would do you good."

She took the diamond to a loan company and borrowed enough for a long cruise. When she got back, she felt renewed in health and spirit and got on well with her book. She called me to tell me how much her trip had helped her and how glad she was that I had thought of borrowing on her diamond, which she was going to redeem soon. But, she added, she had never before heard of a banker's advising that kind of loan.

Probably not. Lending money on jewelry is not a bank's business, and it seldom does it. But whenever someone asks me about a financial problem, especially a personal loan, I recall what Mr. Frissell taught me. True, he always said that before you make a loan you must first ask the borrower if he has a plan for paying it back. But then he also set before me the example of a banker who always considered the personal needs of a client, whether he was a rich businessman or a poor writer. It was not orthodox banking practice to send Miss McGregor to a savings bank out of town to increase the mortgage it held when our bank could have given her a loan. But it worked out well for her, and her account with our bank is now larger than ever and she has become a very valuable client. Not all bankers continue in Mr. Frissell's tradition; it is a hard one to follow in a swiftly changing, highly competitive society, where every businessman feels he must take the quickest profit he can get. But I firmly believe that the more personal and sympathetic your approach to a client, the further you will see into his future—and you will be able to help him more in the long run. And the more prosperous he becomes in the long run, the more valuable he becomes as the bank's customer. Aside from taking satisfaction in being really helpful, a counselor is also building up good will for his bank. The writer who borrowed on her diamond sent to me a very well-to-do friend who opened a large account with us—and now her own account is one we would not wish to lose.

Commercial banks supply loans for a wide variety of needs. A farmer may need money to run his farm and live until his crops are harvested; he has put everything into planting them. He owns his farm, he has good equipment, he is known as a good farmer, and his credit is good. He can go to his local bank and borrow $1,000 against his crops.

Similarly, loans for property improvement are available, and there are also insured education loan plans. Now the federal and state governments have made education loans available to every single person who wants one. Many more kinds of bank loans exist now and are in general use than came within my personal experience, as I was educated in a fairly conservative school of banking, which did not believe in the overextension of credit. Nowadays, charge accounts and installment buying and credit cards make it possible for people with regular incomes and adequate references to spend a great deal of money which they have not yet earned. Most people have to borrow money to buy a house, and they usually do this by taking a mortgage on it (we'll come to this kind of borrowing in another chapter). Now the New York State Legislature has passed a bill which would permit mortgage loans up to 90 per cent—that is, you now need only 10 per cent of the purchase price in order to own a house valued up to $25,000. Mr. Frissell, chairman of our board, who gave me my basic education in banking, would hardly have approved of that from a banker's point of view.

From the spender's point of view it has dangers, too. Sometimes credit—for buying now and paying later—is all too easy to get. You would do well to think twice before availing yourself of all the credit privileges that are offered to you. Remember, first, that you will eventually have to pay for what you buy or lose it and that if you cannot pay you will lose your credit and your good name. And you will also have to pay for the privilege of buying beyond your immediate means in service charges and high interest. Credit offers from merchandisers can be made to look very attractive, but they cost you a great deal more than things that you purchase for cash.

And, from my point of view, nothing could be drearier than working hard all year to pay for last year's vacation—only to have to take next year's vacation on credit.

You will undoubtedly have to buy your first house on credit—indeed, there are advantages to this. But take into account the high cost of retail credit before you buy on it, compare it with bank rates of interest, and do not buy on credit anything you can save for and enjoy without having to pay for it long after its pleasure and usefulness have depreciated.

⚜ ⚜ ⚜

The credit department of a bank is one of its vital nerve centers. Its business is to investigate the reliability of the people with whom the bank and its depositors—including you—have business dealings. If your purpose in seeking credit is legitimate, you need have no misgivings about going to the bank's credit department; and if you have conducted your own affairs efficiently and in good faith, you need not fear for your own credit standing. Everything you tell your bank and all your business affairs are held in strictest confidence. The credit department can be a great help to you if you are a depositor of the bank. You may recall the case of the young man in the previous chapter who lost money gambling in Reno: the credit department of the bank saved his skin, although actually he had risked it rather recklessly.

Bank employees must always be on the watch for bad-check experts and other frauds, who wear a variety of disguises and are sometimes hard to spot.

I remember a day when a nice-looking, well-dressed gentleman came to my desk at the bank during the lunch hour, introduced himself as Dr. Ames, and asked to open an account. He gave me a check for $28,000, drawn on a bank in Texas, and the name of one of our women depositors as a reference. He had dined with her the night before, he said, and she had mentioned my name. He would need a checkbook, he told me, although he probably would not want to draw a check at once, since he had enough cash for his present needs—and he pulled a wad of bills from his pocket as if to prove this. We chatted awhile about New York and Texas, and then he left.

It was a nice sum to open an account, I thought, but something about the man bothered me. He certainly looked respectable, he evidently knew the best people, and he was staying at the Ritz. But why had he come to me in the ladies' department instead of going to one of the men officers? Well, because the lady who knew me had given him my name. I could call her and ask her, of course, but she might resent any inference that a friend of hers was not honest and, anyway, she had done me a favor by sending me a good account. But why hadn't she written a letter of introduction? That was what I should have had.

And then, if he lived in Texas, why did he want a bank account in New York? Or why did he want one at all if, as he said, he wouldn't be drawing any checks right away? Just to be safe, I went to the credit department and asked someone to call the bank in Texas on which his check was drawn. Then I went to lunch.

When I returned, my secretary told me to call the Ritz; it had just received a package for Dr. Ames from Tiffany's—a collect package for $10,000—and he had given the bank as a reference. Our credit man had received the call. It was fortunate that he had phoned the bank in Texas and learned that "Dr. Ames" had no account with them but *was* very well known there: he was wanted by the authorities for passing a number of bad checks.

I was still talking to the manager of the Ritz when "Dr. Ames" reappeared at my desk. I said good-by and hung up casually.

"Miss Armbruster," he said, "I've just bought some jewelry for my wife and I'd like to draw $8,000 against the check I gave you. If it isn't too much trouble. And don't bother our friend Mrs. X about it; it would be embarrassing."

I pressed the button and, in answer, one of our floor men appeared. I asked him if he would take "Dr. Ames" to the credit department. That was the last I saw of him, but he did not go back to Texas unescorted. And how glad I was that the credit department had acted so quickly and had been prepared for the emergency.

The credit department can be of great help to the average individual depositor in advising him on small business propositions. Mrs. Hill, who was a painter—a good one but not a very rich one—once took a vacation in Puerto Rico, where she found the climate and the light so delightful and so stimulating for her creative work that she wished she could spend half her time there. At the hotel where she stayed she met a charming man who shared her enthusiasm for the island, where he had lived for some time. He took her to the roof garden to watch a beautiful sunset and pointed out to her in the distance a tract of land which he was developing as a residential area. This interested her, and when he told her that she could buy a lot for $500 and one of the small houses he was building for $1,500 more she was possessed by the idea of having one as a winter home. She would raise the money, she said, as soon as she got back to New York.

On her return she came to see me. She was going to draw the $2,000 from her savings account to buy a house in Puerto Rico; could I attend to the transfer of the money?

I asked her what her plans were and they sounded ideal for a painter. But, I suggested, we might check on the property, since she still had no papers to show what she was buying. I referred the matter to our credit department, with the name of the real-estate developer, and asked it to make inquiries. The department wrote to our correspondent in Puerto Rico, and in a few days we had a reply. Our correspondent said that it had already had several complaints about the development. There was no such land as the real-estate man had described—it was under water—and no houses were built or even planned.

Mrs. Hill was, of course, disappointed, but she still had the money to put into a real house and lot whenever she found it. A routine inquiry through the credit department had saved her from a heartbreaking loss. Her bank had done her a real service.

Anthony Trollope said, "Credit is a matter so subtle in its essence that, as it may be obtained almost without reason, so, without reason, may it melt away." The real-estate dealer in Puerto Rico had established his "credit" with Mrs. Hill quite easily, but it had vanished as soon as she had checked it with her bank. Mrs. Hill, on the other hand, who had managed her small account responsibly and well, would never have had any difficulty in obtaining credit from our bank. Although you can never expect a bank or anyone else to give you something for nothing, you will find that a good reputation will go a long way in enabling you to get credit when you need it.

CHAPTER FOUR

WHEN YOU TRAVEL: YOUR BANK'S FOREIGN SERVICES

The world is a great book, of which they that never stir from home read only a page.
—St. Augustine

It was about three-thirty on a winter afternoon shortly before Christmas 1925. Most of the customers had left the bank and a hush had fallen over the corridor and the Ladies' Drawing Room. I was sitting alone, busy at my desk, while my secretary, who sat back of me, was finishing the day's mail.

I became aware of a presence in the corridor and saw someone peek around a corner at me; then a wraithlike figure passed my desk and slipped into the "Gold Room" without a glance in my direction. I went on working and did not pay any attention to her; some intuition told me it was better not to make too bold an approach to a woman who seemed so shy. Half an hour must have passed before the woman appeared again, this time smiling timidly. I smiled at her, but still we did not speak. A little later I heard a hesitant cough and turned to see her seated at a little writing table diagonally across the room, beckoning to me. I went over to her.

She was of uncertain age, perhaps about fifty, oddly got up in a high-cut figured dress, with a low-necked black chiffon dress over it, and a tiny, battered black straw hat with a single rose on it. Her eyes were hidden by a short veil. She wore long white kid gloves, creased and dirty; her black cotton stockings and old-fashioned patent leather shoes looked like a little girl's. She was outlandish but so pathetic and frightened that I felt sorry for her.

As I stood beside her she looked up at me and began to tell me about herself. Her name was Mary B. Powers. (I can use her real name now, since her story is a matter of public record.) Her father, who had died when she was twelve, while they were living in a fashionable Fifth Avenue hotel, she scarcely remembered. Her mother, whom she remembered well, had been an unusually shrewd businesswoman, a friend of the famous Hetty Green, who, like her, had made a fortune in real estate in New York and New Jersey. She had handled all her business affairs herself, seldom confiding in her children. Before she had died—in 1911—she had made Miss Powers and her only brother coexecutors and equal heirs of her estate. They had moved to a West Side hotel, where they had lived until her brother's death three months ago. Her brother had handled her mother's estate, discussing major decisions with Miss Powers and obtaining her signature on every transaction. Now that he was dead—she seemed grieved at his death and, at the same time, relieved to have matters in her own hands—she had everything to do herself. Her mother's estate was far from settled and even her father's was not closed. She did not know where to begin. The real estate and mortgages were handled by a lawyer in New Jersey, an old friend of her mother's, but he was not to know of the rest of their holdings, which were far more substantial.

Her brother had never made a will and had advised her not to. She did not want to hire any lawyer and hoped to settle everything herself. Was this possible? Would I help her? I assured her I would help her in every way I could, although it would be impossible for her to do all of it herself. Then I carefully explained how the bank could do almost everything for her. At her request we could apply to the court to be appointed administrator of her brother's estate and take full charge of it and we could assist her as executrix in settling her mother's and father's estates. An executor is appointed by the court and cannot delegate that appointment.

She asked one question after another, all of them intelligent and to the point. Although she was bewildered at the complexity of her affairs, she had a fairly good idea of her situation. She showed clearly that she trusted no one and she never took her eyes off me. But she seemed to lack the courage to make any decision.

If the bank took charge, would there have to be a lawyer as well? Was the bank's lawyer honest and trustworthy? How did I know he was? Would she have to turn over all the property to us? Would she be kept informed of everything we did?

What about these? She held up a dirty brown envelope. They were checks, she said. Not hers. They were dividend checks payable to her brother. What could be done with them? I told her that they could be placed to his account even though he was dead. One can always deposit, though not withdraw. She seemed interested in this and said that if she did decide to deposit them to his account, she would want a receipt for them from the bank.

Of course, I assured her. Inwardly I was praying for the wisdom to say the right thing. I knew who she was. It would be a big account, amounting to millions of dollars. I wanted desperately to secure it. But how could one deal with this timid, frightened woman and gain her confidence? Would she like to meet the president of the bank? He would take a personal interest. No, she said firmly. She had come to me because she had heard I had a heart as well as business acumen. I was a woman like her. She hoped I would be willing to look out for her and assist her.

My secretary had finished the mail and was waiting for me to sign it. Outside it had grown dark and inside the bank was silent as a tomb. There is no place so still as a bank at night. The people are gone; the daylong sounds of movement and conversation, the clicking of coins and machines, and the hum of elevators cease. In the void you become frighteningly conscious of the threat of robbery. Every sound becomes a menace. You want nothing so much as to leave and join the world outside.

She suddenly seemed to become aware of the stillness. "Where are we? What has happened? I must go," she said hastily.

I was relieved; I had stood at her side for two hours.

She walked toward the front door. "Thank you," she said; "you have been very kind. You will hear from me. Please keep everything I've said in strict confidence. I will know if you do not. You don't need to take me to the door. Good night."

The watchman bowed as he opened the door for her. I went back down the corridor feeling limp and exhausted, and I still did not feel that my effort had been to any purpose. When I reached my desk I had another shock. Someone was sitting there.

"Congratulations, Dorothy," a voice said. It was Mr. Hetzler, the president of the bank. "That was good work. Her brother's estate will be a very big account."

"But I haven't got it yet," I said. "I don't believe she'll ever make up her mind."

"I think you have it," he said. "It's the first time she's talked to anyone. I tried to call on her after her brother's death but she kept telling the operator to say she was out. Please come in and talk to me about it tomorrow morning."

I had got some good accounts for the bank but nothing on that scale. It was a turning point in my career. From that time, for nearly twenty-five years, I was to spend at least a day each month with Miss Powers, trying to put her affairs in order.

The immediate result was to be a reward and a promotion. Mr. Hetzler told me the bank felt I deserved something special. Since I would be dealing with important people and large accounts, the officers wanted me to have a title. They debated as to what it should be. Women had never held titles in the bank. Finally I was made Assistant to the President. In recognition of my new status, and for bringing in the Powers account, I was to have a trip to Europe at the bank's expense—a pleasure trip on which I would also have the opportunity of observing foreign banking procedures. I could be of greater service to women who traveled and had business interests abroad.

I began to make preparations to leave the following July. I took three French lessons each week from one of our depositors, and when my family's shock and excitement subsided my mother set to work making me a whole new wardrobe. Before I left, Mr. Hetzler introduced me to old friends of his who were sailing on the same ship, and I was sent off in grand style on the *S.S. Paris,* with my stateroom banked with flowers and filled with *bon voyage* baskets. Both Mr. Foley and Mr. Hetzler came down to see me off, and Mr. Hetzler advised me to make the most of the trip. It could be very important for my future, he said—and he was right. Many of the people I met became my valued clients and some of them close friends.

My travel arrangements were fairly simple. First I bought myself $1,000 worth of traveler's checks for everyday expenses abroad. These are, of course, well known now, but they were less so then, and many a woman still traveled with her cash in a money belt or a bag around her waist—an unsafe as well as an uncomfortable practice. The best known traveler's checks are issued by the American Express Company, but many large banks and other companies issue their own; they come in denominations of $10, $20, $50, $100, and $1,000 and can be bought at banks, at their companies' offices, and at many travel agencies. You sign the checks on a line at the top in the presence of the person who sells them to you. When you cash them, you countersign the checks on a line at the bottom in the presence of the person who cashes them for you. When the two signatures compare, these traveler's checks are as negotiable as currency. It is important not to sign them before you use them: your identity is established by the act of signing before the person who cashes them.

Each traveler's check bears a number, and a record of the numbers is made by the issuing office at the time you buy the checks. On a counterfoil provided for the purpose you may note the number and denomination of each check, and it is wise to mark the checks off as you cash them. Keep this record separate from the checks; if you lose them, notify immediately the nearest agent of the company or bank issuing the checks—or, better still, the bank where you purchased them. Payment will be stopped and in time you will have your money refunded to you.

It is wise, I learned, to take checks of various denominations, always including some small ones. You should not carry large amounts of currency at any time. This precaution can also save you from loss in converting one foreign currency into another when you cross frontiers. When I left Italy and entered France, I managed to have very few lire left—fortunately, since at that time the exchange rate for lire was very unfavorable in France.

One woman on the train was distressed because the day before she had changed a $100 traveler's check into lire and she still had about $90 worth of them left. She took a considerable loss when she had to change them into francs.

Some countries at times may prohibit travelers from bringing in any foreign currency. If you have any with you, you should exchange it at the official rate, which may be very low, or it may be impounded or noted in your passport (in which case you'll have to prove when you leave the country that you have not changed any foreign currency there).

Your bank can tell you before you leave home of the existing currency restrictions in the countries you are going to visit; but even then it is wise to check at every frontier to see if any changes have been made in the regulations.

It is also a good idea to take with you some currency of each country that you enter—enough to provide yourself with cash for tips, customs duties, and taxi fare to your hotel. If you travel by ship, the purser can generally provide you with enough (but if you are on a small freighter, don't depend on this; instead, obtain the necessary foreign currency before sailing). Most international airports now have currency-exchange windows, but I once arrived in Lima, Peru, early in the morning, when they were all closed, and it took a good deal of trouble to cash a check at the hotel at that hour to pay my taxi driver.

In addition to my traveler's checks, I carried a letter of credit for $5,000. This is a letter from a bank, addressed to its correspondent banks abroad, which introduces you and certifies that you may draw drafts on the issuing bank that the foreign banks are to honor up to the amount stated in the letter. Your signature accompanies the letter, on a separate form, and you receive a list of the correspondent banks which are to honor the letter. The signature that you put on the draft when you make a withdrawal must agree with this signature. You should keep the signature card and the list of banks separate from the letter of credit, so that if you lose it the finder will not be able to forge your signature. If you lose the letter of credit, notify the nearest correspondent bank and the bank which issued it.

There are two kinds of letters of credit: those for which you pay cash, the face value plus the service charge, usually about 1 per cent, and those taken on credit, known as a charge letter of credit. These are usually secured by collateral, as in the case of a loan, and as drafts on the foreign banks are presented for payment at your bank they are charged against your account together with the service charge. Letters of credit are usually limited to one year, but if you stay abroad longer than that they may be extended by the bank at your request and sent to a correspondent bank for delivery to you.

One of our depositors, a high government official presumably versed in economic matters, was quite annoyed when I told her that we could not issue her a letter of credit for $10,000 when she had less than $1,000 in the bank and almost no collateral to offer us. Like any other kind of credit, the letter must be paid for or secured sufficiently to guarantee it.

When I traveled abroad I had to learn that banking hours and bank holidays vary widely in different countries. English bank holidays are not found on our calendar; you simply have to learn when they fall and do your banking accordingly. French banks close completely for two hours at noon, so don't count on using your letter of credit during the lunch hour. And the long midday siesta in Italy and Spain, sometimes from noon to four P.M., has made many a traveler miss his train because he could not draw money from the bank to pay for his ticket. The simplest way to cope with this is to make a point of finding out, on your first visit to your foreign bank and/or American Express Company office, what the hours are and noting them then and there. If you rely entirely on your hotel to cash that last-minute check, you may find it without cash or you may be given an unfavorable rate of exchange.

It is a great comfort when traveling in a strange country to be able to rely on your home bank in case of emergency. Miss Foster, an art historian who went often to Europe, found it a blessing to have the bank's help when she lost her handbag, containing her checks and letter of credit, in Barcelona. She merely cabled the bank: "Wire me $5,000 and establish my credit here." We immediately cabled the money, then sent on a new letter of credit to our Barcelona correspondent. She signed it there and resumed her travels after only a minor inconvenience.

Mrs. Wayne, an old lady of seventy who was an indefatigable sight-seer, fell and broke her hip in the Sistine Chapel in Rome and had to be taken to the hospital, where she spent several weeks. Her letter of credit was due to expire just three days after her accident, but, on receipt of a cable from her, we quickly sent her a six-month extension by airmail and she was able to meet her expenses easily.

The bank had planned my trip for me as part of my education in foreign banking, and I was lucky, because I was completely innocent of European banking methods as well as social customs. I learned about foreign currencies as I crossed frontiers. As for finding my way about in strange countries—it turned out to be easy. I was always surrounded by friendly and helpful people. Mr. Acheson, a vice-president of the bank who was in Europe at the time, met me in Paris and introduced me to the bank of Morgan and Company, our correspondent. I spent a few hours each day there, and outside of working hours Mr. Acheson showed me something of Parisian life. I recall particularly a reception given by one of his friends for well-known artists, among them Picasso and Matisse, whom I met and talked to. Modern art was new to me then—I did not grasp it—but Mr. Acheson had previously advised me to look wise and say nothing of what I did not understand. In that way I learned a great deal, and I have since come to appreciate the kind of art that seemed so strange then. Many of the bank's clients collected it, and I was to see a great deal more when I visited their homes. The hostess at the reception was a client of the bank, and years later we settled her estate, which included many priceless paintings and sculptures.

When I left Paris, Mr. Acheson escorted me to the train and saw me safely settled in a compartment occupied by a Swiss couple who spoke to each other in German. I sat on the inside, away from the window, and when the gentleman saw that I was craning my neck to see the scenery he gallantly changed seats with me. Soon we were all speaking English and we became good friends. It seems strange that years later, after the Swiss lady's husband had died and she had come to the United States, I took care of her affairs and that, in addition, the bank settled her estate at her death.

These chance encounters in Europe brought many clients to the bank. I remember especially an American couple, the Maxwells, whom I met in Paris. They had stayed on at their country home in France during the First World War. The Germans had occupied their house—far to the east of Paris—and had let them stay but had virtually made servants of them. Mr. Maxwell, a dignified gentleman, had had to shine the officers' shoes; Mrs. Maxwell, a well-born lady of great culture, had become their cook and housemaid. Years later I helped them to reinvest their money and they placed their securities in a custody account with us.

In northern Italy I missed my stop for the Villa d'Este, Cernobbio, and got off at Como; from there I called the hotel on the telephone, and it sent a yacht across Lake Como to bring me back. I visited Milan, where I saw Leonardo's "Last Supper," worshiped at the cathedral, and attended a performance at La Scala; then I went on to Nice and Monte Carlo. There I was induced to try my luck at the casino. I think I rather dashed my friends by playing just once and quitting while I was ahead. It may have been unsporting, but I did not think that the representative of an American bank would inspire confidence by spending too much time at the roulette wheel. With my small winnings I made a side trip to the monastery of St. Bernard in the Alps, saw the famous dogs, and particularly enjoyed eating *fraises des bois* and *petits suisses*.

I was glad I had not been tempted to stay long at the casino when, some time later, one of our depositors, Mrs. Holmes, who had a passion for gambling and played regularly at Monte Carlo each time she went abroad, sent me a desperate cable. She had lost heavily, she was $5,000 in debt, and she could not ask her husband for it, as he had threatened to leave her if she did not stop gambling. I knew that the bank would never approve a loan and that she had very little in her account. I thought of calling her sister, who could have lent her the money, but I remembered that I was sworn to secrecy. Finally, in going over Mrs. Holmes's affairs, I found that the accumulated income from a trust fund of which she was beneficiary could be advanced to her and would cover the debt. I cabled her the money, to her immense relief, and after that she never went near the casino again.

I returned to Paris, then flew to London, on one of the first scheduled cross-channel flights, in a small plane that was long overdue before we were in sight of the airport. In a moment of anxiety I wrote a post card to my mother, telling her that my last thoughts were of her; but soon we were safely on the ground and I was being met by a representative of Hambro's bank, our correspondent in London.

Hambro's was and is one of the foremost of the English merchant banks, financing commercial enterprises in England and abroad and acting as intermediary for foreign banks. It had been our correspondent ever since our bank was founded. I spent two weeks in its offices in a beautiful old building in Trafalgar Square, at the heart of what was then the financial center of the world, studying various aspects of foreign banking.

At that time the settlement of England's war debt to the United States had become a controversial issue. The English bankers I met thought it should be canceled and told me so. The United States was pressing for payment. I thought it would be unbecoming for a young woman banker to have a flat opinion, but finally I had the temerity to say that the United States had gained nothing from the war and at least had the right to be repaid a debt. The English bankers looked a little shocked, then politely agreed with me—but more out of gallantry than conviction. That was 1926. Now the British and American banking communities have grown so close that Hambro's is allied with one of the oldest of the American mercantile banks.

International banking is a complex matter, since banks not only serve their depositors when they are abroad but also make loans to foreign enterprises, invest capital abroad, underwrite foreign bond issues in this country, and perform a number of services that are indispensable to international finance. These large transactions are seldom of immediate concern to the average depositor. More important to him are the ways in which banks can expedite the transfer of money from one country to another.

As you know, if you have traveled abroad and observed that the buying power of your dollar varies from one country to another, foreign currencies fluctuate in value. There are several factors that influence this fluctuation—political conditions, balance of trade, and currency manipulation. Since gold is no longer the international currency standard, a government may arbitrarily fix the value of its own currency in relation to other currencies. The United States devalued the dollar in the thirties so that foreign currencies would buy more goods here and thus stimulate trade. Similarly, Mexico devalued the peso from twelve and one half to eight cents. (I was there at the time and saw at first hand what a difference it made to tourists.) We could buy more goods with our dollars, but it was hard on the shopkeepers. I recall a day after the Second World War when I sat in the council room of the Bank of England, looking out on the bomb-shattered St. Paul's cathedral, reflecting that the church had suffered from the bombs intended for the bank. That day the British Government devalued the pound to $2.80 to stimulate foreign trade.

Such are the factors that cause the fluctuations, and you can observe them yourself if you read the reports on foreign currencies on the financial pages of the newspapers. Because of these variations and the regulations which governments impose on the transfer of their currencies, the services of the bank are essential if you want to transfer money abroad.

If you want to buy a dress in Paris, your bank will sell you a draft in francs to pay for it; if you want to send to England for books, your bank can provide you with a draft in sterling. If you want to send money to friends and relatives in a foreign country, the bank can do it for you, provided it can be done at all. Since the last war, currency restrictions are so numerous and changes so frequent that you should seek information on them from your bank before sending money abroad. All banks can provide you with information and service through their correspondents and can put you in touch with banking and commercial interests all over the world.

Many of our depositors sent regular remittances to relatives or employees abroad. Mrs. Cross had a sister in Berne, Switzerland, whom she supported. Her instructions to the bank would read: "On the 3rd day of each month until further notice please send a draft for the equivalent of $200 in Swiss francs to my sister, Miss X, and the equivalent of $500 at Christmas and on her birthday, June 10." Under those instructions the bank would make the transfer through its correspondent in Berne, charge the cost of the draft and the service charge against Mrs. Cross's checking account, and advise her. On receiving the advice, Mrs. Cross would make the record of the withdrawal in her checkbook, just as she would if she had written the check herself. If there were drastic changes in the relative value of the currencies, we would advise her and she would revise her instructions to meet the situation.

At Christmas time the foreign-exchange window was the busiest spot in the bank as people bought drafts to send to friends and relatives abroad. Many people send money abroad at Christmas, and many make the mistake of sending currency in the mail with a Christmas card or package. It has little chance of ever reaching its destination. One rather needy depositor told me she had bought some foreign currency in a place that had had it for sale "at bargain rates"—presumably black-market rates. But her relatives in Europe never got it (assuming it was worth anything); it was confiscated by postal authorities or simply looted.

There are some countries with which the United States does not have normal commercial relations. If you want to send money to relatives in these countries, by all means consult your bank first. If there is any way of doing it, the bank can do it for you and you will have some assurance that your money will reach its destination.

Beginning with the elementary procedures that I learned on my first European trip and lessons I learned from Morgan and from Hambro's, I found that the foreign banking service I was asked to provide for clients could become very complicated indeed. One of our depositors was a distinguished American woman who had married, as her first husband, a national of a Baltic country that had later come under the domination of Soviet Russia. She had had two sons by him: one had emigrated to England, where he had become a prominent political figure of the Left, and the other had kept his native citizenship and become an eminent diplomat and an authority on international affairs. After the death of her first husband, this lady had married a Frenchman and they had returned to America to live. When she died, her two sons by her first husband inherited her estate, which was settled by our bank.

Shortly before the Second World War, the two sons came with their families to receive their inheritance. Out of it they purchased an annuity for their mother's American housekeeper, of whom she had been very fond. They planned to take their securities and money back to Europe with them, and as they had only a few days before sailing I was hard pressed to settle their affairs in time for their departure. Then they changed their minds. The war in Europe seemed inevitable and they decided that their money would be safer here. So they opened accounts in the bank for their wives and placed their securities in custody accounts in their own names. They rewarded me for my feverish efforts by bringing to the bank as a gift a bronze statue of a gladiator, one of their mother's cherished possessions. Then they left for their respective homes abroad.

During the war it was easy enough for us to send money to the British politician, but it was impossible to transfer any to the diplomat who had returned to his native land. Through the diplomatic pouch I received from him an urgent request for food; he and his family were literally starving. After consulting the president of the bank, who agreed that it was not orthodox banking procedure but something which had to be done anyway, I arranged for food parcels to be sent to the diplomat throughout the war, and they kept him and his family alive.

After the war, the Englishman had to transfer all his holdings to England, according to new regulations. The diplomat came to America to live but decided that it was not a safe place for his money and had us transfer $25,000 to a Swiss bank, since he thought the Swiss franc a more stable currency. The entire estate required services that only a bank could perform. It was fortunate that the boys' mother had made the bank her executor; otherwise a fortune might have been lost in the disorder of the war.

On later trips to England I visited the British politician, who had become something of a Left-Wing firebrand. One day I handed the hall porter of my hotel in London a list of my appointments for the day and asked him to look up the telephone numbers. When he saw that I was seeing a radical Member of Parliament and an extremely conservative member of the House of Lords, who had inherited one of the oldest titles in the realm, he shook his head and warned me not to tell either one of them that I knew the other.

When I returned from my first trip to Europe aboard the *Leviathan,* I was seated at the same table as Dr. Bernard, a well-known surgeon, and his wife. The doctor had gone to England to perform a heart operation, and as his fee he had received a check for £1,000 and some bonds of Great Britain. He had not the slightest knowledge of financial affairs, and he asked me how he should handle these foreign matters. Cashing the check was simple enough. As for the bonds, he could either sell them through our bank's special foreign broker or keep them until they matured and put the coupons in the collections department of our bank, to be collected, as they became due, at the rate of exchange that prevailed on the day they were due.

Later he brought to me his investments to be reviewed. He and his wife had invested heavily in foreign bonds because they paid a high rate of interest, but now they were worried about their value. The bonds included issues by the governments of Peru and Bolivia, the transit system of Rio de Janeiro, and other foreign issues. There were many thousand dollars' worth, at face value, but the bonds were declining in market value to sixty cents on the dollar and lower and some were about to default. With the bank's help, the doctor sold them all for the best price he could get and then reinvested in safer securities. The bank's knowledge of foreign investments saved him from a heavy loss and helped him to rebuild his holdings.

I sometimes went to dinner at the Bernards', and on one occasion I remarked how good the green turtle soup was. Dr. and Mrs. Bernard were obviously pleased that I liked it. After dinner they took me down to the basement and turned on the light. There, row on row, sat dozens of live turtles, each waiting its turn to go into the soup. Somehow I never ate it again with as much relish.

⚜ ⚜ ⚜

When I returned from my European trip, with a new title, my status at the bank seemed to have changed. I was no longer just a young girl who worked there but, rather, the friend and confidante of many of our clients—and I began to handle more and more of their affairs. I had a new assurance and an additional understanding of finance, and I began to be more involved in what was to be my major function as a counselor—assisting women depositors in investing their money.

CHAPTER FIVE

PUTTING YOUR MONEY TO WORK

For riches certainly make themselves wings.
—Proverbs

During my first years in the ladies' department, the women who came to me usually asked me questions about routine banking matters: how to open an account, how to keep a checkbook, how to carry money abroad when they traveled. Few of them ever asked me about investments. At that time women of property had their holdings in real estate, mortgages, or high-grade bonds, given to them by, or inherited from, their fathers or husbands. These were long-term investments—the women had only to collect the interest —and when the time came to reinvest money they were more likely to consult their lawyers or real-estate dealers than the bank. But in the early twenties more and more investors began to buy stocks in corporations and women became aware of a field of investment that was new to them and that could bring them much larger returns than their old conservative securities. When more and more women started asking me about stocks, a whole new area of banking procedure opened up to me; I spent more time with our investment officers and studied the entire range of corporate investments exhaustively. Eventually investing money for women became the most important part of my work.

Still I stayed at my desk outside the "Gold Room": there I was more accessible to the women who wanted to consult me and I could keep up a more intimate contact with them.

One day a woman who looked familiar approached my desk. She was Miss Altschul, who had been one of my teachers in high school twelve years before. She looked somewhat as I remembered her—tall and thin, wearing a white shirtwaist and tie, her red hair coiled on her head—and she still made the emphatic pointing gestures that sometimes become second nature to schoolteachers. I had a kindly recollection of her, because she had, without much justification, passed me in German, allaying my apprehension about my father's reaction to my low grade by saying, "I'm sure you'll learn to do better." Far from being a figure of authority, she was shy and nervous. She told me that she had read in the paper that I had been made an officer of the bank and that she had come to me for advice.

It is always gratifying to have your old schoolteacher come to you for advice; it gives you a pleasant feeling of achievement. But I did not press her; she seemed so uneasy. She wanted to open a checking account but she did not know how to go about it and had never learned to keep a checkbook. She drew something from her handbag and clutched it to her; it was, she said, a very large check, and she seemed reluctant to part with it. But—she smiled—we were old friends, both of the same German community; so she handed me a check for $11,000. It represented her inheritance from her mother. She wanted to do something with it that would keep it absolutely safe but would provide her with some income. She could continue to live on her teacher's salary, but it was so small that she had never been able to save very much. I let her tell me her problem in her own way without interrupting her, and after a while she was quite at ease and we began to consider how we might handle her money.

First we opened a checking account. She demurred a little at the $1,000 minimum balance but was finally convinced that it was worth while.

Next we took $2,500 and added it to her small savings account. Since her income was so small, it would be wise to keep something on hand in case of emergency, without having to liquidate securities, possibly at an inopportune time, and it would also be a good idea to have money in reserve to invest if an unusually good opportunity came up.

Next we set aside $5,000 to invest in the highest grade preferred stocks that would guarantee an annual 5 per cent interest. Since her account was small and her future security depended on it, a conservative investment that would bring a good income seemed prudent for the time being. We chose preferred stocks issued at a fixed par value and paying a fixed rate of interest for as long as the owner wished to keep them—that is, they could not be called in by the company that issued them. Miss Altschul was too inexperienced to know how to handle anything but the simplest kind of stock.

It was also important for Miss Altschul to increase her holdings. So we earmarked the remaining $2,500 to invest in *growth stocks*, in this case the common stocks of leading industries which could be expected to expand. I offered her the names of five or six such companies and she selected three—American Telephone & Telegraph, General Electric, and Standard Oil of New Jersey. On her instructions the bank purchased the stocks in her name through its broker, charging her only the fixed brokerage fee and a small service charge to cover the costs of the transfer and delivery of the stocks. Thus Miss Altschul had a small, secure portfolio of stock and some money in reserve.

She came to me in 1933, early in the depression, when some of our common stocks had fallen in market value below the price she had paid for them. She came in and complained that her investments were deteriorating. I showed her that her preferred stocks (the larger part of her portfolio) had risen in value, that she was not in an alarming situation. In fact, I recommended that she take one half of her savings account and buy more of the same common stocks while the price was low, pointing out that (in the case of A. T. & T.) people could be expected to use more and more telephones eventually, that (in the case of General Electric) the use of electrical appliances was destined to increase, and that the prospect of the widespread use of oil heating would tend to make oil stocks more valuable. I said that such shares would increase in value despite this temporary drop. By this time Miss Altschul had confidence in me, and she bought the additional shares. And I think that she was beginning to enjoy the game of investing. Indeed, she later became so enthusiastic about it that I felt that I should restrain her tactfully from following some of her more adventurous impulses. A bank cannot and will not tell you what to buy or what not to—it is your money—but a bank will try to advise you against an investment that seems too risky or unsuitable to your needs and will make suggestions.

The dividends from Miss Altschul's securities were paid directly into her account in the bank and she was notified of each sum as it was received. She soon found that her income was a good deal more than she had ever expected. Moreover, she had become quite knowledgeable about investing and was quick to learn how to handle her own affairs—in fact, rather quicker than I had been at German.

One day she brought her father in to see me. An elderly, white-haired man, he thanked me graciously for all I had done for him and his daughter. For him? I wondered. I had not thought he was dependent on her. Then he explained that he had had a small amount of money too, that each transaction that Miss Altschul had made through the bank had been duplicated for him—unbeknownst to me—and that he had enjoyed a similar increase of fortune. This was foresighted of Miss Altschul, for she later inherited his estate, and that, plus her own holdings, enabled her to realize the dream of her life: to travel as she pleased.

When she retired from teaching and went on her travels, she left her affairs in the hands of the bank by opening a custody account: she left her stocks and bonds in the bank's care. The bank clipped the coupons of her bonds at the proper times and deposited the interest in her account. She also had some callable stocks—that is, stock that the issuing corporation could call in by repaying the principal. When such stocks were called, the bank redeemed them and added the principal to Miss Altschul's account. It acted as a financial secretary while Miss Altschul was away, and she did not have to worry about her securities.

Thus Miss Altschul's modest inheritance was built into a substantial sum that enabled her to travel at will and, at her death, to leave a respectable estate, which the bank administered under the terms of her will, drawn by her attorney, naming the bank as executor.

⚜ ⚜ ⚜

Miss Langham, who was also a schoolteacher in her middle years, had a somewhat different problem. Like Miss Altschul, she was rather shy and reluctant to entrust her financial affairs to anyone. She had been a depositor of the bank for many years and we knew her well by sight, but she had never spoken to anyone except the teller who accepted her deposits. She was unprepossessing in appearance and self-effacing. When she finally decided to speak to me, it was because she had learned something that would drastically alter her plans for the future. Her doctor had just told her that she would have to work less and guard her health and that she would never be very well again.

She was nervous, and she trembled as she told me her story. Her parents, both teachers, had had two children, herself and a brother, a successful engineer who had had the burden of an invalid wife and two children of his own. Her father had been injured in a fall, and the care of him and her aging mother had fallen to her. They had had a fine old house near a small village upstate, filled with valuable antiques and heirlooms. After both her parents and her brother had died, she had sold it, realizing about $14,000 from the property and from those family treasures she had not kept for herself. She had settled in a small apartment in New York City, where she taught in a college.

Over a period of years she had saved about $20,000, which was deposited in various savings accounts at interests varying from 2½ to 4 per cent. Now that she had the money from the sale of the house, her friends had told her that she should invest it in stocks that would bring 5 or 6 per cent.

She had nephews and nieces of whom she was very fond, but her greatest desire was to be independent and to have something to leave to them. In three years she would retire on a small pension, but because of her health it would not be adequate.

Our first task, then, was to invest the $14,000. We put one half of it in preferred stocks for income and the other half in growth stocks to increase her principal. Her investments increased substantially. Her savings remained untouched. (In view of her possible needs and her family's, she wanted them to be secure and accessible.)

The day came when the doctor told her she would have to enter the sanitarium near her home town for an indefinite stay. She rented her apartment to a friend, who paid the rent into her bank account, and she left her savings account passbooks with the banks, with signed drafts in case the money was needed while she was away. Her dividends on stock would be sent directly to the bank to be credited to her account. The bank would pay her bills as I approved them, in case she might not be able to sign a check. Although her situation was not happy, at least she had the peace of mind of knowing that her affairs were completely taken care of.

Several months later the floor man at the bank came to me and said that a distinguished-looking gentleman who declined to give his name wanted to speak to me. I had him shown in and recognized him before he told me who he was: he was the president of one of the largest corporations in the country and well known for his philanthropies. He told me he had recently been appointed a trustee of the sanitarium in his home town and, on a list of new patients, had seen the name of a childhood friend—Miss Langham. He remembered her well—she had been a pretty child, lively and determined—and although he had pursued her with attentions, she had never given him any encouragement.

"You see," he said, "I wanted to sit next to her in school because I was dumb and she was smart and I wanted to copy her papers."

It was hard to think of poor Miss Langham as anyone's childhood sweetheart and impossible to think that this successful man had once had to copy her papers to get through school. But when I thought of the money my clients had made on the stock of his company I was very grateful that he had.

He wanted to know the state of her finances: if she needed help, he would give it, without telling her, because she was still firmly independent. I told him that I could not tell him anything about her affairs, but I assured him that she had enough money for her needs. He wanted to know some of the companies in which she had stock and was pleased when I told him that she had done well with the stock of his company. When he left he gave me his private phone number and asked me to tell him if she ever needed anything.

Without letting her know, he had her room at the sanitarium changed so that she could have a view of the western hills that she had always been so fond of; and he visited her regularly until her death. When she died he wrote me a letter thanking me for having helped her.

The bank settled Miss Langham's estate, and after all her debts were paid there was enough left for a substantial bequest to each member of her family. She had been able to spend her last days in comfort, after having had a rather hard life. But I have always regretted that she did not go to a banker twenty years earlier: she might easily have been well to do long before her last illness. For years her savings had been kept in many small accounts, bringing little income. One of them had been in the bank in her home town, which had also held a mortgage for $10,000 on her house, on which she had paid 6 per cent interest for many years. If she had gone to her local banker for advice and told him that she had savings that would pay off the mortgage and still leave her a margin of security, he would undoubtedly have advised her to rid herself of the burden of 6 per cent interest and to invest what she could in preferred stocks for income or good common stocks for growth. In those twenty years—the 1930s to the 1950s—which were wasted as far as her finances were concerned, she could have increased her principal tenfold. She came to the bank in time to provide for her last illness and her estate, but I have always been sorry for the years of hard work and the strain of caring for her parents; it could so easily have been different.

⚜ ⚜ ⚜

Miss Altschul and Miss Langham were both single women of small salaries and limited means. But Mrs. Nelson, as I will call her, was married to a wealthy man who gave her a great deal more money than she needed for herself. She had a special reason for wishing to establish an independent bank account, and she came to me to discuss it.

The daughter of poor parents, she was born in a southern town. At the age of eighteen she married a young man who was also without education or means. They had one son, and shortly after the boy was born her husband was killed in an accident. She was still young and attractive when a lawyer from New York came to town on business and fell in love with her. He wanted to marry her and she hesitated because of the child, but finally he persuaded her and she went to New York with him. Their early years together were happy; he worked hard and became one of the most successful lawyers in New York. As his wealth and social position increased she saw less and less of him, but sometimes they traveled abroad together and they frequently entertained his business friends. Still she felt that she had failed to keep up with him. He increased her allowance far beyond her needs, and each time she entertained his friends he gave her an emerald necklace, a diamond bracelet, or a ring; her jewelry was beautiful and immensely valuable. They had a town house and a country estate, both filled with fine paintings, furniture, and objects of art. She had all the servants her position demanded. But their lives grew more and more apart and she suffered from the estrangement. In addition, her husband had never liked her son, who was a grown man with children of his own, and she knew that he would never leave the young man anything in his will and that her son would never earn much money himself.

When she came to me she wanted to accumulate some money for her son without her husband's knowledge. This was a problem, because he made a joint income tax return and her earnings would have to be reported. So we collected from various accounts in her name a quarter of a million dollars, all of it saved from her allowance and gifts from her husband, and we put it into New York State and other New York municipal bonds. These were tax-free and the income would not have to be reported.

Later her husband gave her gifts in the form of securities, about which she knew nothing, and she brought them to me to have them explained. As a result, since her husband knew that she owned taxable securities, she was free to acquire others, keeping the tax-free investments for her son.

Mrs. Nelson and I became great friends. She told me the story of her life, of her relationship with her husband, and of her son, with whom she spent one day a week. I had lunch with her frequently at her home and spent weekends at her country house, a huge estate overlooking the ocean. One Sunday before lunch a Rolls-Royce with a liveried chauffeur and footman brought an English stockbroker and his wife to the door. When I was introduced as a banker he gave me a withering look, as if to indicate that only *nouveau riche* Americans would have a woman banker around. Some years later I was very gratified to have him call on me, to help him with a particularly difficult problem involving a trust, and he became a regular client. That day, however, he ignored me. Mr. Nelson subjected me to a daunting third-degree questioning after lunch, but I must have passed it creditably because he later told his wife that I was a good friend to her and that he liked me—and I continued to help Mrs. Nelson with her affairs.

She liked to take her bonds home from the bank and clip the coupons in bed. She would take as much as $100,000 worth at a time, put the bonds in a little black bag, and walk a few blocks home with them. Bearer bonds are negotiable by anyone into whose hands they fall, and a richly dressed woman leaving a bank with a little black bag is an open invitation to robbery. I remonstrated with her, but she was stubborn; so I consulted Mr. Foley. Thereafter, whenever Mrs. Nelson left the bank carrying bonds, a bank guard unobtrusively followed her to see that she got home safely.

One day when I was having lunch with her at her house she told me that she had in her wall safe about $20,000 in bonds that had matured and asked if I would take them back to the bank for collection. But she had mislaid the combination to the safe; she would have to call the safe company and find it out, then bring the bonds to the bank. At this point her Japanese butler, who was standing behind her chair, said, "Madame, the combination is zero, turn twice left to ten, right once to eighty-six, left to fifteen, and right to zero." We looked at him in astonishment. "I have watched you open it often," he said. "I thought you might need to know the combination some day."

This was touching but also a little sinister. It convinced Mrs. Nelson that it was risky to keep bonds in the house, and I persuaded her to open a custodian account at the bank. After that the bank took care of the bonds and the coupons.

Her account continued to grow; when her husband gave her stock, she bought more of the same kind. She made a will in which she left her entire estate to her son, in trust for his lifetime, and then to his children for their lifetime. After that, the principal was to go outright to his grandchildren. Of course she did not tell her husband about it.

When she was ill for several months, at the end of her life, her husband brought her a will and asked her to sign it. It left her whole estate to him and named him executor. She showed him the will she had already made. (She told me later that he cried like a child: Hadn't he given her everything she ever wanted? What would people think if her money didn't return to him?) He assured her that he would carry out her wishes regarding her son, and rather than have any further unhappiness about it—she had already suffered a great deal from the distance between them—she signed it. It was, she told me, really all his money anyway. Certainly it had been, I reflected, but it was her care that had increased it, and surely she was entitled to make some provision for her son. But there was nothing to be done about it then. Years earlier Mrs. Nelson might have taken another course—but that comes in another chapter.

When she died her estate amounted to about a million and a half dollars; she had come to me with a quarter of a million. The half of this which we put into tax-free bonds amounted to only one sixth of the estate; the other five sixths represented the increase made by investing in stocks over a period of twenty years—a striking example of the different results that you can obtain by different kinds of investment.

I have never known if Mr. Nelson made any provision for his stepson.

⚜ ⚜ ⚜

Most women sooner or later find themselves obliged to plan for the future of their children or perhaps aged parents or an invalid husband.

Mrs. Sanford was one of these; she found herself a widow with two adolescent children who had nearly reached the age when their education would become an acute and costly problem. Still a young woman, of an aristocratic bearing and outlook far beyond her actual means, she had maintained a small account with our bank for a long time. (Because her brother was a broker who kept his firm's account with us, we had accepted hers without a minimum balance requirement.) When her husband, a fine doctor, but one who had never earned or saved a great deal of money, died, her son was sixteen and her daughter fourteen. She owned a large and very old house in Washington; it had been in the family for generations and she did not want to part with it. Besides the house, which, with its upkeep, was a potential liability, she had a little less than $20,000—and she could not count on any help from relatives.

A house, whether it is an ancestral home or one you have built yourself, has a value in your life that cannot be reckoned in purely financial terms. Mrs. Sanford loved her house; it represented her whole background, her social position, her children's future. It was obviously a financial burden, and I would have been tempted to advise her to sell it at once. But nothing is ever that easy for a bank counselor. I could only tell her that to keep it would require sacrifices on her part and the children's. She was willing to make them.

The house had one advantage: it was in the Capitol Hill section of Washington and could easily be rented. Otherwise it would have been too hard to keep.

Mrs. Sanford took a job in a doctor's office and even supplemented her small earnings by baby-sitting. She rented the house, sometimes for a six-month period and once for a year for $10,000, and took smaller quarters or stayed at the Y.W.C.A. or with friends.

Of her ready cash we put $5,000 in a savings account for emergencies—and, as it turned out, it was needed. The other $15,000 we put into stocks. I made up a list of twenty high-grade common stocks in leading companies of various industries, and she took it to her brother, who chose specific ones to buy. The shares were purchased through his firm.

For most women who were inexperienced in handling securities I recommended a custody account, but Mrs. Sanford's income was so small and the demands on it so great that I was reluctant to add any additional charges. She was a young and energetic woman and I wanted her to learn for herself how to handle her affairs.

Her son was given a scholarship to go to college and was able to finance his medical training with a loan from a foundation, to which the bank had directed him. At the time he finished medical school the United States entered World War II, and he went into the service as a surgeon. When he came back he still had to repay the loan to the foundation. In time he did, and he is now an eminently successful young doctor.

Mrs. Sanford's daughter went to a two-year college. Then she had a serious injury which required expensive surgery. This and Mrs. Sanford's own spells of illness exhausted her savings account and made inroads on her investments. At times it seemed that she would have to let the house go. Nevertheless, by the time her son was established in practice and her daughter was married, her investments were still worth $30,000 and she still had her house. At one time her investments had been valued at $41,000, but illness had reduced them. The house, however, had increased in value, and what had once been a liability had become an asset.

The house will remain in the family—and without Mrs. Sanford's feeling for it, I don't think she could have accomplished her aim: to bring up her children in the family tradition. But it took a great deal of management, and she always said she could not have come through without the counsel she got from the bank.

Here were four women, with very different needs and ambitions, whose financial problems required different solutions. Yet the solutions all involved two common factors—safe investments and counsel when they needed it.

⚜ ⚜ ⚜

From these cases and many others I learned what the basic types of investment are and how they must be understood in order to build a profitable portfolio.

The oldest type of investment is the mortgage. Almost everyone who has bought a house knows what this is: it is the pledging of property as security for a loan. It runs for a fixed period of years at a fixed rate of interest and usually provides for an annual payment to reduce the amount of the loan. Let's see how it works from the investor's point of view.

You may recall from an earlier chapter the Misses Adams, one of whom kept her cash in the books of her library. Most of their investments were in mortgages: they had about $75,000 in fifteen different ones. Some of them had run for as long as forty years, and they were constantly being renewed. These were the only investments they had and the only kind they trusted. Since mortgages are not easily salable, the Misses Adams needed a cash reserve for current expenses. That is why the older sister kept her money in her books: it was too much trouble to come to the bank to withdraw money.

One of the mortgages they held—on a piece of farm property in Vermont—had been renewed many times. Then the owner of the farm paid it off—the entire sum, $10,000 (called the principal). Most people would be delighted to have an old debt repaid, but to these ladies the payment was a calamity: they had been receiving 6 per cent interest on it, $600 a year, and no payments on the principal had been made.

So they came to the bank to deposit a check for $10,150, the principal and the last quarter's interest, and to discuss with me the misfortune of having $10,000 to reinvest. I suggested that they place it in U. S. Government bonds; a particularly good issue was available, and it paid 4¼ per cent interest. This was too low for them, and they did not want to bother to clip the coupons to collect the interest. I suggested stocks; they frowned. Their father, a conservative Vermonter who had believed only in land as an investment, had told them that buying stocks was gambling. Nothing would do but another mortgage at 6 per cent on an individual property. They would not consider participation shares in a large corporate loan.

The bank knew of no such opportunity at the moment, but I called the Adamses' lawyer, who had drawn the papers for their other mortgages, and he had just heard from another client who had a valuable property on which he wanted to raise money; so another 6 per cent mortgage was arranged for them.

The Misses Adams did not want to have annual payments made on the principal. These payments are called amortization, and they reduce the value of the mortgage progressively until, at the end of a specified term, part or all of the principal is paid off. Interest is paid only on the remaining sum, so the income from such a mortgage diminishes. Here is an example of how it works:

One of my clients, Mrs. Fenton, a broker's wife, had inherited her husband's estate. Among his securities was a mortgage for $50,000, on a midtown office building, paying 6 per cent. Her lawyer wrote her that the mortgage was coming due—that is, it had to be paid off or else renewed. Because of its location, the building seemed to be declining in value. The lawyer advised that before renewing the mortgage Mrs. Fenton ask for a $10,000 payment on the principal and for yearly amortization payments of $2,000. The new mortgage would be for $40,000, to run for ten years at 5½ per cent interest, the principal to be reduced each year by $2,000. Thus, at the end of ten years the mortgage would be for $20,000, and the interest payments would decrease by $110 each year as the amortization payments were made. This arrangement suited Mrs. Fenton; she did not mind having $2,000 a year to reinvest, and although the income was smaller the mortgage was still a very secure investment.

The Adams ladies, however, would not have liked that; they preferred receiving a straight 6 per cent year after year. Many of the mortgages they held had long since run their term: they were "open," and the holders could call them in for payment at any time. But as long as the interest was paid and the value of the property did not decline, it was to their advantage to let the mortgages run and receive the income.

If the person whose property is mortgaged cannot pay the principal when the mortgage is due or called, then the holder of the mortgage may foreclose—that is, take possession of the property, sometimes at a loss if the value of the property has declined.

Mortgages pay a relatively high interest rate for long periods, and in times and localities where property values are stable they are a secure investment. Many investors who have money that they do not have to keep readily available find that a 6 per cent mortgage is a good investment, especially if the property is worth a good deal more than the amount of the mortgage. But since mortgages are not easily marketable, they have a limited place in a small portfolio, although they constitute an important part of the assets of banks and building and loan associations.

If you hold a mortgage on real estate, you must watch the property to see that its value is maintained, that the taxes on it are paid. A new zoning law, a new highway, or any other public improvement can alter the property's value drastically. Nowadays mortgages are a rather special kind of investment and the most common investments are stocks and bonds.

When a group of people wants to start a business—a manufacturing company, a railroad, an airline, a public utility, or whatever—it sets up a corporation. In order to get the money it needs for equipment, raw material, and operating expenses, the group raises outside money by issuing bonds and stock, which are purchased by the public. These are of various types, and they are issued under the conditions stipulated in the original charter of the company, which is drawn up according to state laws. When the corporation issues bonds, it is borrowing money; when it issues stock, it is selling shares of ownership in the company. A bond represents a loan of capital by an investor to a corporation, with a promise to repay when the bond becomes due. It pays a fixed rate of interest during its term regardless of the company's earnings. Bondholders, as creditors of the company, have a prior claim over its earnings and assets: that is, a bondholder must be paid his interest before a stockholder can be paid his share of the company's profits and he must be repaid his principal when it is due.

Mrs. Fenton, who inherited her husband's estate, had holdings that included nearly every kind of security there is. When she came to see me after her husband's death, her affairs were somewhat disordered; they had been neglected during her husband's illness, and she was at a loss to know what to do about them. She consulted me about everything, and in the process of advising her I learned a great deal about the whole field of investment. She was a charming, generous, forthright person, quite honest in her admission of complete ignorance, willing to confess her mistakes, to acknowledge her losses philosophically, and to learn new ways of investing her money. She kept nothing from me, and although her affairs were sometimes complicated, they were easy to handle.

Her husband, a broker, had had about one third of his holdings in bonds, which he had considered the safest kind of investment. He had particularly favored first-mortgage bonds. These are secured by a mortgage against a company's property and assets, either against the whole or against a specified part. They carry a good rate of interest, which the owner collects by clipping the coupons attached to the bond certificate. Each coupon is dated and should be turned in to the bank at the proper time so that the bank can collect the interest from the paying agent. Mrs. Fenton knew nothing of this and, as a result, she irretrievably lost some interest that she might have collected.

Bonds usually run for a fixed term, and the principal is repaid only when that term has expired and the bonds have matured. But other bonds may be *callable*. A corporation that is paying a high rate of interest on bonds does not wish to pay that rate any longer than necessary, so when it is in a position to repay the principal it calls in the bonds. Mrs. Fenton, who had learned that coupons must be clipped and presented for collection, brought me twenty-five coupons worth $25 each—a little too late. The bonds had been called six months previously. Mrs. Fenton got back her principal, but the interest—$625—was lost to her forever. However, she accepted this loss cheerfully—and never let it happen again. Corporations show this possible call on the bonds and notify bondholders when bonds are called by publishing a notice in the call lists that appear periodically on the financial pages of newspapers. The bank follows these lists, and if we had known that Mrs. Fenton had those bonds, we would have told her what to do.

She also had a number of debenture bonds, and she brought them to me, asking what they were. A debenture bond is issued with only the good will of the company as security; it is not a loan against any real asset. Debentures pay a higher rate of interest and are only as good as the company's financial standing. Mrs. Fenton understood at once why her husband had bought these: his grandfather had been president of the company that had issued them. Thus, her husband had known the firm's history and had been perfectly sure of its solvency.

He had also bought some *convertible* bonds—that is, bonds that can be converted into other securities of the company, if the bondholder chooses to convert them, or that can be held until the principal is repaid. Mrs. Fenton's convertible bonds were good for one and a half shares of the company's preferred stock (par value $100) for each $100 bond. Since the preferred stock paid a higher interest rate than the bonds—even though it was less secure as an investment—Mrs. Fenton accepted it.

Mrs. Fenton had relatively few stocks, but she soon acquired more, both preferred and common. A share of stock is a share of ownership in a company; the stockholder's proportionate ownership is shown by the number of shares he holds. Stock is not so secure as bonds of the same company, since it represents ownership of the *net* assets of a company—that is, its assets after its creditors, such as bondholders, have been provided for. At most a stockholder can lose only the amount of his investment; he is not further liable for the company's debts. He does, however, share in its growth. The dividend on preferred stock is usually at a fixed rate and must be paid before the dividend on common stock; if it is cumulative and the company misses a dividend, it must be paid before common stockholders receive their dividend. Preferred stock is less risky than common, but it usually does not offer as good an opportunity for increasing the investor's holdings.

Mrs. Fenton also had some sound common stock that she had inherited from her husband. Both the earnings and the market value of common stock fluctuate more widely than those of preferred. A company declares its dividends on common stock on the basis of its net profit for the year; if business has been very good, the dividend may be very high. This will increase the market value of the stock, and a share with a par value of $100 may go up to $150 or more on the market. It is the increase in the market value of the common stock of an expanding industry which makes it a *growth stock*—that is, one that increases the total market value of your holdings.

Mrs. Fenton's common stocks were largely in railroads. At one time railroads were a good growth stock; now they are less so, since railroads are no longer an expanding industry. In fact, by the time Mrs. Fenton brought her affairs to the bank, railroad common stocks were no longer as promising or as safe as they had once been, and so Mrs. Fenton chose to diversify her holdings by selling some of her railroad stock and reinvesting the money in the common stock of public utilities and electrical appliance corporations, which were then expanding rapidly. She was so pleased with the results that she undertook further diversification and enjoyed spreading her holdings out over as many different corporations as was consistent with security. One day she came into the bank and said she wanted to buy some common stock in a large food corporation because she had just had a pleasant lunch with the wife of its president. This is usually a very poor reason for investing in a stock; however, in this case our investment department had looked into the company quite thoroughly and had found it very good, so I did nothing to discourage Mrs. Fenton. She bought the stock at about $100, and when it went up to $150 she sent me two dozen roses to thank me—for what, after all, had been her own idea.

Mrs. Fenton had spread her holdings over so many companies that she was always receiving notices from them that were, to her, incomprehensible. But after her experience with the callable bonds on which she had lost the interest she saved all letters from corporations carefully and brought them to me to be explained. "I thought I knew everything," she would say; "but now what's *this*?" One notice concerned "rights" in a new issue of stock by one of the corporations Mrs. Fenton had invested in. She had bought twenty shares of its stock at $100 per share. Its market value had risen to $150 per share, but the company, which wanted to raise more capital for its expanding operations, had issued more stock and given its stockholders the right to buy one share at $100 for each ten shares they owned. Thus Mrs. Fenton had the right to subscribe to two shares at $100 each: she could either take advantage of these rights or sell them. She chose to acquire the shares and, thus, had twenty-two—which had cost her $2,200, but which had a market value of $3,300.

Mrs. Fenton was the least avaricious of women; she really enjoyed investing her money. She had never handled money before, and it gave her the satisfaction that learning to do something well can bring to anyone. She was fairly wealthy and had no reason to worry about her investments. A good deal of her money was invested in bonds and preferred stock that paid a good income without involving much risk. But, aside from deriving pleasure, she wanted to increase her money for two reasons: to assure future security for her husband's sister, whom she had taken into her home at the time of her marriage and who was her closest friend and only dependent, and, at her sister-in-law's death, to leave a handsome endowment to both her husband's college, as a memorial to him, and to her own college.

So she watched the increase and the income from her principal carefully. She had bought ten shares of a good common stock at $100 a share. Its market price dropped, but, instead of being discouraged, Mrs. Fenton bought ten more shares at $80 per share. Thus she owned twenty shares, which had cost her $1,800, or $90 per share. The dividend which the company was paying to its stockholders was $3.60 per share. So the return on her shares was 3.60 (the dividend) divided by 90 (the cost per share to her), a *yield* of 4 per cent. When she took advantage of the right to buy a share of a new issue by the company for $86, she had twenty-one shares. The cost per share became $89.80. The dividend per share was still 3.60, so her yield had increased to a little better than 4 per cent. The market price of the stock at that time was $120 per share, so investors who paid that price for it and received a dividend of 3.60 per share were receiving a yield of only 3 per cent. And the market price of the shares for which she had paid $1,886 had become $2,520.

Since Mrs. Fenton could afford to take some chances with new issues of stock, she did so without undue haste and accepted temporary reverses without panic. Once she learned something about investments, she never repeated past mistakes, and although her holdings were widespread and complex, they were a model of clarity and good sense. She was a wonderful example to me of how a woman can handle finances profitably and enjoy herself. And her college and her husband's are eventually to receive very large endowments.

Mrs. Fenton diversified her portfolio—that is, she spread her holdings out over a wide variety of securities—for two reasons. First she wanted to maintain her income so that it would be adequate for the needs of herself and her sister-in-law. This she accomplished by keeping, or reinvesting, some of her principal in high-grade bonds and preferred stock, which paid a fixed rate of interest and did not fluctuate much in market value. Then she wanted to increase her principal also. So she disposed of some common railroad stocks that no longer held much possibility of growth and reinvested in the common stocks of industries that were expanding—utilities, electrical appliances, food corporations. This was a simple kind of diversification of funds that suited her purpose and reflected the changing times.

Another of my clients, Mrs. Stagg, had a different problem. She had inherited a considerable estate from her husband, a Canadian banker, who had invested his money wisely and conservatively. But these investments had become totally unsuitable to Mrs. Stagg's needs. She came to me with questions about them, and, being a very cautious lady, she inquired carefully into my qualifications. One day she suggested that she drive me home after work. She called for me in a chauffeur-driven Packard and took me out to Sherwood Park. Then she asked to meet my father and mother. I think she wanted to size up my family background before entrusting her business affairs to me. She invited us all to go for a drive, and we rode around Westchester for hours, getting hungrier all the time. Finally, when she brought us home at ten o'clock in the evening, Mother asked her in to have something to eat.

"No, thank you," Mrs. Stagg said. "I eat only one meal a day, at noon, and the rest of the time I just live on fresh air."

I took care not to make any evening engagements with her after that.

Mrs. Stagg came close to living on fresh air out of necessity, since her investments were not bringing her an adequate income. At our next meeting in the bank she showed me a list of her securities, all inherited from her husband seven years before. Her holdings consisted partly of Canadian Government bonds, which would have been tax-free to a Canadian citizen living in Canada but were taxable to her because she was an American citizen living in the United States. She also had shares of common stock in two Canadian banks; her husband had been a director of one of them and an officer of the other. Then she had some shares in a Canadian mining company that were paying her no income at all by that time. In addition, she had $15,000 in savings banks in Canada.

This is how her portfolio looked when she came to me:

VALUE AT HUSBAND'S DEATH	SECURITIES	MARKET VALUE	INCOME	
$50,000	Canadian Govt. bonds	$45,000	$1,500	(taxable)
14,000	Canadian Bank A stock	35,000	1,050	"
15,000	Canadian Bank B stock	40,000	2,250	"
	Savings account	15,000	450	"
44,000	Gold mines, Alberta	22,000	none	
			$5,250	

What Mrs. Stagg needed was a little more income—and she wanted to take as little risk as possible, especially after seeing what had happened with her husband's flier in gold mining stock. Her requirements were quite simple, in spite of the impression she gave of living on a lordly scale. Her car was paid for, and she hired the driver for only a few hours a week. Her rent, in a residential hotel on West End Avenue, where she had a small apartment with a kitchenette, was $85 a month. (These, I need hardly say, were the good old days.) Her expenses were small, and she distrusted anything speculative.

First we sold all her Canadian Government bonds—at a loss below their former value of $50,000—in order to invest the money in securities that would bring a higher return and to eliminate Canadian taxes. We disposed of the 11,000 shares of mining stock at $2.00 a share (on a par value of $10); they were bringing in nothing, and the chances that they would ever pay dividends were nil. The loss was $22,000 to her. Although the shares were valued at $44,000 at the time of his death, her husband had originally paid $84,000 for them; it had been his one indiscretion. But the sale of one half of the Canadian bank stock brought a gain of $23,000, which offset the loss on the mining stock.

Next we took the $45,000 from the sale of Canadian Government bonds plus $5,000 of her savings, making $50,000 in all, and put $35,000 into bonds that paid 5 per cent interest and $15,000 into preferred stock that paid 6 per cent.

From the sale of half the bank stock we had $37,500 to reinvest. We put $20,000 in high-grade preferred stock that paid 5 per cent and $17,500 in common stock at 5½ per cent. At that point her portfolio looked like this:

VALUE		YIELD	INCOME
$35,000	Bonds	5%	$1,750.00
15,000	Preferred stock	6%	900.00
20,000	" "	5%	1,000.00
17,500	Common stock	5½%	962.50
37,500	Canadian bank stock	3%	1,125.00
10,000	Savings	3%	300.00
			$6,037.50

Thus we increased Mrs. Stagg's income by nearly $800. And she had a far different portfolio, containing securities of fixed value to meet any cash requirements that might arise, with greater diversification, a better tax position, and an opportunity for growth.

Every investor strives for a balanced portfolio—one that contains bonds for stable market values and fixed income, as well as shares of stock in companies of various industries: preferred shares chosen for income and common stocks in demand at the time they are bought because they show possibilities of growth. It is easy enough for a large investor—someone who has, say, $100,000 to invest—to keep his portfolio diversified; but it is not easy for a small investor. How does a small investor—the woman, for example, who has only $1,000 to start with—distribute her holdings so that she may have the possibility of increasing her principal with growth stock? A good growth stock at the moment—let us say International Business Machines—may sell on the market for $650 per share, and the dividends may not be bringing a high income. Thus the small investor who wants to participate in the gains of a high-priced growth stock hasn't much chance.

It was to serve such small investors that mutual funds were established. They have two advantages: they enable the investor to share in a balanced and diversified group of securities and they are ideal for the investor who is too inexperienced or lacks the time or interest to manage his own portfolio.

A mutual fund is set up by a group of people—often stockbrokers or investment counselors—to invest money in a wide variety of profitable securities. Suppose you have $1,000 to invest. You could buy only one share—or, at any rate, only a very few shares—of stock for that sum, and if you kept buying and selling very often in an effort to increase it, stockbrokers' commissions and taxes would reduce your small gains considerably. But if the managers of a mutual fund can find 10,000 people with $1,000 each to invest, they have $10,000,000 to work with from the start and can invest in a wide variety of securities to make the fund grow and bring good income. They then sell units in the fund to small investors. You may buy units of the fund, paying for each unit a price based on the market value of the securities the fund holds at the time of purchase, plus a fee—a percentage of your investment—to pay for the cost of managing the fund. The management is composed of experts in investment; they avail themselves of the best market research and bring all their experience to their task of increasing the fund and producing income. As the fund grows, the owners' units increase in value; as its income increases, so do the dividends; and when the fund makes money, the owners of units share in the capital gains.

Management fees charged by different funds may vary; in general, 15 per cent of your principal at the time you make an investment goes for management and there is an annual running charge of from 1 to 3 per cent of the income you receive.

⚜ ⚜ ⚜

One day a charming woman with snow-white hair and lively blue eyes came to my desk and presented a letter of introduction from one of our depositors. Her name was Miss Fairchild, and from the letter, and from our subsequent talks, I learned that she was a very distinguished woman. She was an expert in the designing and weaving of textiles: she had studied in France, Italy, and Sweden; her work was often exhibited in galleries and museums; and she had written an authoritative book on the subject. She had also devoted a great deal of time and skill to the teaching of weaving as occupational therapy for mentally disturbed people, and many neurologists recognized her achievement in this field.

"I'm afraid you won't want to be bothered with my account—it's so small," she said; "but I hope you'll take me under your wing."

In those days the bank waived the minimum balance requirement for such worthy people as Miss Fairchild, and so we opened a checking account with the $350 that she had on hand. Her other assets were a small annuity that she had purchased from her savings and some realty bonds, which had dropped in value from the $16,000 that she had paid for them to $9,800 and which were paying no income at all. From her work she made very little, possibly $75 a month; she had always been devoted to weaving as an art and had not looked to it for financial rewards.

It was sad to see the meager savings of such a dedicated life wasted on such poor bonds. We sold them for $9,800—none too soon, as the realty company was dissolved shortly afterward. We put $5,000 in a savings account. (It seemed necessary for a frail woman of her age to have some cash reserve.) This left us $4,800 to invest for income. Miss Fairchild's annuity brought only $600 a year; the interest on the savings would be about $150 and her income from her work would bring about $900. Even though she lived modestly in an inexpensive women's residential hotel, it was very little.

I showed her some lists of stocks and soon realized that Miss Fairchild would never understand how to select them. She was all artistic temperament, and while it is not always true that artistic people have no head for business, it was certainly true in her case. She would have to be guided all the way.

I suggested that we buy ten shares of A. T. & T. at $140 per share; it was a good growth stock, always one of my favorites, and at that time it paid a 5 per cent dividend. The $3,400 we had left I suggested putting into a mutual fund of diversified securities that would bring 5 per cent and that had a good growth potential.

This fund was one of the earliest of the mutual funds designed to meet the needs of small investors. It was perfectly balanced, holding a large block of bonds and preferred stocks as well as common stocks. A unit in this company sold for $34, and Miss Fairchild bought 100 units. Each paid a dividend of $1.38 a year, or a yield of 4 per cent; and, in addition, each year the fund made a capital gains distribution of thirty-six cents, making the total yield 5 per cent. The fund had showed continual growth from the start, and the management had shown an uncanny flair for buying the right stocks at the right time. It could do Miss Fairchild's financial thinking for her. The cost per unit included a 15 per cent management charge, and the running charge was low. Miss Fairchild would now "own" fractions of several hundred companies, and she would probably never even know their names or the market value of their securities. But she could easily follow the progress of her own mutual fund units by looking at the financial pages of the newspapers.

Her A. T. & T. stock added $70 a year to her income, and her mutual fund units $174. Instead of $1,650 a year, she had $1,894—a small gain, but an important one to a woman in her circumstances. (In a few years her principal had increased 50 per cent, and in twenty years it had doubled.) She was very proud of her small "ready-made" portfolio and watched it with loving care, although she never had to do anything about it and she was spared any worry. Her income from her work doubled the following year, perhaps because she was able to devote herself to the work without other preoccupations, and she invested further savings in the mutual fund. When she died, at the age of eighty, she had received every honor in her field; but she seemed proudest of all of the growing investments that had dispelled her fear that she might become a burden to her only relative, a nephew—and she had enjoyed visiting his home each year because she had known that she was independent.

⚜ ⚜ ⚜

Small investors are not the only ones to whom mutual funds are advantageous. Mrs. Black, a depositor for many years, was the wife of a lawyer, and on his death she inherited his estate and received a check for $250,000 from his life insurance. Her husband's business partner suggested to her that she invest the check in a mutual fund for which her husband had been counsel—although he himself had owned no units in it. She brought the check to the bank and asked my advice.

A mutual fund is as good as the men who run it. The one which Mrs. Black was considering was operated by an old, successful, and highly respected firm of stockbrokers. Associated with it were top men in public affairs and finance. Mrs. Black was anxious to invest in the fund, since her husband's best friend was high in the management. She had no interest in handling money and no intention of learning, and so it was without doubt the best way for her to invest. The fund had four kinds of portfolios: (1) a "legal" fund, all bonds; (2) a diversified fund; (3) a fund for preferred and common stocks for income; and (4) a common stock fund for growth. Mrs. Black invested one quarter of her $250,000 in each. At first her return was 4 per cent, or $10,000; later she received $15,000. After ten years her original investment had doubled, and now she is more than a millionaire.

Her units are in a custody account with us and her lawyer has a power of attorney over the account. Dividends are paid into her account, and she does not have to do anything about the care of her investments.

Mutual funds are a relatively new kind of investment, but they have proved themselves and their popularity is increasing. Some of them are listed on stock exchanges, but most of them are traded "over the counter." The market prices of the units of the leading funds are listed daily in the financial pages of newspapers; the value of a fund is, of course, based on the market values of the securities that make it up.

As an example of the growth potential of a mutual fund, one large fund cites figures in a recent report that indicate that an investment of $10,000 in 1951 was worth nearly $40,000 at the end of 1960, including capital gains distributed to unit owners. This does not include the income received by shareholders over the ten-year period. Not all funds, however, have such an excellent record.

Mutual funds have become a powerful force in the financial world. Twenty-four leading funds control $10,000,000,000 of capital. When funds like these decide to buy a certain security, its market value goes up; if they sell a security, its market value drops.

Many mutual funds are highly successful, but, like other kinds of investment, they do vary. Some are well managed; some are less so. I seldom recommended mutual funds except in such special cases as Miss Fairchild's or Mrs. Black's—and then I did so only after our investment department had investigated them thoroughly and found them to be satisfactory.

For women who cannot or do not want to learn how to manage securities, mutual funds have their merits. But a woman who takes an interest in investment and is willing to give it time and thought and to seek the necessary advice when she needs it can do better, at lower cost, by managing her own portfolio. Managing is not so difficult as it may seem at first, and most women who apply themselves can learn to invest and handle securities very quickly and easily and can derive great satisfaction and pride as well as financial gain.

CHAPTER SIX

HOW SECURITIES ARE BOUGHT AND SOLD

> *There is nothing so useful to man in general, nor so beneficial to particular societies and individuals, as* trade. *This is that* alma mater *at whose plentiful breast all mankind are nourished.*
>
> Fielding

Mrs. Billings was the wife of a famous journalist, a foreign correspondent and roving reporter, and she spent most of her time traveling all over the world with him. She took care of the money in the family. Her husband was so generous that, although he was highly paid, he found it difficult to hold onto his money: he was always picking up everyone's check and giving handouts to writers who were down on their luck. So Mrs. Billings kept a firm grip on all his business affairs and left him free to concentrate on his writing.

She had a fair-sized account in the bank and a safe-deposit box, where she kept her few securities, mostly long-term bonds. When she was in New York she often came in to talk to me. Once when she had just returned from Europe by boat and had sat at the captain's table during the voyage she was full of enthusiasm for a stock which she had heard some businessmen discussing at dinner and she thought that she would like to buy some. I warned her that a tip overheard at dinner is not a sound basis for investment: the financial status of the corporation, the volume of its business, the dividends it paid, its possibilities for growth, the men who ran the company—all those should be considered.

But when she told me that she had been talking to the vice-president of Union Carbide, who had told her of the company's plans for growth, I could make no objection. I already knew the stock and had suggested it for other clients. That day she asked me to buy 100 shares of it at 39⅝, or $39.63 per share. She gave me a written order to purchase these shares and charge the cost of them to her account. I sent the order to the bank's trading department, which had a direct telephone wire to one of the bank's stockbrokers. He in turn gave the order to his floor man at the stock exchange, who went to the trading post on the floor where that stock was traded and asked for the price. The price was the same as Mrs. Billings was willing to pay, so the shares were bought, and in a few days the certificates, in the "street name" (that is, registered and endorsed and guaranteed by a bank or broker—in negotiable form), were delivered to the bank. The bank then sent them to the banking house that had been designated by the corporation as the transfer agent. There the shares were made out in Mrs. Billings' name. They were then picked up by the bank's messenger and brought to the bank, where they later were turned over to Mrs. Billings, who put them in her safe-deposit box. In a month she began to receive dividends; according to her instructions, these were sent to the bank and credited to her account, and the bank sent her a notice of each dividend payment received.

Her account was charged $3,962.50 for the stock, plue $10 for the broker's commission and $7.00 for state and federal taxes. The federal tax on a purchase of stock was four cents and the New York State tax was three cents per share (state taxes vary). To this the bank added $1.50 service charge to cover the cost of the messenger to deliver the stock. There was no other charge for the bank's service. (These charges have risen since that time, and they vary in different banks. Ask your bank what its charges are; if they are too high, you may wish to deal directly with your broker.) So the total cost to Mrs. Billings was $3,981. This was in 1934. Today those 100 shares purchased at that price have become 300 shares, worth about $36,000—not because Mrs. Billings bought more shares, but because several times in the intervening years Union Carbide has given its stockholders dividends in additional shares of stock.

Mrs. Billings had no idea at the time what would eventually happen to the value of the stock; she was more preoccupied with its day-to-day fluctuation, what caused it, why people traded in stock, and how it was done. I had visited the New York Stock Exchange, so I was able to give her a firsthand account of what went on there.

My younger brother Raymond had quit high school before his senior year—over the family's protests—and had gone to work as a runner on the floor of the Stock Exchange. One of the traders he had known was Mike Meehan, a colorful figure whom many people considered a rogue and everyone conceded to be a shrewd operator. Raymond had arranged for me to visit the exchange as Mr. Meehan's guest.

From the visitors' gallery I had looked down on a scene that had resembled Grand Central Station during the rush hour. Throngs of men had stood about at various trading posts or moved back and forth between them, while runners had darted about carrying orders. It had been impossible to conceive of that bedlam as a normal business routine without understanding how it was organized; and so I explained it to Mrs. Billings as Mike Meehan had explained it to me.

The Stock Exchange is an organization of stockbrokers who become members by buying a "seat" on the exchange—an investment that requires a large sum of money. The membership is limited—there are now about 1,366 members—and the members are bound by the rules for trading in securities which the exchange has set up. Only a member of the exchange can deal in the stocks that are listed there; thus, if anyone wants to buy a listed stock, he must do so through a stockbroker. The exchange has strict requirements for every stock that it lists: it investigates the issuing company to be sure that it is financially sound and that the shares have been legally issued.

There are now over 1,500 securities listed on the exchange, and each one is assigned to a "trading post" on the floor of the exchange.

(There are eighteen of these, each handling about eighty listed securities, which can be traded only at that post.) When a broker wants to buy a certain stock, he telephones or teletypes the order to his floor man on the exchange, who then goes to the post where that stock is traded and asks to have a price quoted. At this point some bargaining takes place: so much is bid and so much asked until an agreement is reached and an order placed.

Now while the value of a stock is basically and ultimately determined by the soundness and the growth of the corporation that issues it, there are periodic fluctuations in its market value because on the Stock Exchange, as in every other kind of market place, prices are influenced by supply and demand. If many shares of a certain stock are available, the price will be relatively low; if brokers begin buying the shares, they will become more scarce and the price will rise.

Thus the daily trading in securities causes the market values to fluctuate. Each stock has a par value specified by the corporation that has issued it, but once it has been issued and listed the corporation has no control over its sale and resale. A share is worth on the market what a buyer is willing to pay for it and what a seller is willing to accept.

So when Mrs. Billings' Union Carbide shares dropped from 39⅝ to 39, or rose to 40, it was simply because they were being traded at a public auction and their market price depended on the bid and asked prices.

Trading in stock is the business of the broker; the investor's interest is in the income he can receive from his shares and the growth of his capital. Mrs. Billings was thrilled by the increase in the value of her Union Carbide, so she wanted to try another good common stock—in this case A. T. & T., which at that time (1934) was selling for $120 per share. She did not have enough cash in reserve to buy 100 shares: she wanted to buy only twenty at 120. She put in an order at the bank, just as she had done for her first purchase. She did not want to pay 120½ or 121, as she might have to in view of the fluctuation, so she stipulated that she would buy only at 120. The bank then put through what is known as a limited order: it instructed its broker to buy the twenty shares only when they could be bought for 120. In a few days the broker was able to obtain them at that price. The bank received the shares and, in turn, sent them to be registered in Mrs. Billings' name and returned to the bank, where she called to receive them.

Most shares are traded on the New York Stock Exchange in lots of 100; if you want fewer than 100, the broker must buy them from an odd-lot man, whose function is trading in lots of 100 and then breaking them up into smaller lots for smaller investors. The odd-lot man charges a small additional fee. (The fee is set by the Stock Exchange; in New York it is one eighth of a point, or twelve and one half cents, for shares under $40 and one quarter of a point, or twenty-five cents, for shares over $40. When Mrs. Billings wanted to buy at 120, the broker had to wait until the price dropped to 119¾.)

Mrs. Billings never returned from a foreign trip without having heard of some new investment that sounded desirable. In many cases investments which I would have been impelled to discourage turned out, on investigation, to be very sound: Mrs. Billings, because her husband was a famous journalist, moved in circles where she met prominent businessmen whose ideas on the values of securities were based on a solid knowledge of the companies that issued them and the business factors that would influence their growth. Nevertheless, she placed her orders through the bank and often asked for counsel. She and her husband once made a trip far up the Amazon into the interior of Brazil, a most unlikely place for her to learn of any new investment opportunities, I thought. But she did, and she asked me if I knew anything about the Amazon Oil Development Company, let us call it. It was not listed on the New York Stock Exchange or any other that she knew of. Did that mean that it was no good?

Not at all, I told her. There are hundreds of good stocks that are not listed on any exchange but are sold "over the counter." They are dealt in privately by brokers instead of being bought and sold at auction on the floor of an exchange. Bank stocks, insurance company stocks, Government bonds, and securities of many large and well-known companies are bought and sold in this way. While the New York Stock Exchange investigates any securities it lists, the fact that a security is not listed does not mean that it is not a good one.

Mrs. Billings asked me to find out what I could about the Amazon Oil Development Company. I turned her inquiry over to our investment research department, which called one of the bank's brokers and learned that he could buy Amazon Oil over the counter. By further inquiry, the department found that Amazon Oil was a new subsidiary of a large oil company and that it was very promising and was managed by experienced and responsible oilmen. It could be bought for $8.00 per share, plus the broker's fee—determined in over-the-counter transactions by negotiation between the brokers rather than by a Stock Exchange regulation. I passed this information on to Mrs. Billings, who asked us to buy for her 100 shares for $800, plus a commission of $3.00.

In the course of years of traveling, Mrs. Billings encountered many good investments in little-known over-the-counter stocks: she had excellent sources of information about new enterprises, she learned to evaluate them intelligently, and she became a wizard at selecting good securities. I often wished I had followed some of the suggestions that she benefited from.

Mrs. Billings developed a keen instinct and a passionate enthusiasm for investing: she knew that her husband's peak earning years would be limited and she wanted to let him indulge his generosity as much as he wished and still leave them some security. So she wanted to see if she could make some money in trading in order to buy him an annuity which would give him an income to spend just as he pleased without upsetting her plans for their future.

Now trading is not the function of a bank; it is for speculators who look for large gains in short-term speculations: they buy stocks not to keep them for income or for growth but to turn them over as often as possible to make a quick profit on the fluctuation in market value. I told Mrs. Billings that she was doing so well with her investments that she had no need to resort to trading, but she wanted to try it. So I advised her to risk no more than she could afford to lose. I suggested that she limit herself to $10,000 and recommended a broker who had an office that was convenient for her and who had begun to cater especially to women. She had $10,000 transferred from her checking account to the broker and opened an account with him, and every day for a week she sat in his office watching the ticker tape. Sometimes the increase in the value of the stocks she already owned tempted her to trade them in, but she had promised to use no more than the $10,000 and to let her securities alone.

First she bought 100 shares of Commonwealth & Southern, a utilities holding company (that is, a company that controls the shares of various utility companies) at $30 a share. The broker placed her order by telephone, sent her an advice of the transaction and the cost, including commission and taxes, and kept the shares in his office in the street name. A few days later the shares went up to 32 and she told her broker to sell. He did so and sent her an advice of the sale, the commission and the taxes. After deducting her costs, Mrs. Billings had made a profit of $166; this was a capital gain, and she was required to report it on her income tax return.

She bought stocks and sold them in this way for several months while she was in New York and had the leisure to visit her broker's office. Each month she received a statement of her account from her broker, which showed in detail every transaction she had made, with the exact cash balance remaining at the close of the month, and a listing of the securities in the broker's hands. She felt quite pleased with the profit she had made; her $10,000 was now worth $13,000 in market value. Her cash balance was exhausted, and since she had resolved not to draw any more cash, she could continue to trade only by buying on margin. This meant that the broker would buy stock for her up to the value of—let us say—30 per cent more than the value of her account. She would pay for 70 per cent and the 30 per cent would be a loan from her broker, at the current bank rate of interest. And so Mrs. Billings bought more stock in this way.

But a drop in the market eventually reduced the value of her securities, so that they were worth less than 70 per cent of what she owed the broker. Since margin accounts are regulated by the

Federal Reserve Bank, the broker was required by law to have this difference covered; otherwise he would have to sell out enough of Mrs. Billings' stocks for what he could get to protect the account and she would have to take whatever loss was incurred.

In this case there were two things to do: put up more securities as collateral for the loan or put up the cash required to bring her account into balance. She came to the bank and told me a little sheepishly what she had done, adding, "I knew you wouldn't like it." I was already familiar with such risks; I had seen other investors take them and lose far more heavily than Mrs. Billings. Fortunately she had enough cash to spare to cover the margin without disturbing the thriving portfolio of securities in her safe-deposit box.

Another time she came in to see me, quite puzzled by a transaction she had made at her broker's suggestion. He had advised her to "sell" 100 shares of a certain stock. Surprised, she had told him that she did not have any of it. Then it would be a good idea, the broker had said, for her to acquire some, since it was going to go down. He had heard on good authority that the corporation that issued it was about to make public an adverse financial statement and that the stock was expected to fall in market value. He had said that he would "sell" some of this stock for her and that when the shares fell in value she could buy them at the lower figure and return them to him. She wanted to know what all this meant.

This, I told her, was short selling. In effect, she had sold some stock she did not own. The broker had "loaned" her the stock to sell at, say, 120, and the transaction had credited her account with $12,000. If, in a few days, I told her, the stock dropped to 100 per share and she bought a hundred shares for $10,000, her account would show a $2,000 profit.

And this is what happened. In this case, the broker's information had been correct: the stock soon dropped and Mrs. Billings made a profit. The next time, however, she was not so lucky. The stock remained steady. Mrs. Billings had had to buy a hundred shares, and instead of making a profit she merely came out even—minus, of course, the broker's commission and the taxes on the "sale" and the purchase. I pointed out that she would have been in worse trouble if the stock had risen and she had been compelled to purchase it at a higher price to repay her broker. She foreswore any further buying on margin or short selling.

At that point, since she was about to go on another long trip with her husband, she closed her brokerage account and turned over her affairs to the bank to handle in her absence. When she did this, she took the securities that the broker had held for her in the street name and had them sent to the proper transfer agents to be registered in her own name and then sent to the bank. Otherwise she would not have received dividends, which are paid by the company only to the owner registered on the stock certificates. If she had left them in the street name, she would have had to claim her dividends from the broker in whose name the stock was registered. Her only considerable loss had occurred when she had bought on margin. This had happened not because she was an inexperienced investor or because her broker was unreliable—he was a very good broker and what he had done for her was common practice—but because her flier in trading had caused her a loss that could have happened to anyone who was buying on margin at that time.

I have always discouraged depositors who came to me for counsel from carrying margin accounts with brokers. It means that they are risking more than they can afford to lose. The stock market crash of 1929 was disastrous because so many people bought on such wide margin. Since then, regulations have limited margin accounts and they are not so widely used as they once were. No small investor who is investing for the future should have one—and none should try short selling either. Your bank cannot buy stock for you on margin or carry out a short-selling transaction, but it can perform for you every other investment service that you may require.

Mrs. Billings made so much money from her investments that she was able to buy her husband the annuity she had always wanted for him, and it was a large one. Unfortunately he did not live to enjoy it long. Financially, it might have seemed a poor investment, but the pleasure she had in giving it to him, and his pleasure in spending it, for the short time he lived, were worth more than can be calculated in terms of money.

Today Mrs. Billings is a very wealthy widow; her selections of securities have always been shrewd, and she has taken very few losses. She had a certain advantage over the average investor—through her husband's connections she had access to reliable sources of information on stocks before the public became aware of those stocks—yet even the average investor can do very well with the information that is available to him through news reports, his bank, his broker, and the increasing variety of market reports that are current today. I think Mrs. Billings would have been a very sound investor even if she had not learned of special investments.

Recently I read the annual report of the Union Carbide Corporation and recalled Mrs. Billings' first stock purchase in 1934. No one had to be an insider to buy Union Carbide then; it was a well-known company and its future growth could be foreseen. Its sustained growth over a period of years has been phenomenal. It has paid many stock dividends, and now these split shares are selling at over 100 and paying a dividend of $3.60 per share. Moreover, the company's growth is hardly finished. The firm is one of the most widely diversified in the chemical industry, with many subsidiary divisions in many fields.

When Mrs. Billings began to invest, the old-favorite stocks—railroads and coal—were on the wane. After them, utilities and oil and motor stocks rose. Now the new emphasis in industrial growth stocks is on chemicals and electronics. Yet the sound old growth stocks are not done for. Mrs. Billings' portfolio proves that the stock market is a barometer of industry. She once reminded me, at a time when General Electric was selling at $80, that she had bought it at $2.00. And when IBM was $448 per share, she was considering buying more of it, although she had first bought it at $15. It is now far beyond $500 and is still generally regarded as an excellent growth stock. She knew that a long time ago, and she knows that industries that have grown phenomenally for thirty years still have great possibilities.

Aviation and electronics are the new favorite growth industries. The conquest of space has opened up vast possibilities to both of them. The glass industries—allied to chemicals—have profited from new trends in architecture in which buildings are made largely of glass. Supply and demand govern the growth of securities on the market and, in turn, these are governed by the times and their needs. New discoveries, new technological areas bring new opportunities. These are determined by what people want and need and can buy, and anyone who is reasonably well informed on his own times can choose a sound industry in which to invest.

It is the course of history over a period of years that really determines the rise and fall of industries. But in shorter periods of time other factors can influence the stock market. Elections have their effect, and the effects of war are obvious enough: armaments and food are in great demand and wars stimulate production generally and are usually followed by low periods of readjustment before another boom begins. The weather, too, can influence the market; a long cold winter hurts the construction industry and steel and allied materials are apt to suffer.

Other man-made factors also play a part. Today the existence of huge pension funds which have to be invested have a great influence on the market. Stocks bought by these large funds may go up. We have already noticed the effect of the actions of the trustees of large mutual funds. The mergers of large corporations may affect the market. And a recent sale of stock rights in A. T. & T., by which the corporation raised $900,000,000 merely by offering rights to its stockholders, is credited with having momentarily depressed the market for other stocks by taking that much capital out of the market.

But, in general, in a reasonably stable and expanding economy, the stocks of well-managed companies in basic industries are the best growth stocks. I emphasize "well-managed" because it is the forward-looking corporation that, through careful scientific research and imaginative policy, sees into the future, expands its activities, explores new needs and the means of satisfying them, and continues to grow long after its original product has become commonplace. Thus large oil companies carry on chemical research that may revolutionize metallurgy, an electrical company discovers a process that may have profound effects on agriculture and that opens new fields of endeavor, and Bell Telephone's research leads it far into outer space. The soundness of the long-term growth stocks in Mrs. Billings' portfolio shows that the stocks' possibilities are far from exhausted.

⚜ ⚜ ⚜

Jean Williams was an attractive young woman who had for several years been secretary to one of the vice-presidents of the bank. She told me that she was going with a young man who worked for a brokerage firm and that he was urging her to take advantage of the new Monthly Investment Plan for investors that the New York Stock Exchange had set up. By this plan she could pay the broker as little as $40 every three months for any stock she wanted to buy. If a share cost more than $40, then she could buy a fraction of a share. Her young man was going to buy stock this way. Was it a good idea?

Regular saving and investment is an excellent idea at any time, and on several occasions I have recommended the Monthly Investment Plan to investors who I thought were unlikely to save in any other way. I know a hairdresser who has built up a nice small portfolio through this plan, which provided her with the incentive she needed to save. But I told Jean that there was a better way for her to buy stock. I said that she should save up whatever she could each month until she had enough to buy a whole share of stock. On the Monthly Investment Plan the broker's commission for the purchase of stock under $100 is a flat 6 per cent, whereas on ordinary stock purchases the average fee is a little over 2 per cent. Like all other kinds of installment buying, the plan involves extra cost.

"Since you work in the bank," I told her, "your savings account is no inconvenience. And you can have all the counsel you want." Her boss was, in fact, head of the investment department. "Why don't you just consult him?" I asked her.

"My savings would be such a small amount," she said. "I thought I'd ask you about it first, rather than him." She added, "Ken says

I'd never save the money if I didn't have a monthly payment to make. And on my salary it would be a pretty small one."

"Do you remember Annabel," I asked her, "who used to be the maid in the Ladies' Drawing Room?" She did, and I told her how Annabel had managed to save money even on her small salary.

After I had occupied my desk just outside the "Gold Room" for a short time, we had become great friends and Annabel had brought her small savings to me to invest. I had made her keep a sufficient amount in her savings account for emergencies; after that, whenever she had saved up $300 she had brought it to me and I had advised her how to invest it. We had bought good common stocks for growth. On her thirtieth anniversary with the bank I had given her a diamond ring, which she had cherished more than anything else she owned. But when she retired on her fiftieth anniversary what gave her the most pride were the securities she had bought with her small savings—they were worth over $20,000 and the income would supplement her pension so that she could live in comfort.

"You know about what Annabel's salary must have been," I told Jean. "You can easily spare more than that. I'll make a bet with you."

So we made a bet with a lunch at the Ritz as the stake. She and her young man would invest the same amount of money each month, he through the Monthly Investment Plan and she with a savings account. He would invest through the brokerage house where he worked; Jean would consult her boss on investments and buy securities out of her savings. At the end of two years they would compare the values of their portfolios, and their costs, and if she was not ahead I'd stand her a lunch at the Ritz.

It took some sacrifice, but Jean decided she could save $40 a month, as her young man intended to do. I used to remind her from time to time that if she failed to put $40 each month in her savings account I'd automatically win the bet—and she would smile mysteriously but never say how she was getting along. At the end of the two years, when I was about to retire from the bank, she called me and announced happily that she owed me a lunch.

There she showed me the diamond engagement ring her young man had just given her, and then she told me how their accounts stood. His portfolio was worth a little over $1,100, while hers was worth nearly $1,300—and her costs had been slightly lower. She had had no reverses, while he had taken a slightly greater risk.

Today they are married. Each of them has a separate bank account and a separate portfolio, and they make a friendly game of comparing their gains and following the financial pages of the newspapers. I know of few young couples whose marriages have begun on a better economic basis—and Ken need never worry for fear that his wife will not know what to do in case anything happens to him. Their children will have twice the security and a much more prosperous home than they could expect if only one of their parents knew how to manage money.

These young people had no problem in choosing a stockbroker: he was employed by one of the finest brokerage firms in the country, which had been a pioneer in using the Exchange's Monthly Investment Plan, and he hoped to become a partner. She was secretary to the head of the bank's investment department. Both of them knew the pitfalls into which young investors could fall and knew that it was wise for them to buy stocks of well-established companies; and if they were interested in the securities of a newer company, they knew they could find out about its financial status, the experience and responsibility of its management, and its prospects for the future by going to the research department of the broker or the bank.

If you do not have such personal contacts, then your bank can help you. If you do not want to buy your stock through the bank, then ask for the name of a reliable broker: the bank can give you several such names chosen with care to suit your requirement. Its credit department is aware of brokers' business histories and financial standings.

There are large brokerage firms that operate in every part of the United States: nearly 700 brokerage firms have seats on the New York Stock Exchange (and usually several other metropolitan exchanges as well) and maintain 2,500 branch offices in 650 cities.

Other firms may be members of the smaller stock exchanges, but almost all brokerage firms have connections with brokers on the New York Exchange and can obtain almost any stock for you that exists.

Do not give your brokerage business to a firm that offers to make you rich overnight, offers "free" services to which charges or conditions actually may be attached, or advertises by means of charts or graphs that show stocks perpetually rising but never falling or partial graphs or figures that are unrelated to any sound economic index. The Securities and Exchange Commission (a federal agency) and the New York Stock Exchange have framed regulations that govern investment advisers, and they warn specifically against extravagant claims and misleading advertising. Your best safeguard against being misled, if you are a beginner, is to rely on your banker's advice.

But there is no safeguard as reliable as learning for yourself how the stock market functions, examining the history of corporations whose securities you buy, and maintaining a rigidly skeptical attitude until you are satisfied of their reliability and the reliability of the person or company that wishes to sell them to you.

Recently I received an urgent phone call from a woman whom I had counseled before I retired from the bank. There was nothing wrong with her affairs, but her mother's were in frightful disorder and she asked my help in straightening them out. I recalled her mother vaguely—Mrs. Green, who had inherited a considerable estate from her own family and from her husband and who lived in a small New England town, where a local broker was in charge of her investments. This brokerage firm was well established and known to Mrs. Green's bank. There was nothing wrong with its credit; it was not a member of any stock exchange but it cleared through a brokerage firm that was a member of the New York Stock Exchange. It seemed eminently respectable, and Mrs. Green, whose husband had been an active investor, considered herself experienced in such matters.

She had been warmly welcomed by the senior partner of the firm when she had first gone there, with a portfolio valued at about $75,000, and the young account executive assigned to assist her had been agreeable and attentive. He had often asked her to lunch and had knowledgeably discussed changes in her portfolio. He had felt that it was rather "old-fashioned," that it represented industries which were declining. She had felt that they were sound investments —her husband had chosen them—but that, nevertheless, the young man might have a point, since times were changing. So on his advice she had bought new stocks, in industries that she had never heard of and that made products she knew nothing about, at prices so low that she could buy hundreds of shares.

The daughter had known nothing about the mother's affairs, and the mother had offered no information. Over a period of seven years Mrs. Green had never mentioned them to anyone. Finally a neighbor and friend in her small New England town had noticed that Mrs. Green's standard of living had noticeably declined and that the old lady was quite anxious about her financial affairs. So she had written to Mrs. Green's daughter, who had looked into them and then called me.

Mrs. Green came to New York and I went to see her and her daughter and looked over her portfolio. It told its own story—and a very sorry one. In seven years it had declined in value from about \$75,000 to a little over \$30,000, and her income had dropped from \$6,100 a year to \$358. The list of stocks she now owned was entirely new, and there were thousands of shares.

During the years, she had taken out about \$18,000 in profits; in one year she had paid a capital gains tax on \$14,000. This had represented profit on her "old-fashioned" securities—such growth stocks as Mrs. Billings held—which her broker had disposed of to buy newer ones. This had gone on until nothing had remained of her original portfolio, and the stocks her broker had bought her had been turned over and over constantly, providing him with commissions and steadily reducing the value of the portfolio and her income. Most of the securities had been bought very cheaply by the hundreds of shares; most were in dubious corporations, some of which were close to dissolution; and nearly all of them had declined steadily. No wonder they had been cheap!

Needless to say, she was quite willing to close her account with that broker. She realized that he was a supersalesman who had taken her in, flattered her with attention, and persuaded her into risky ventures. She had not turned to anyone else for advice because she had thought herself an experienced investor and had liked to act independently. Even when she had known that she had been duped she had not told her daughter because she had hesitated to reveal how stupid she had been to let her affairs deteriorate so far before calling for help.

I advised her to get rid of all the securities at the best price she could and to reinvest in sound, established ones. When her broker learned that she had sought advice and that her portfolio had been appraised, he sold out her holdings without taking any commission. Now her banker takes a personal interest in her new portfolio, which will bring her income up to $1,400 a year. But it is doubtful that it will increase much during her lifetime—she is eighty-one—and now she must live with her daughter and she has lost the independence which, like so many elderly people, she had always guarded with pride.

What had she done wrong? The broker's credit standing was good and the bank would not have hesitated to refer a client to him. Yet if Mrs. Green's banker had been asked to examine her portfolio, he would undoubtedly have been horrified at the risky ventures, the constant turnover, the drop in income. And so would many another broker, perhaps even another member of the same firm.

Her first mistake was not in the selection of a brokerage firm: she went through the proper steps. Her first error was allowing herself to be persuaded to sell reliable, familiar securities and to buy securities of which she knew nothing, while seeking no other advice. Her fundamental errors were letting herself be persuaded to buy stocks of which she knew nothing and not seeking outside counsel soon enough after her affairs began to go wrong.

There were several danger signals that might have warned her. When her broker sold out her "old-fashioned" securities at a large profit, she might well have wondered what was so old-fashioned about them. Then she paid a large capital gains tax in a single year, and this reduced her profit. Her income then declined steadily. Since at her age income was what she needed most, she should have reviewed her situation sooner.

The answer to a problem like Mrs. Green's is to know your own portfolio, learn how to handle it, review it monthly, and keep an eye fixed on your objectives. Do not be beguiled by zealous and attentive salesmen who are working for commissions. The only reason for buying a security is that you have studied it, and the company that issues it, and believe it to be a good one.

CHAPTER SEVEN

HANDLING YOUR OWN PORTFOLIO

Truly wisdom is the pearl of great price.
—Proberbs

When I counseled women who came to the bank for help in their investment problems, I always tried to give them suggestions that enabled them to build the portfolio that suited their individual needs. For women who could not or would not learn how to handle their own securities, I recommended the kind of investment that would require a minimum of care and attention on their part: long-term highest grade bonds, sound noncallable preferred stocks, or capital stock of well-regarded companies that had little, if any, debt. I much preferred to see my clients learn to handle their own securities—so that disasters like the one that befell Mrs. Green could be averted.

When I suggested to these women that they could easily learn how to care for securities, to buy and sell them, to diversify their holdings according to their income requirements, to read the financial pages and follow the stock market, many of them simply shrugged and brushed aside the suggestion: it was too complicated. "I could never get all those figures straight," they would say. This reflects the traditional attitude that finance is a man's world; it is deeply ingrained not only in men but in women themselves. But when a few simple beginning steps were explained to them, these same women found them easy enough to understand, and once they became really interested they studied and learned with great enthusiasm and pleasure.

The initial advice was always the same. To invest, you must have cash first of all—cash to spare, beyond the minimum savings account balance for emergencies. People's circumstances vary, but I have always insisted that for self-dependent women, elderly women, women in uncertain health, or women with dependents, $5,000 should always be kept in reserve. When you have more than that, then you can begin to invest. Saving for investment should be a part of your budget.

Then, too, you must have credit. If you deal through a stockbroker and place orders by telephone, he will check your credit rating thoroughly. If you buy stock through your bank, the bank will want to know what your financial position is. Here your checking account with a minimum balance helps establish your responsibility.

Then you must size up your financial situation and decide how much you can afford to invest, after all your living expenses and all your primary obligations are met. And you must decide whether you want to invest for income now, or growth for the future, or both. Tell your counselor (either banker or broker) just what your situation is and what your objectives are—and tell him the whole truth. Otherwise he will not be able to act in your best interest. If your situation changes so that you need more income or can do with less in favor of future gains, then tell him of the change.

One of my clients was Miss Marston, a nurse, who first came to the bank to ask for the name of a broker through whom she could make investments. She was a woman in her fifties who had been nursing for twenty years, and by that time she was able to get very good jobs because of her experience and she usually had work. Initially she wanted to supplement her income by investing her savings. We recommended a broker and she went to him, and I did not see her again for several years. Then she came to see me, quite indignant that the bank had sent her to a broker who was not doing at all what she'd expected. I knew the brokerage firm—and it was an excellent one—and I looked over the list of her securities while she fumed with anger at our credit department, which she somehow blamed for the broker's alleged inadequacy.

The broker had suggested to her twelve good preferred stocks that paid 6 per cent. Some of them had dropped a little in market value, some had gained a little, so there was no over-all increase in the value of her portfolio.

I said I thought it was a very good list.

"But I haven't made any money. I've only had interest," she complained.

I pointed out that her portfolio was planned for that—and well planned, too.

"But I make enough income now," she said. "It's the future I have to provide for."

"But when you first came to us you said you wanted income," I pointed out; "and that is what you must have told the broker, since he's done very well by you."

She realized then that her objective had changed and calmed down. I suggested that she go back to her broker and ask him to sell some railroad stock that showed a slight decline and to buy the common stock of a very good utility company in the Southwest, located in a region that was showing a phenomenal industrial growth because atomic research installations had been built there. Little by little she changed her preferred stocks into common growth stocks, and she was very satisfied with the increase. Once she began to take an interest in her own securities, she watched her portfolio, studied the financial pages, and was on the alert for new investment opportunities. Her dissatisfaction with her broker was not his fault, she realized; she had failed to tell him just what she wanted.

She had been steadily employed for some time by a well-to-do woman who was an invalid. One day she came to me and said, "I'm going to buy a foreign stock. The lady I'm with has all her money in it; it's the coming thing."

As I've said before, I distrust market tips like these; they should always be checked. Miss Marston added that she had watched the stock—International Nickel—for some time; in five years it had risen twenty points and had never fallen back. I pointed out that it was a Canadian stock and that the dividends would be subject to a Canadian tax, deducted before she received them. That did not matter, she said; she wanted increase.

"You used to say you wanted 6 per cent," I reminded her.

"Not now," she said. She pointed to one of the 5 per cent preferred stocks that remained in her portfolio. "Those ten shares show a loss of $180. I'll sell them and take that loss and report it on my income tax."

"There are still some good 5½ per cent preferreds," I said.

"No," she said. "International Nickel. My landlord just installed a new Monel metal sink, and I notice that it's being used everywhere."

Miss Marston obviously wasn't just taking a casual tip. She had studied the security and checked it with her bank and her broker, and she knew what she was doing. She was dropping preferred stocks for growth stocks, and she was doing very well. She was extremely pleased with her portfolio, with her broker, and particularly with herself, because she could watch her own affairs with a knowing eye.

⚜ ⚜ ⚜

Professor and Mrs. Mitchell—they were both professors at a large university near New York—came to me in the early 1940s completely innocent of any knowledge of financial matters beyond the alternate checking account they had kept in the bank for a number of years. They had always been careful of money: they had even purchased a small annuity. But in the past few years their circumstances had changed: they had four sons—there were twins, aged seven, and two boys, four and five—and it had dawned on them that in several years these boys would all be in college, at almost the same time, and that they had made no provision for their education. Although neither of them had any detailed grasp of money matters, they started with the advantage of knowing exactly what they wanted and what they could afford to invest. Their next step was to learn how the stock market worked and how they could keep informed of the value of the stocks they would buy.

Besides the annuity, they had one share of Christiana Corporation, an unlisted stock of a holding company that controlled the vast interests of a very rich family. It had been a present from Mrs. Mitchell's mother when it cost $800 a share, and it had risen considerably. I suggested that they keep it. (I would not have suggested that they buy it to start with: it was too high a price per share for a small investor and it was unlisted.) They would learn more about the market by buying listed stock, but Christiana was a good security and they were lucky to have it.

Professor Mitchell made $12,000 a year and his wife $8,000. It was agreed that he would pay for most of the household expenses out of his salary, while she would reserve one quarter of hers to invest. They decided at once that she would handle the investments, buy the stock in her name, and have the dividends paid into their alternate account in the bank. Neither of them knew anything about finance, and I thought Mrs. Mitchell, although somewhat vague and untrained in anything but teaching English poetry, would be a more diligent student. The professor was inclined to be impulsive.

He said right away that he would like to buy some shares in a certain chemical corporation since his brother worked for it. I suggested that they first study the history of the company, starting by looking it up in the *Wall Street Journal* or the financial pages of the New York *Times.* (Metropolitan newspapers all over the country have financial sections; there is no one who cannot have access to some daily financial reports, no matter where he lives.)

That day the report on the stock read like this:

STOCK AND DIV. IN $	SALES IN 100S	OPEN	HIGH	LOW	CLOSE	NET CHANGE
CHEM. CO.						
1.6	120	39½	41	39	40	½

This meant that the Chemical Company paid $1.60 a year in dividends; that 12,000 shares had been traded the day before; that the high for the day had been 41, the low 39; and that the stock had closed at $40 per share. The net change for the day was one half of a point.

Then I got for them the most recent financial report of the company and told them what I had learned of the firm from our research department: it was a large company, it had the finest research laboratories in the world, and its possibilities for growth were enormous. The professor, striding about the room enthusiastically, wanted to buy 100 shares at once; Mrs. Mitchell looked approving when I suggested that they not put everything into one stock, that they start with 50 shares—which they did. These 50 shares at $40 per share, or $2,000, would bring them a 4 per cent return, as compared with the 2½ they were getting on savings.

"Only 4 per cent," Mrs. Mitchell said. "We get 5 from our annuity."

"Yes, but the principal will never increase and it will be gone when you die," I said.

Mrs. Mitchell became a devoted reader of the financial pages and knew exactly what she owned. Twice a year she and her husband came into the bank to invest $1,000. Their next purchase was Socony Mobil, because Mrs. Mitchell had a friend who owned some. I suggested that she watch the stock in the papers and read the company's financial statements before buying. She did—and she told me a little while later that she thought it would be a good investment. Her reasons seemed to me very sound, I told her, and she made the purchase. The next time she bought another common stock in a completely different industrial field, keeping her investments diversified over a wide area. Sometimes she picked up rights offered on a stock she already owned.

That portfolio put all four sons through college and fulfilled their objective. It is conceivable that, by systematic saving, they might have got together enough money to educate their boys in the ten years between the time they began to invest and the time when the twins entered college. But it would have meant a severe struggle and much sacrifice, and it would have left them in middle age with no resources but their salaries, which looked small enough by that time and which they could never expect to increase greatly. By investing, they had made enough money to put their sons through school and still have a substantial nest egg. Mrs. Mitchell, who at first had seemed to me the most unlikely businesswoman I could imagine, with her mind almost always on teaching and scholarship, had become a very good investor and thoroughly enjoyed herself.

⚜ ⚜ ⚜

Once you have a portfolio you must learn to handle it. A portfolio is a list of all the securities you own—and this includes savings account passbooks, which represent money in the bank that earns interest. So, first of all, you must remember to present your passbooks at least once a year for interest—preferably quarterly, since in most savings banks interest is computed every three months. The accumulated interest is income and must be reported on your income tax return.

One of my clients, Mrs. Wooley, came to the bank and turned over to me four passbooks, totaling $33,000 in savings. She was going to present her newly married son with a house, and it was a proud moment for her. As I arranged to collect the money I remarked that the passbooks showed no entry of interest for the past three years.

"No," Mrs. Wooley agreed, "it's just been accumulating. I have no idea how much it is."

The annual interest was well over $1,000. Mrs. Wooley had to revise her last three state and federal income tax returns, report the interest, and pay the tax on it, plus a penalty, plus interest on the unpaid tax. It caused her a good deal of trouble and took the edge off her fine elation.

If you have mortgages in your portfolio, you must make sure that you receive the interest payments when they are due, and if amortization payments are due, you must watch for these. You will then find yourself with some of your principal returned to you and will have to decide how to reinvest it. And when the whole mortgage is paid, you must take care of that principal too.

If you have bonds, you must clip the coupons attached to the certificate, each one stating the date due and the value. You should do this twice a year and put the coupons of each company in a special envelope provided by the bank for identification and turn them in to the bank for collection, with instructions that they be paid into your account. Coupons are payable to the bearer—that is, whoever has possession of them. When they are due, they are as good as cash and should be treated as carefully. Coupons are not payable until they become due, and if you clip them in advance you must deposit them for collection when due. If you accidentally clip the wrong coupon—one that is not yet due—the bond will not be marketable unless the coupon is restored to its proper place.

Coupons must be clipped correctly; a mutilated coupon may be invalid. I remember my own first experience at clipping coupons. One of our depositors stopped at my desk and left with me 200 $1,000 bonds of the Erie Railroad, asking me to clip the coupons and deposit them for her. As I was in a hurry to get to a luncheon engagement, I tried to save time by cutting the coupons off in lots of twenty-five instead of individually. I had just finished when Mr. Frissell, chairman of the board, stopped by my desk and spoke to the lady, an old friend of his. He glanced down at the strips of coupons and picked one up. A look of dismay came over his face: every coupon was mutilated. It took two men from the collections department the whole afternoon to put them into negotiable shape.

"Carelessness," Mr. Frissell told me, "is an unforgivable sin in this business"—a mild enough rebuke, but one I never forgot. He might justifiably have fired me; instead he apologized to the depositor for me.

If you have callable bonds, you will have to watch the call lists published in the financial pages of the newspapers to see if any of them are called; and when they are you should turn them over to the bank to be redeemed. If a bond has been called, any coupons uncollected after the call are no longer valid: you may recall Mrs. Fenton, who, when she was new at handling her portfolio, lost $625 because she did not know that some of her bonds had been called. You must watch these call lists, because the company will not notify you: since most bonds are issued to bearer, the company does not know who holds them.

Some bonds, including state and municipal, may be in registered form—that is, issued to the person whose name appears on them. In this case, payment will be made by check at specified intervals and you must make sure that it is made. If you do not receive a payment, it may have been lost in the mail; in that case, you notify the company to stop payment on the check and to issue a new one.

But if a payment is missed, either by check or coupon, something may be wrong: perhaps the company is in bad financial condition and is not meeting its obligations. If this is the case, you must decide whether to hold the bond without income or go with the company through bankruptcy proceedings. At this point you would do well to ask your banker or broker for advice.

If you own bonds, you must watch the bond price quotations in the financial pages. It is wise to check them at least twice a year. If the bond is declining in value, ask your banker or broker what to do. Usually it is not wise to hold a bond that is deteriorating in value, because the drop may indicate that the company is failing. Bonds are meant to provide steady income and full repayment of principal; they are not for gambling. It is usually better to sell them when they start to decline and to buy another bond or a good common stock if you wish to regain what you may have lost.

Mrs. Fenton, like many women of her generation, owned a good many railroad bonds, once considered a very safe investment. She learned to check bond quotations, and over a period of eighteen months she noticed a steady decline in the second-mortgage bonds of the Michigan Central Railroad, whose securities were once very sound. She asked me why this was and I consulted our investment department and learned that the traffic on the railroad's Michigan division had fallen off. (At that time railroads were beginning to lose business to motor traffic.) She did not quite understand this phenomenon; the Michigan Central had been a famous money-maker. A short time later she told me that she had talked to a young cousin who was hoping to attend a Michigan college on a scholarship. The scholarship fund was invested almost entirely in

Michigan Central securities, and now the scholarships were much fewer and smaller. This demonstrated to Mrs. Fenton quite concretely that the securities were losing ground. She sold her bonds and put the money into nontaxable State of Michigan bonds, which held a sentimental interest for her and also were very sound. She lost $100 on each bond, but she would have lost much more if she had held on to them. Her loss in income was somewhat compensated by her improved tax position on the tax-free state bonds. And, as she was generous and very interested in her Michigan relatives, she made up the deficiency in her cousin's scholarship. Eventually she sold all of her railroad securities.

Mrs. Fenton also held convertible bonds, which she converted into preferred stock at the proper time—that is, as stipulated on the bond by the company and at a time when this brought her a desirable increase in income. If you own a convertible bond, you may convert it or you may hold it for the full repayment of the principal when it comes due. If a bond is convertible after a certain date into one and a half shares of preferred stock paying a certain rate of interest, then you should look up the market value of the preferred stock and compare the stock's price and its yield with that of the bond. If the preferred stock brings an increase of principal and a higher rate of interest, then you may wish to convert it. This is the kind of decision you must make in the light of your own objective and the balance of your portfolio.

If you have preferred stock, you will receive the interest on it by check at a fixed time, usually quarterly. If you do not receive it, then you should follow through—find out the reason, as you would in the case of a registered bond.

⚜ ⚜ ⚜

Miss Griffin was a librarian who made a very small salary and had to take care of her aged mother. She needed income and was opposed to taking any unnecessary risk. So when she brought her savings to me to ask my help in investing them I suggested putting the money into preferred stocks that paid 5 or 6 per cent.

Her portfolio consisted of four types of preferred stock: non-callable, callable, convertible and callable-convertible. She still has her noncallable preferred stock, but, contrary to her original intentions, she now also has some common stock.

She came to me in consternation one day to tell me that the July 1 dividend on ten shares of preferred stock had been passed—at least she had not received it. Was the company insolvent? I looked up the stock and found that the issue had been called in April. She should have received a notice. She produced a letter from her handbag and showed it to me; she had not understood what it meant. I explained it to her and showed her that the conditions under which the stock might be called were stated on the certificates. The stock, which had been issued with a par value of $100 per share, had been called at $120. She endorsed the certificates and turned them over to the bank for collection, and she received $1,200. This was a nice gain, but she was very irked that the $15 interest she had expected to receive in July was lost to her.

After that she learned to examine her stock certificates and to pay close attention to the mail she received regarding them. One of her stocks was a convertible preferred issue: after she had held it for two years it was convertible into common stock of the same corporation. The par value of the preferred stock was $100, callable at $125, and convertible after that year into two shares of common stock, which paid only a slightly lower dividend than the preferred. The preferred stock was selling at $125 and the common at $135 per share. So, swallowing her scruples against common stock, Miss Griffin elected to make the conversion, thus increasing her principal.

She had a third preferred stock that was callable and/or convertible—that is, she could redeem it when it was called or she could take the privilege of converting it after 1950 but before it was called. Usually, when such a stock is called, the stockholder has no choice but to redeem it: the issue ceases to exist and will pay no further interest. She brought me the letter notifying her of the call and we reviewed her portfolio. She decided immediately to convert the preferred into common stock of the same company: it was a good mining company located in the state of her birth, and we knew it to be sound. The terms of the conversion were to her advantage: for each share of 5 per cent preferred stock (par value $100), which was being called at $110, she could subscribe to two shares of common stock (no par), valued at $80 a share and paying a $3 annual dividend per share. So, instead of owning ten shares of preferred, paying an annual dividend of $50, she would own twenty shares of common, valued at $1,600 and paying an annual dividend of $60. She realized that her risk was greater but, since the company was reliable, she was willing to assume it. By this time she had tasted the pleasure of seeing her principal increase.

On common stock the dividends are declared by the directors of the corporation, announced in the financial pages of the newspapers, and sent to those stockholders who are on record as owning the company's stock as of a certain date. Dividends are not necessarily declared at any fixed time, and if a dividend has been passed it does not mean that the company is in bad financial condition. The corporation may, on the other hand, have made a good profit in the past year and chosen to put it into research or plant expansion, which might well increase the future potential of the stock. This does not make the stock too attractive to the public—especially to investors who want a steady return on their money—but the management generally has a good reason for it. Stockholders of record receive a financial statement annually, which tells them of the company's status and its plans.

Professor and Mrs. Mitchell once bought fifty shares of common stock that paid $1.60 per share per year, or forty cents each quarter. They bought it in May and expected a dividend on June 1. When they didn't receive it, Mrs. Mitchell asked me what was wrong. I said that before they had purchased the stock it had been designated "ex-dividend," or without dividend. In other words, on May 15 the company had closed its books and sent dividends to the stockholders on record as of that date. Therefore, purchasers of the stock who had not been on record on the day that the stock was declared "ex-dividend" had received no dividend for that quarter. Professor Mitchell said he would never again buy a stock that was ex-dividend—it had cost him $20—but Mrs. Mitchell, who was somewhat wiser than her husband in the ways of the stock market, said that that was nonsense, that they'd bought the stock at a good price and it was steadily rising, and that even though they had missed a dividend, their potential capital gain was still good.

Mrs. Mitchell once asked about a dividend that she had expected to receive in July and that hadn't come. When we looked it up, we found that the dividend had been moved to August. There was nothing wrong whatever; the change was merely a bookkeeping convenience for the corporation.

⚜ ⚜ ⚜

An annuity is also part of a portfolio. It pays you a certain amount each year for life. At your death, the principal is gone; it cannot pass on to your heirs. As in the Mitchells' case, a joint annuity extends for the lives of both beneficiaries. The return from an annuity is calculated by the insurance company that issues it on the basis of mortality tables—statistics that indicate the life expectancy of the average person. You may recall that Mrs. Billings bought an annuity for her husband after she had made a good deal of money on investments and could afford it. It cost her $100,000, and he lived to enjoy it for only six months; so it was very costly. She would have been wiser to buy a refund annuity. This would have given Mr. Billings a somewhat lower income, but when he died his estate would have received from the insurance company the original purchase price minus the payments that had been made.

Mrs. Almond, on the other hand, made a very good investment when she bought an annuity. Her husband left her his entire estate of about $100,000, stipulating in his will that she should buy an annuity. She was sixty-four years old at the time, and the annuity brought her $6,000 a year for the rest of her life—quite an adequate sum for her needs. She spent her old age comfortably, reading Tolstoi and attending the Metropolitan Opera, of which she was the oldest living subscriber at the time. She even found it possible to give to a few friends U. S. Savings Bonds bearing the portrait of Franklin D. Roosevelt—because she admired him so much. Each month she received a check for $500, which she had to endorse herself, as proof to the insurance company that she was still alive and entitled to the payment. And each month her endorsed check came across my desk. Eventually she signed her name and added, "So sorry"—for she lived to be 104 years old! For her $100,000 she received $240,000, and the directors of the insurance company must have been chewing up their actuarial tables in anxiety, awaiting her demise.

The care of a portfolio is quite simple once you have learned it step by step. The best way to handle it is to set aside a definite time each month to balance your checkbook, check your income, review your investments, and read all the communications you have received from any corporation you have stock in, including financial statements. Then if you have questions you cannot answer for yourself, go to the bank (or to your broker) with them. If you have stocks or bonds that have been called or may be converted, arrange to take the certificates out of your safe-deposit box and turn them over to the bank for collection, properly endorsed and with instructions.

It is important not to overlook any communications from companies in which you own stock, even though they may look like advertising matter. And be sure to read the corporation's annual statements. These used to be dry financial reports; now they are more likely to be elaborate illustrated brochures that explain the company's policies and its plans for the future and give you an account of its earnings and expenditures. Reading the statements of such companies as A. T. & T., Union Carbide, or Eastman Kodak is a financial education, and it can be as exciting and informative as a good newspaper feature. Moreover, a statement is your company's management's report to you, one of the owners, and you should keep abreast with the firm and its progress or retrogression.

Mrs. Mitchell once came to me with a list of her holdings and some questions, including one of taking up rights to subscribe to additional shares in A. T. & T. When I complimented her on the neat and systematic way she had kept her portfolio, she laughed and said, "I amaze myself. My family always told me that I had no head for business, that I always had my nose in a book, and my husband doesn't quite believe that I really manage these things. I wish you'd tell him." She sighed, "I never knew I could handle business affairs because I never tried. Now I find it's easy. I'm even handling my sister's affairs for her. I wonder how many other talents I have neglected just because I never thought of using them."

Her system was to set aside a morning in the first week of each month when she had no classes. By that time she would have received her bank statements, annuity check, and any dividends that were due. She would shut herself up in her study and forbid anyone in the house to disturb her. She declared that she enjoyed these mornings very much and went back to her work refreshed. "Teaching literature involves a lot of indefinite and tentative speculation—and then you never know if it's getting through to the students," she said. "There's something nice and concrete and reassuring about figures. Now I find myself reading the financial page of the *Herald Tribune* every morning."

⚜ ⚜ ⚜

There is one other important aspect of the care of your portfolio which does not concern immediate income or growth but which should not be neglected. As an owner of a corporation, you have a voice in its policies; each share of stock you own entitles you to a vote.

Once a year the annual stockholders' meeting of the corporation is held. If the firm is a large one with many stockholders, a statement outlining the meeting's agenda is usually sent in advance to each one. Stockholders are widely scattered all over the country. Many of them attend the meeting, but those who do not attend may still cast their votes—which are equal to the number of shares they own—by signing and sending in to the company a written power of attorney, called a proxy, in favor of a person designated therein to cast their ballots. Such a proxy can be revoked at any time before the meeting and the stockholder may appear in person to cast his vote. Usually the majority of votes rules; if one person owns a majority of the shares of stock, then one person may cast the majority of votes and control the meeting.

Like other elections, these stockholders' meetings are decisive in electing the directors and endorsing certain policies. If you do not approve of any of these policies, you may vote against them. This lets the management know that a number of stockholders disapprove of the new policies. If they are approved by a majority of votes, the policies will be adopted, but a substantial number of negative votes may cause the directors to reconsider the policies or amend them. The president of a corporation was once given a large salary increase by a small majority of votes, but in view of the number of dissenting votes he chose not to accept it.

At a recent stockholders' meeting of a large corporation, 90 per cent of the company's outstanding stock was represented either in person or by proxy and nearly half of the votes were cast by women. The company dedicated a new research laboratory, where the meeting was held so that the stockholders could have a firsthand view of the company's progress in research and plans for the future. The items on the agenda were the election of fifteen directors for the ensuing year (stockholders elect directors and directors appoint the management), a split of the corporation's capital stock among current shareholders, a resolution covering the adoption of a stock-purchase plan for employees, and a resolution to adopt a stock option plan (to give executives and other employees the opportunity to buy stock at advantageous prices).

Any of these issues might have a considerable effect on the long-term policies of the company. The issues were set forth in a statement published prior to the meeting and the views of management and the persons designated in the proxies were made known, so that the stockholder, in signing over his vote, would know how he was voting on each issue.

When securities are left with the bank in a custody account, the bank generally votes the proxies on routine matters, unless it has other instructions. But if a major policy change is involved, it will ask the owner how he wants to vote.

I have often been asked what I do with my proxies. I think that every woman who owns stock should read her proxy statement carefully and, if she has no definite objection to any proposal, should give the management her votes, no matter how few they may be. A great many small holdings voted in this way give the management the assurance that its policies have the approval of these shareholders.

If you think well enough of a company to put your money into it and your investment is satisfactory to you, then your best course is to give the directors your votes. If a very drastic change in policy appears on the agenda for the meeting, then you should ask your banker or broker what its effect on your holdings might be and give your proxy according to the advice you receive.

Be sure you give your proxy to a person or a group whose policies you clearly understand: do not ever give it to anyone you do not know and who does not take a clear position on major issues affecting the corporation.

If you own stock in a corporation whose policies are not clear, whose financial position is dubious, then it is better to get your money out of it and invest it elsewhere.

When you decide to invest money, do not be afraid to go to your bank to ask for advice. Your banker will not think you are ignorant if you ask legitimate questions: he has seen persons of considerable wealth who are far more ignorant than you. Most banks have women counselors who are friendly, well informed, and especially knowledgeable about women's personal and family financial problems.

If you get advice on investment from any source other than your bank or broker, consult an expert before you act on it. A tip overheard on a train, well-meaning but uninformed advice from friends or relatives, or the label on a product you like is not reliable investment counsel. Don't invest in a corporation merely because you know someone on the board of directors or because it sponsors a good television show. Even if it is a sound company, it may not be the right kind of investment for you. And do not be influenced by any sentiment when you are investing.

I hardly know what to make of Miss Fitzgerald, a little woman with intelligent, penetrating eyes who came to see me about investments.

"Miss Armbruster," she said, "are you familiar with the symbols used on the stock exchange?"

I thought she was trying to test me. I assured her I was.

"What does X stand for?"

"U. S. Steel."

"Then will you buy me 100 shares and charge the cost to my account? And if I were you," she added in a friendly way, "I'd buy some too, if you have the money."

From time to time she asked me to buy stock for her, always using the symbol, never the name. She never asked advice; she only gave instructions. Her purchases were sound, and they always rose in value. One day I remarked that she certainly had good advice on her investments and asked whom she consulted.

She seemed a little flustered and said, "Don't ask me. I can't tell you that. I promise you I'll do nothing the bank wouldn't approve of, but I can't tell you the source of my information. I know I can trust you. That's why I come to you instead of a broker or the men in the bank."

Some time later I made a list of her securities, at her request, and was astonished at their growth. Again I said so, and she told me, "If you'll promise me—and I know I can trust you—never to tell anyone while I'm alive, I'll tell you."

Her mother and her sister had run a famous hairdresser's salon in New York, and when her mother died Miss Fitzgerald inherited her savings, about $80,000. Her mother had told her she should invest it in stocks, about which she knew nothing. Shortly after, Miss Fitzgerald told me, she began to have visits from her deceased mother, who instructed her to buy stocks by symbols. If she did not buy a stock, her mother reproached her on the next visit. Each time Miss Fitzgerald came to the bank and gave me the instructions. (In addition, each year at Christmas Miss Fitzgerald gave me a tortoise-shell comb from her mother's collection.)

"So you see," she told me, "this is my mother's portfolio. I haven't the slightest idea what is in it, but I know her advice must have been good."

I was too dumfounded to speak.

"Why don't you laugh?" she asked me. "Anyone else would. It *is* a crazy story."

I could only say that the advice had been impeccable. The original sum invested had multiplied five times. Now that Miss Fitzgerald is dead, and the trust fund she set up helps to support eight descendants of her deceased sister, I can tell the story.

The method worked for Miss Fitzgerald, but I don't recommend it for the average investor. If the investments Miss Fitzgerald had asked me to make had been very poor ones, I would have felt compelled to tell her so—and I do not know what her reaction would have been.

I am frequently asked when is the best time to invest. The only answer is "when you have the money." The market will always fluctuate, and when you have the money to invest you do not stand to gain by waiting for a supposedly opportune time. The time to begin is when—having taken care of your living expenses, your family obligations, and a reserve for emergencies—you have a surplus.

There is no investment that is totally without risk. Some women have asked me to put their money in securities that would involve no risk whatever. This is like asking for the Philosopher's Stone, the secret substance by which medieval alchemists hoped to change base metals into gold. There is no such thing. But if you invest wisely, learn what you are doing, and seek reliable advice, then your risk will be small and the possibilities of gain considerable.

When you invest money, do not expect to get something for nothing. In the twenties and thirties many people made fabulous sums of money in a short time, and we still hear legends about them. A great many more also lost large sums and were completely ruined. Nowadays the stock market is more rigidly controlled both by the government and the Stock Exchange itself; the dividends and gains are not as spectacular as those of the legends, and many more small investors now participate in them. But as long as we have an expanding economy there are gains to be made by investment, if you know your own situation and your objectives and take pains in selecting the securities you buy—either the old, reliable, well-established stocks or the newer ones which you have thoroughly investigated with expert help.

There is nothing so gratifying as spending money that has been earned, saved, and wisely increased. I have seen hundreds of women made happy by having money when they needed it. I remember one woman of modest circumstances who had a small portfolio. Her husband had been offered a new and much better job, but to take it he had to have a car, and they had never owned one. She gladly sold a few securities and surprised him by turning over to him the money he didn't know they had—because they had always lived so close to their budget.

"But why didn't you ever get the clothes you wanted to have if you had this money put away?" he asked.

She explained that she had foregone those extra luxuries just so they would have the money for something more important. Her small sacrifices had made possible this portfolio, which became the cornerstone of their lives. They later used it in buying a house and investing for their first child's education. If this woman took an almost sacred pride in her investments, she was entitled to it—and she was more than repaid for her self-denial by the happiness and prosperity of her family.

CHAPTER EIGHT

PLANNING YOUR FUTURE

For they say, if money go before, all ways lie open.

—Shakespeare

Before I had spent very many years as a counselor in the bank, I had already seen dozens of women come in to ask advice on urgent problems: one had suddenly found herself a widow, without the slightest knowledge of how to handle the estate which her husband had left her; another had faced a serious operation, which would change her life completely, and had had no ready money to see her through; another had had a portfolio which had once been good but, through neglect or mismanagement or the illusion that such matters take care of themselves, had declined to a fraction of its former value.

One of the earliest lessons I learned—and one that I have always tried to impress on clients—is "Don't wait until you are in trouble before looking for a way out of it." Nothing is more certain than the fact that you will need ready surplus money to meet the emergencies of life as well as its normal events. And many of these events are easily foreseeable.

When Jean Williams, secretary to the head of the investment department, married her fiancé, the young broker Kenneth Taylor, she talked to me about their financial arrangements. As far as investment counsel was concerned, she could have it readily from her boss; but women like to talk to other women about personal problems, and we had become good friends. For the time being, she did not foresee any great change in her situation, although she knew it was untrue that two can live as cheaply as one. She intended to keep on working, and with both their salaries they would be quite well off. But the time would come when they would have children and would want to buy a house; and they had other family obligations that would require readjustment. She was not relaxing her savings habits or her periodic purchases of securities, but she was keeping a larger margin of ready cash in her savings account.

About two years after her marriage, Jean resigned from the bank because she was going to have a baby. After the usual farewell luncheon, she made a date to have tea with me alone the following week; she had some new problems, and she and her husband were not entirely in agreement on how to solve them. When I saw her, she told me that she'd started a special savings account for the baby, for the clothes and other things that she would need. She'd taken up the rights offered on some common stock she owned, but aside from that she was not going to invest in any more securities until her doctor bills were taken care of and they'd bought a house. They'd been looking at houses and they'd found two that they liked. They couldn't quite decide which one to buy.

One was in a new development on Long Island: it cost $15,000, and they would pay $3,000 down and take a mortgage for $12,000, to run ten years. She asked me about the financing, and I looked over the proposal that the real-estate dealer had made. The mortgage would be held by a good savings bank. Jean told me that she'd figured out the cost: with interest on the mortgage, property taxes, amortization at $100 a month, and insurance on the house, they'd be paying out $2,400 a year—twice what they'd paid in rent for their small apartment in Jackson Heights. But Ken had had two raises, and they could manage that.

The other house—one that she'd fallen in love with—was an old house in Connecticut that cost $20,000. It had a $12,000 mortgage which they could assume, paying $8,000 down. It was in the country, somewhat isolated, and quite far from New York. Ken's commuting expense would be twice as much as from Long Island. They could get the house if she and Ken sold some of their securities and took their profit, and their annual expense would come to something over $2,500. In this case they'd have to have a lawyer draw up the papers; it was not all arranged for, as it was in the new development on Long Island. I reminded her that they would need a lawyer in any case. Once you own anything, you should have a lawyer—and you must have one if you buy real property. Even though a real-estate dealer has had a title searched, your own lawyer should examine it. The fee will be well worth it.

Jean wanted to know if the bank on Long Island that would hold the mortgage would confirm the title before lending the money.

Yes, I said; but I added that although a bank can do almost everything for you, it cannot draw up legal documents for you; in fact, there is a severe penalty for doing so. You must have your own lawyer for that—and you should choose him as carefully as your doctor or your broker, since he will have a good deal of influence in dealing with your affairs. And do not leave vital matters up to someone else's lawyer. Have a lawyer of your own who counsels with you and acts only in your interest.

I told her of the case of Mrs. Brewer, who had come to me in great agitation some months after the death of her father, a wealthy California lumberman. He had made a will, leaving one half of his estate to his wife of three months (who had formerly been his nurse) and the other half in equal amounts to Mrs. Brewer and her two children. Her share had been about half a million dollars. She had thought that the new wife's share, under the circumstances, was unduly large and had decided to contest the will. On the train to California, where she had gone to investigate her affairs, she had talked to a woman who had recommended a lawyer in Brooklyn. She had not known him, but she had gone to him on her return and had taken his advice *not* to contest the will. He had also suggested that she give him a power of attorney so that he would have full competence to handle her affairs. They then had traveled together to California to bring back all her securities, which he had kept for her. One day she had received a letter from him advising her that he was selling $60,000 in bonds to put into mortgages on houses on Long Island. Suddenly she had realized that she did not have the faintest idea of what he was doing with her securities, and so she had come to me for advice.

I had looked over the papers she had brought and noticed that the mortgages into which the lawyer was putting the money from her bonds were of a realty company of which he was an officer. This had alarmed me, and she had been quick to notice that; she had dimly suspected that he had been acting in his own interest more than hers. I had reassured her and explained what I thought should be done. I had suggested that she get her securities back and keep them in her own safe-deposit box and revoke the power of attorney. She had agreed, and I had called the lawyer, who had answered the telephone himself. I had told him that I had been instructed by his client, Mrs. Brewer, to have her securities turned over to the bank's messenger. He had refused, citing his power of attorney, and had said that he could deliver them only to her personally. He had also said that the papers on the mortgages were not yet ready. I had then advised Mrs. Brewer to accompany the bank's messenger—a competent trust clerk—to retrieve her securities and demand complete information on the mortgages. This she had done; and she had then placed the securities in the bank—all but the $60,000 that had been put into three mortgages. Of these, two had eventually been paid off; the third had had to be foreclosed at a loss to Mrs. Brewer—but she had felt that it had been a small price to pay for her folly. And by that time I had hardly needed to point out to her that she should not have gone to a lawyer of whom she had heard only through a casual acquaintance.

When I told Jean this story, she agreed that they must have a lawyer—and one whom they knew well. Her husband's college roommate was now practicing law with a well-known firm. He could draw up the title and also their wills.

As for the question of which house to buy—the Connecticut house certainly had more charm, but Ken hated to sell his securities. He had great confidence in them: they had already increased in value since he'd bought them and they were linked to his work and his career.

Then there was the problem of his mother. He sent her $30 a month to supplement her small income—the same as her other children contributed—and they would have this obligation for years to come.

I told her that I thought that this was the point in their lives when she and Ken should plan their future in every detail, even though they might have to revise these plans later, and so she told me exactly what their resources were and what their obligations would be.

They both had good savings accounts—several thousand dollars each—but since they were starting a family they did not want to deplete these reserves too far. They could sell securities to make the down payment on the Connecticut house and take a profit, but then they'd have to pay a capital gains tax and give up investments that were very promising for the future.

Jean had recently received a legacy of $6,000 from an aunt. She suggested that this might be used to provide for Ken's mother, though she doubted that Ken would agree. But he might use his savings account, she suggested, to help his mother, and she would keep her legacy in cash.

"I've seldom suggested annuities," I told her, "but, in this case, if Ken bought his mother an annuity, the rate of return at her age would probably be 6 per cent on $6,000, or $360 a year; and since he's pledged to do this for her lifetime, I think you could settle it once and for all. You might be tempted later to change the arrangements for some need of your own. This way she'll always have the income and it will be off Ken's mind."

Then there was the question of establishing an educational fund for the child. Ken thought it unimportant. Nowadays, he said, state and federal plans make it possible for anyone who wants a college education to have it. Jean thought differently: who knew what such plans would be worth in twenty years? She'd looked into an educational endowment policy; the weekly cost of it would be so little that she could manage it out of her household budget. Or, better yet, she'd just earmark the dividends from one of her stocks, which would cover the cost and cause no drain on their joint funds. That was the nice part about having your own portfolio, she added; if you and your husband didn't always see eye to eye, you could just go ahead and do something you really believed in yourself, without argument and without hurting anyone. And so she started the policy.

As for the house, I suggested that it wasn't necessarily the last house they'd ever buy. (This child probably wouldn't be the last child either.) The Connecticut house was old and needed repair. It was also isolated, which would make it difficult for her, and Ken would have very little time for home jobs while he was working so hard at his career. There would be more than enough for him to do around a new house.

Eventually they decided on the Long Island house. (They live there now with two small children and a third on the way. But they're looking for a larger house, which they can afford, because the one they now own, in a good suburban district which has developed rapidly, has appreciated in value and they can get a good price for it. And they still have Ken's portfolio and hers—if they need them—to help with the down payment on the new house.)

As for insurance, they knew that everyone who has dependents and a mortgaged property must carry it. Ken's was part of a group plan that he participated in through his company, and while it had no cash value it was adequate protection and cost relatively little. (If he had not had that kind of insurance, he would have had to take out a policy on his own and it would have cost him more. In that case it would have had a cash value—a paid-up insurance policy is good as collateral for a loan—on which he could have fallen back in an emergency.)

Ken's lawyer friend drew up the title of their house—a joint title, with the property to pass to the survivor in case of death.

Recently I had dinner with the Taylors and we went to the theater. He boasted that his portfolio was a good deal larger than Jean's, and she pointed out that he'd taken an awful chance on the last stock he'd bought and said that she'd stick to her dependable growth stocks. Besides growing, they were now financing *three* twenty-year endowment policies for the children's education. And she'd sold one stock to buy a cemetery lot. He hadn't shown much interest in that—he thought it a little gruesome of her—but she wanted to have *everything* settled. He smiled and went on to speak of a motorboat he was going to have when they got a new house—close enough to Long Island Sound to make it worth while.

The way the Taylors arranged their affairs is not necessarily the way for everyone—different circumstances call for different solutions—but as I thought it over it appeared to me to be a very good way. They had started to save and invest while they were young. They had thought of everything: his mother's annuity, the children's education, a savings account for each child, insurance, tax advantages, their wills, and their estates. They were, of course, ideally situated to obtain sound financial advice and to realize early the need to foresee the future. But any young couple can easily have the same counsel and service as the Taylors if they are only wise enough to seek it.

⚜ ⚜ ⚜

Barbara Goodwin was a young woman who needed quite different counsel. The Goodwins had been depositors for many years. He was a minor department store executive who made possibly $7,500 a year, and they lived in Montclair, New Jersey, where they owned their own home. The summer after Barbara got out of college she took a secretarial job with a publishing firm. That same summer Mr. Goodwin died of a stroke while he was working in his garden. Mrs. Goodwin and Barbara decided that because of her job it would be more convenient for them to live in New York, and so they sold the house and took a small apartment in the city. Two years later Mrs. Goodwin was injured in an automobile accident and was disabled for life. Living in New York became too difficult for her, and her doctor thought she would keep in better health if she lived in the country. She and Barbara found a small house in New Jersey, from which Barbara could commute to work, leaving her mother in the care of a part-time companion who was also a practical nurse.

Barbara's problem was very trying for a young girl. Her mother was by nature demanding, and she became no less so when she was an invalid. Barbara foresaw years of having to live with her and contribute to her support—and she was making only $3,500 a year. She was quite unhappy when she came to talk to me. As I had handled several matters for Mrs. Goodwin, I knew what her financial circumstances were. She had her husband's insurance money, $15,000, plus the money she had received from selling the house in Montclair; a few securities, which would bring about enough income to pay her nurse-companion; and $10,000 in a savings account, which she insisted on keeping at that level. The savings were particularly necessary because of her health, and she had medical bills and other small expenses to meet.

Mrs. Goodwin had insisted on buying the house in her own name. Since the title was not a joint one, I suggested that she make a will leaving it to Barbara so that there would be no legal difficulties in the event of her death. For these two matters they needed a lawyer, and Mrs. Goodwin wanted to deal with the lawyer herself. She was unable to come into New York, so I asked the bank in the small town near their new home—a bank with which we had frequent dealings—to recommend a local lawyer who could easily keep in touch with Mrs. Goodwin personally. (He has taken care of Mrs. Goodwin's legal affairs very satisfactorily.)

When the problems of the house and Mrs. Goodwin's care were settled, it remained for Barbara to make some provision for an uncertain future. Most of her salary would go to keeping up the house and supporting her mother and herself. But I advised her to put aside 10 per cent of it regularly and to invest it in sound common stocks for profit. She did not take out any insurance, choosing instead to put everything she could spare into investments. As her salary increased, she put aside more, and now she has a very nice portfolio in her own name. Mrs. Goodwin is still alive—elderly and crippled but tenacious—and Barbara has had to devote many years to her support and to her own career, which has turned out to be a distinguished one. When her mother dies she will have the house, and when she retires her portfolio will guarantee her some comfort

—and perhaps some luxuries to compensate for the sacrifices she was required to make.

Every week young people came to me for counsel in planning their future, and each case was different. The young women often brought their husbands with them. In fact, some of our fussier old ladies began to complain that my time was too much taken up with young men. Some of these men were able to take advantage of federal housing loans and other financial assistance available to veterans; others began with gifts from their families or bequests; still others had only small salaries to start with and had to make their way by diligent saving and budgeting.

Some young people have special advantages. If a young man is employed by any well-established and growing company, he probably will have an opportunity to join his own company's stock purchase plan. Most of these plans are set up so that the stock is bought by regular salary deductions and, often, at a cost below market value. Make every use of this advantage. Besides being an excellent investment opportunity, it may sway the personnel officers in their choice for a good opening because it shows your sincere belief in the company by which you are employed.

The means by which I tried to solve young people's problems were varied, but one basic rule holds for every case: start saving while you are young and seek advice when you need it.

As for my part in helping young people to plan their future, there was one principle I always followed: a successful banker must understand his client's most personal needs and aspirations and base his counsel upon them. I have suggested plans for some people which would have been absolute folly for others. Sometimes I trembled at the chances I took when a young person's whole happiness might have been at stake—and I prayed for the wisdom to give the counsel that would be best for her. A counselor cannot guarantee the financial success of his plans any more than a doctor can guarantee the efficacy of a medical treatment, but he can do his best with full knowledge of the responsibility he takes; and sometimes he is able, through a personal sympathy and understanding of his client's individual problem, to open up visions and possibilities the client had never seen before, to help him assess his own situation, and to inspire him to work, save, and invest wisely.

Again and again I fell back on what Mr. Frissell had taught me about banking: to see each woman I dealt with as a human being with a unique problem. When I think of the legacy of faith and good will that he left me, it seems to me more than ever incumbent upon a bank counselor to possess that personal feeling for people and to cultivate it. And it is equally important for a client to seek the counselor who has it.

CHAPTER NINE

IF YOU CAN'T DO IT YOURSELF: THE TRUST DEPARTMENT

Money is a handmaiden, if thou knowest how to use it, a mistress if thou knowest not.

—Horace

I was never more aware of the responsibility Mr. Frissell had given me, as well as of his confidence in me, as on the day he sent for me to come to see him at his apartment. He had been an invalid for several months and could not come to the bank. When I went in, he smiled and said to his nurse, "Take a good look at this young lady and tell me I'm not making a mistake." His nurse smiled as I sat down, ill at ease, hardly knowing what to expect.

"Dorothy," he said, "I don't believe I'll be coming back to the bank, and so I wanted to have a visit with you here. At a directors' committee this morning we decided to recommend to the directors' meeting in January that you be made an assistant cashier of the bank. Mr. Hetzler and I are very proud of you and I wanted to tell you myself. I know I can trust you to continue my policies. God bless you."

I never saw him again—he died shortly after that—and I have never ceased to feel his loss and to remember what he instilled in me: the obligation of personal service as well as sound banking practice.

In January 1933 Mr. Hetzler called me into his office, where some of the officers of the bank were assembled, and, kissing me on the forehead, said, "You are as of this moment assistant cashier of this bank. It was Mr. Frissell's last wish, and we are all very happy about it."

I was not only happy but also utterly astonished. Women bank officers were virtually unheard of—especially in a staid old institution like The Fifth Avenue Bank.

Both my parents were still living to take pleasure in my promotion, and my father's quiet pride brought me one of the greatest satisfactions I've ever known. It was he who had first suggested that I go to work for the bank, who had allowed me to make my own choice about staying there, and who had supported me with his constant faith. My mother was just as pleased; she had always hoped that I would have some compensation for having given up my education and my early missionary ambition.

Now my work, which had led me through various phases of banking, brought me into contact more and more with the working of the bank's trust department. It is here that a bank assumes its greatest responsibility toward its clients and that careful personal planning is most essential.

At one time the credit department of a bank was the one that made the most money for it, by lending out money at interest or investing it. Nowadays in a commercial bank the trust department may be the chief source of revenue. It is the department that takes care of your money or your investments for you when you cannot do it yourself, because of illness or absence or the lack of time or experience. While I always advised women to handle their own affairs—because of the money they can save and the security and satisfaction they can derive from it—when such a course was clearly against their own interests or too great a burden I suggested that they turn to the trust department.

One of our depositors was Mrs. Westbury, a sweet, gracious, and very independent woman who came of a wealthy Quaker family. She had inherited her parents' money as well as her husband's, and he had taught her to handle her affairs herself, to be conservative and economical. Most of her money was in high-grade bonds, which she kept in a safe-deposit box in a downtown vault. Each month her chauffeur would drive her from her Long Island home to the corner of Lexington Avenue and Thirty-fourth Street, leave her there, and call for her at our bank at four in the afternoon. In the interim she would go to the safe-deposit box, traveling by subway, cut the coupons that were payable, and bring them to me, along with any bonds that had matured or been called, for collection and deposit in her account. I never understood why she observed this ritual, and I warned her that it was unsafe for her to carry bonds and coupons with her. I asked why she didn't give up her downtown vault and rent a safe-deposit box in our bank.

"That was the safe-deposit box my father chose for me," she said. "I could never give it up." When I suggested that she put her securities in a custody account, she replied that it was wasteful, that she had been taught to handle them herself.

When she did not appear for about six months, I began to worry about her. I knew she had some convertible bonds which should be brought in, and so I telephoned to her. She had been ill, she told me, and it was still hard for her to get about; she didn't know quite what to do. I suggested again that she open a custody account, and she agreed to come in and discuss it.

She came in, assisted by a nurse, and I explained to her what a custody account was and what it would cost. Under such an account she could turn over her securities to the bank to be held for convenience and safekeeping and instruct the bank to act as her financial secretary: to clip coupons and collect them, to watch for calls on stocks and bonds, to advise her when rights were issued, to advise her of mergers or changes of any nature in corporate structure that might affect her holdings, to exchange temporary certificates for permanent ones at the proper time, and to deposit all money due her to her account and to send her a statement. Aside from handling these routine matters, the bank would act on any additional instructions she gave us—for example, on a bond or a stock.

The transfer of bonds is simple. Most of them are in bearer form—that is, they are not registered in the name of an individual and may be sold by anyone who has them in his possession. Stock certificates, however, are registered in the name of the owner, and in order to transfer them the owner must put his signature to the assignment on the back of the certificate and have it witnessed. The certificate is then sent to the transfer agent for that stock, who issues a new certificate in the name of the new owner.

To avoid having to come to the bank herself to attend to such matters, Mrs. Westbury could have the stock registered in the name of the bank's nominee. The bank's nominee is merely a name that the bank has adopted for registering its clients' securities. (The name has been registered with the state as a corporation formed for that purpose.) When a stock is registered in the name of the bank's nominee, the bank may transfer it without requiring the signature of the actual owner; the bank, of course, is responsible for the transaction, which in the case of custody accounts is made only on the owner's instructions.

It was difficult for Mrs. Westbury to give up the habits of a lifetime. "What if the bank fails?" she asked me. Her securities would not be part of the bank's assets, I told her; they would be kept separately from all others and she would be given a detailed receipt identifying every security she placed in the bank's care. She would be totally protected in the unlikely event that the bank failed, and she could always close the account at any time if she did not need it. No other person need have access to her securities.

I told her of the time Enrico Caruso had stopped by my desk and said, "It's easy to sing in Rio de Janeiro when you know your bonds are being taken care of by your bank in New York," and this seemed to impress her. But her habits of thrift were deeply ingrained and she feared that the service would be costly.

She had about $200,000 worth of bonds, of twelve different issues, and the cost of the account would be about 1/10 of 1 per cent, or a little over $200 a year. (Such charges vary with time and place.) She was already paying $20 a year for a safe-deposit box she would no longer need. The visits to town cost her something—about $10 a month, she figured—aside from the inconvenience and the danger to her health. And, I pointed out, the clerical work on preparing her income tax return would be simplified. Instead of itemizing every bond and coupon herself, she could merely submit the bank's statement of her income and capital gains.

She jotted down a few figures, then said, "Why, it will really be costing me nothing at all." I went with her in her car to bring her securities back to the bank.

"I am relieved," she said as we rode downtown. "I was afraid I would have to turn over everything to my daughter to take care of, and I didn't really want to. She is a wonderful girl but hasn't much sense about money. Sometimes I worry about her. I wanted to talk to you about her."

I suggested that she at least give her daughter a power of attorney in case she became completely disabled, and she agreed. She told me no more about her daughter at that time, but I was later to remember what she had said.

For the time being a custody account provided Mrs. Westbury with all the service that she required. But in case she were to become too ill to attend to the details of watching her portfolio, the bank could also provide an investment review service. The bank would review and analyze her portfolio periodically, submit a semiannual report on the value of her securities and their yield, and make suggestions to her on any special situations that, in the bank's judgment, required action on her part. She would still retain full ownership and control; the bank would act only on her instructions.

If she wished to be entirely free of any care regarding changes in her portfolio or the reinvestment of money, the bank could provide an investment counsel service. Her investments would all be subject to constant scrutiny, with her own personal requirements and objectives in mind, and the bank would give advice on such changes as it thought advantageous to her.

These services would cost more than a simple custody account. Since Mrs. Westbury was interested in financial matters and able to follow them herself, she decided that the custody account alone would serve her purpose. So the bank took care of her securities for her and she seldom had to pay us a visit.

Custody accounts have advantages that extend beyond the routine care of portfolios. One morning the manager of a mid-town hotel called me and told me that one of its residents, Mrs. Woods, had been found unconscious on the floor by her bed by the maid who had taken in her breakfast tray. On the mirror over her dresser he had found my business card with this message: "Call Miss Armbruster in case of emergency." In a few minutes I stood at her bedside with her doctor, and she was soon on her way to a hospital, still in a coma.

Mrs. Woods was an elderly widow with no living relatives. For months she remained unconscious and, acting under the emergency instructions she had given, the bank paid her hospital bills, as I approved them, out of the income from her securities. We could do this much because she had sufficient funds and had given us instructions to use them for her benefit if necessary. But we could do no more than this. We could not break the lease on her apartment, buy or sell securities, or make an income tax return for her.

It became apparent that Mrs. Woods was never going to recover her faculties, and so the bank had to have more authority to act on her behalf. According to law, people who are unable to act for themselves have the right to be taken care of in a manner conforming to their station in life and according to their means. Therefore, the bank petitioned the court to appoint one of the friends mentioned in her will "committee of the person" and the bank "committee of the property." Thus her friend could take charge of her personal needs and the bank could take complete charge of her property.

The court granted this petition, and Mrs. Woods was adjudged an incompetent—that is, one not capable of managing her own affairs or understanding the effect of any property arrangement she might make. Thus the two "committees" were given complete authority to do everything necessary for Mrs. Woods and her property. I testified before the jury that heard the petition, and afterwards one of its members—it was John D. Rockefeller, Sr.—expressed his admiration for the way in which the bank concerned itself with the welfare of its client far beyond its actual responsibility. We were able to do this because of Mrs. Woods' custody account, her instructions, and her will; evidently she had intended the bank to take full charge of matters. She had placed her securities in a custody account and given the bank instructions to use them for her care in case of emergency. The bank also had her will in its safekeeping: after certain bequests to charities, friends were named as residual legatees, and the bank was named executor of the will.

Usually the procedure of appointing committees is reserved for cases of mentally deficient persons. One of our clients, Mrs. Jamison, had a son who was mentally incompetent. When her husband died he made her, according to his will, a guardian of the son. She, in turn, provided, by her will, for the appointment of another committee, or guardian, of her son's person and named the bank guardian of his property. The same kind of legal provision was necessary in the case of Mrs. Woods because she never regained consciousness although she lived two years after her stroke. At her death the bank settled her estate as her executor, as provided by the terms of her will.

Although Mrs. Woods had made a reasonable enough provision for her care in case of emergency, she would have done better to have had her attorney draw up an agreement whereby she would have turned over her securities to the bank to hold for her lifetime, paying her the income while she was competent and applying the income for her care and benefit when she became incompetent. She might have stipulated the kind of investment the bank could make for her and given it power to use the principal if it became necessary. Under such an agreement she could have indicated the disposition of the trust fund at her death, just as she had done in her will. If the bank had agreed to accept the trust under the conditions she laid down, it would not have been necessary to apply to the court for a committeeship to care for her when she became incompetent. This kind of agreement is known as a living, or voluntary, trust; the fees are a little higher than for a custody account (they are fixed by law and vary in different states), but they are reasonable for the service and protection they provide.

The purposes of trusts are to conserve property and keep the principal safe, to provide income suitable to the beneficiary's needs, to keep the principal invested in securities that are readily marketable, and to take advantage, within the existing laws, of certain tax privileges.

Judith Morrison set up a living trust for herself because she did not want to handle her husband's estate. She was a beautiful young woman, married to a prosperous lawyer to whom she was devoted. Every time she passed my desk she stopped and spoke of him. Her bracelets were all gifts from him, the perfume she used was his favorite, her life seemed to revolve around him, and she never missed a chance to tell me about him. They lived in a lovely house in a fashionable community, they had no children, and her only interest outside Bob, her husband, was her garden.

One day she came to my desk and asked if she could speak to me alone. She seemed utterly changed, lifeless, and crushed by grief. I led her at once to a conference room and closed the door behind her.

"Bob is dead," she said. "He dropped dead without any warning while we were having lunch in a restaurant." She described the shock of his death, of having to wait in the restaurant until the coroner came, of the days of grief that had followed. The day before the funeral the butler had handed her the morning mail; with it had been a letter addressed to him, and she had laid it aside. (They had never even looked at each other's mail.) Then she had realized that she would have to open his letters from then on. This one had been from a woman who asked him to meet her in two days at the Waldorf; she said that she had missed him so and that Paris hadn't been the same after he'd left.

Mrs. Morrison had tried to recall when Bob had been in Paris. He'd been away for a fortnight about two months earlier, and he might have gone to Paris then. Anyway, there had been the letter. She had somehow got through the funeral, which she scarcely remembered, and had kept the luncheon date at the Waldorf, which she would never forget. Then she had gone home, where she had sat brooding vacantly over Bob's infidelity.

When her attorney had called—he was Bob's business partner—to tell her about Bob's will, she had taken no interest in it. She was named executrix and sole beneficiary. The day we talked she asked me what that meant. It meant, I told her, that she could settle all his affairs and claim all his possessions. She had never handled any business affairs; she had always left them all to Bob—even her own personal property.

Fortunately she had a good lawyer, and he settled the estate promptly while she merely signed the necessary documents mechanically as they were presented to her. She wanted nothing to do with the estate. According to my suggestion, she created a living trust at the bank; that way I could watch her interests for her, she said.

Her attorney drew the trust agreement and the bank accepted it: the bank was sole trustee and the income was to be paid to her or applied to her care and benefit for her lifetime. When she died, one half of the principal would remain in trust and that income would go to her mother for her lifetime—after that, the principal would go in equal shares to five cousins, who were her closest blood relations—and the other half of the principal would go to her college, Bob's college, and the charity he had represented as attorney for many years. She, her attorney, and I planned the trust in our conference room; her main wish was to have the money safe and to receive the best possible income. She had no heart for doing anything more about it.

Her own securities, bequests from her father or gifts from Bob, she kept separately in a custody account. At one time she sold five bonds to help out friends in England whose income had been sharply reduced after the war.

"It's a good thing I kept my own securities separate from the trust," she said, "or I would not have been able to help my friends."

I realized then that she had never even read the trust agreement, which contained a clause whereby she could invade the principal if she wished. I urged her to read it carefully so that she would know where she stood; her attorney had been aware of the emotional paralysis that had afflicted her and had carefully drawn the agreement to anticipate her every possible need. In eight years the bank has not made a single change in the securities in which the funds are invested, and the principal has grown tremendously and the income has increased.

Judith Morrison established this trust because she was emotionally and temperamentally incapable of dealing with her husband's affairs after she learned of his infidelity. Once it was created, she never took any active part in administering it, although she handled her own securities capably enough. It was a strange reason for creating a trust, but it worked out well for her.

This was a living trust, and Judith Morrison could have altered it if she had chosen to do so. A testamentary trust—one which is created by a will—cannot be altered.

Mrs. Levy was the beneficiary of such a trust through her husband's will, and when she found that her income was diminishing rapidly she came to me to ask me what could be done. I asked to see the will and read it: it provided that her husband's attorney would be trustee, that when he died the trusteeship would pass to her brother, and that when her brother died a cousin would be trustee. The first two had died, and her cousin, the present trustee, was old, infirm, and blind. As each trustee had died, an accounting had been made and paid for out of the principal, and that had been costly; bonds had been sold to pay for it, and so the fund had diminished. In addition, at that time the state laws provided that trust funds could not be invested in stocks—only in bonds and mortgages. As bond interest had decreased, so had Mrs. Levy's income. And yet it had been a wise provision; her first trustee had died penniless, and if he had been permitted to invest in legal securities he might have invested the trust fund as badly as he had invested his own money.

Mrs. Levy felt bitter toward her first two trustees and very apprehensive about the third. She was happy to learn that her cousin could resign his trusteeship and that the bank could be appointed trustee by the court. A trustee cannot delegate his authority; a court order is necessary to make a new appointment.

Under a change in the law, the bank could invest a part of the fund in stocks, and by a careful selection of growth stocks it could build up Mrs. Levy's principal. And the bank's charge for acting as trustee was no higher than the charges of individual trustees. (Both are regulated by state laws. But, of course, they vary, so it is important, when creating a trust, to ascertain the conditions and charges imposed by the laws of your state.) Ultimately, after the bank took over, it was able to increase Mrs. Levy's income as well as her principal.

Mrs. Levy had never read her husband's will, and she had also been ignorant of what course might be open to her until she came to the bank. When you are beneficiary of a trust—and, more especially, if you are creating one—be sure that both you and the bank understand and are in complete agreement on all its terms. Have your own lawyer draw the trust agreement, to make the most of all the tax advantages that the law permits. And, above all, be sure that it contains the provisions you want.

Miss Kingsley, one of our depositors, came to me with a trust agreement that her lawyer had drawn for her to ask me if it met her requirements and if the bank would accept the trust. I asked our trust officer to sit in on the conference, and we found that it was generally acceptable but that it did not really conform to Miss Kingsley's intentions. By suggesting certain revisions, we were able to help her plan a trust agreement that gave her maximum tax benefits and, at the same time, fulfilled her wishes for her family.

A successful designer at the peak of her career, Miss Kingsley was unmarried, and her only dependent was her elderly mother, who lived with her and managed the household. In addition to supporting her mother, she also gave her about $100 a month for personal expenses. (Aside from the interest on a few tax-free municipal bonds, this was all the income her mother had.) Miss Kingsley also had a sister, of whom she was very fond, and she wanted to do something for her and her children.

The agreement she brought to me seemed to express most of her intentions. She was making a very good income, and she had securities and savings accounts to the value of $120,000. According to federal law, any person may make one gift in his lifetime of $30,000 tax free; in addition, he may make gifts of $3,000 per year to as many people as he wishes without paying gift tax.

So Miss Kingsley proposed to establish a trust of $33,000 for her mother (the $30,000 plus one annual gift of $3,000), who would receive the income from it for life. At 4 per cent this would bring her mother $1,320 a year, or a net of about $1,200 a year after trust fees and other expenses were deducted. Her mother had two income tax exemptions of $600 each—one normal one and another because she was over sixty-five—so she would not have to pay any tax on the $1,200.

This arrangement brought two benefits. According to federal law, the first $60,000 of an inheritance is tax free. After that, the rates rise sharply on a graduated scale from 3 per cent to 77 per cent. Before she made the trust agreement, Miss Kingsley's taxable estate was $60,000. She might reasonably expect that $10,000 could be deducted from it for funeral expenses, lawyer's fees, executor's fees, and debts, leaving $50,000. But she had also provided a bequest to charity of $5,000, so only $45,000 was left taxable. By taking $33,000 from this and putting it in a trust, she reduced her taxable estate to $12,000—eliminating the tax at the highest bracket to which the estate would be subject. She also removed the $1,320 from the highest bracket of her income tax. And she no longer had to give her mother the $100 a month allowance.

That far it was an excellent arrangement. But the lawyer had made her sister's husband the trustee, with the bank to come in at his death, and Miss Kingsley wanted the bank to be sole trustee—the simplest and most economical procedure. She did not want her mother to be subject to her brother-in-law's control—there was no love lost between them—and she wanted to avoid the cost of an accounting of the trusteeship in the event of her brother-in-law's death.

At her mother's death, the principal of the trust was to pass outright to Miss Kingsley's sister—and here we made another suggestion for Miss Kingsley to take back to her lawyer. We advised that, instead of having the principal pass outright to her sister at her mother's death, the trust continue and her sister receive the income from it for her lifetime (after which the principal would pass outright to the children). By this arrangement the principal would not be part of the sister's taxable estate at her death. If the children were still minors, the bank could continue to manage their money as guardian of this property (until they became 21 years of age) and the principal would not be taxed until each child's estate became subject to inheritance tax.

But this brought up a further question. Miss Kingsley's sister was married to a fairly well-to-do man whose fortunes were on the increase. She did not really need the money under these circumstances. And since her husband was paying a large income tax he would perhaps prefer to claim his children as dependents on his income tax return. (Each dependent has an exemption of $600.) He couldn't do this if they were receiving an income from the trust of over $600 a year each. But the income from the trust could be allowed to accumulate until the children were twenty-one, and the income tax return could be made by each of the children's trusts, which also would have a tax exemption. This way the income and inheritance taxes on the trust funds could be kept at a minimum, and although the sister would benefit from the trust in her lifetime, it would add no extra tax burden to her estate at her death.

Miss Kingsley took these suggestions to her attorney and had him revise the agreement and then brought it back to the bank. In its revised form it embodied Miss Kingsley's intentions precisely and included tax advantages which neither she nor her lawyer had envisaged.

She had profited, then, from the bank's scrutiny of her trust agreement and the changes and further provisions we had suggested. The bank, on its side, had some minor reservations. (A living trust must be accepted by the trustee before it can be created, and a bank makes some conditions for such acceptance. A bank wants to know what securities will be placed in a trust, and if there are unreliable securities that the bank doesn't approve of, it will not want to accept any responsibility for a decline in their value and may suggest that they be sold.) Miss Kingsley had some securities that the bank did not want to put into the trust, but this difficulty was easily surmounted. She had savings accounts, and she simply took $33,000 from them to establish the trust.

A bank generally insists on one full trustee's commission. Since a trust department must be staffed by highly skilled and experienced officers and personnel, it does not pay a bank to accept less than a full commission; so even if it is named cotrustee it will still want the full commission.

New York State and other states have inheritance tax laws, while some do not, and taxes, trustees' commissions, and regulations concerning the investment of trust funds are regulated by the states; hence, they vary somewhat. Your bank can give you full information on these matters very quickly.

According to common practice in New York City, when a bank accepts a trust under $100,000 it invests the funds in one or more of the bank's common trust funds. These are investment funds administered by the trust investment committee of the trust department on the same general principles as those of mutual funds, and the types of investments in them conform to the state laws regarding the investments that trustees can make. There are various kinds—for income and growth—and a small trust like Miss Kingsley's may buy units in them and thus benefit from a much wider diversification than her small trust fund could have afforded.

Grandparents often create educational trusts for their grandchildren, either because they enjoy doing it or because they are afraid the parents will not provide for them adequately. Mrs. Ellis was such a grandparent. Her daughter had six children, and since Mrs. Ellis knew that the young woman was extravagant and improvident she came to me and asked how she might assure the children a proper start in life. I explained to her how she might give $30,000 tax free at one time—$5,000 for each child—and add $3,000 per year for each child and said that the money could be invested in the bank's common funds, which are a great boon to small educational trusts. She started the six trusts, and each year she added $3,000 as a Christmas gift to her grandchildren, the oldest of whom was ten and the youngest two. The income accumulated and was invested in common funds, according to the terms of the instrument. By the time the oldest boy was twenty-one, the funds Mrs. Ellis had put into the trust had doubled in value. The boy was then permitted to take his principal outright or leave it in the trust and take the income.

Mrs. Ellis's provisions proved to be very wise. She had stipulated that the funds could be used at the parents' discretion for educational purposes only. When her daughter's husband divorced her and married another woman, leaving her an inadequate income, funds were available for the children's prep school expenses—but they did not affect the agreement whereby the father had to support his children.

Sometimes trusteeships come into being without a specific legal agreement. For example, if you buy stock for your minor children it must be registered in your name as custodian for the child, making you a trustee. State laws on this point vary, and you would be wise to consult a lawyer before buying stock for minors. Another good way of providing for your children's future is buying them U. S. Government Savings Bonds, registered in the children's names and held by you as custodian. The interest on such bonds is in the increase in their value at maturity; it is not paid periodically.

⚜ ⚜ ⚜

Mrs. Westbury, who had told me of her misgivings about her daughter, Hannah Putnam, when she opened her custody account, came to see me one day on a personal matter. Hannah, she said, had just lost her husband and was in desperate grief. She was now far richer than Mrs. Westbury, who had been worried about what would become of Hannah when she died. She asked me to promise, after her death, to get in touch with Mrs. Putnam and somehow gain her confidence. She would need help, Mrs. Westbury said; in spite of her stubborn independence, she was very sensitive, and Mrs. Westbury felt that she would have many burdens to bear.

Mrs. Westbury seemed well enough that day, but not long after she died suddenly—to my sorrow, as I had become very fond of her. I could not go to the funeral, since it was private, but I wrote Mrs. Putnam a letter of condolence and received an engraved acknowledgment. Six weeks later Mrs. Putnam, who was the beneficiary and executrix of her mother's will, came into the bank and opened the estate account, but she did not come to me. Since her husband had been a close friend of the bank's president, she went to him. I recalled the promise that I had made to Mrs. Westbury and felt conscience-stricken because I could not carry it out. But the door seemed closed.

Then some months later she came to my desk and introduced herself. "I don't need any help now, but I found this note with my mother's papers," she said. "What does it mean?" She showed me a slip of paper on which was written, in Mrs. Westbury's hand, "Ask Miss Armbruster not to forget."

I was taken aback. "It was something your mother asked me to do," I said, "and I won't forget. I loved her dearly and miss her. I'll get busy on this at once, and when it is accomplished I'll let you know. Won't you stop and remind me from time to time? It's something very personal." Then I added, "Your mother always told me that you were very self-sufficient and I could learn a good deal from you. I hope we'll get to know each other better."

This was the beginning of one of the most precious friendships of my life. Mrs. Putnam lost nearly everyone dear to her in a short period of time—her husband's mother, her husband, her own mother, her brother, and her brother's wife. She was left completely alone, with enormous responsibilities. From all these estates new securities came to her, quite different from her mother's conservative investments, and she had no experience in handling them. Her husband had left large blocks of railroad stock, real-estate holdings, farms, cattle, race horses, and a huge country estate with greenhouses full of rare plants. She was so overburdened with cares that she began to stop at my desk often just to tell me what she was doing. When her grief weighed on her too heavily, she would plan a trip, tell me when she was going, and dictate a letter of instruction for the bank to follow in her absence. These letters were usually canceled when she returned. The president had authorized me to carry out any requests she made.

When her brother's widow died, Mrs. Putnam found herself the guardian of her sixteen-year-old niece. In such a case, one has a trusteeship thrust upon him and cannot delegate the authority without a court's permission. The entire estate consisted of common stocks, but according to the law at that time a guardian could not invest a ward's funds in stock; in addition, the will gave her no discretionary power to hold the securities. She asked me what she could do. I realized that she would have to sell all the stocks and reinvest them according to law, but since legal advice should properly come from a lawyer, I sent her back to her attorney, who advised her to put all the securities into a custody account, with the income payable to an account in her name as guardian, and to instruct the bank to sell all the stock and reinvest the proceeds in legal securities—that is, those securities that the law permitted guardians and trustees to invest in. When this was done, the income from the securities was insufficient for her niece's needs and Mrs. Putnam had to contribute to her support.

The niece came into her inheritance when she reached the age of twenty-one. Mrs. Putnam made an accounting of her guardianship to the court and was relieved of her responsibility. The custody account was closed and the securities in it were transferred to a new account in the niece's own name. The girl then asked us to help her reinvest her funds in a portfolio that would bring her an income suitable to her needs.

One morning Mrs. Putnam came to my desk beaming with pleasure. "Now I am a banker like you," she announced. "I've taken my late husband's place on the board of directors of our bank upstate."

I could not help noticing how this headstrong woman who had refused all help and counsel and had protested at every stroke of fate had matured into a calm and responsible woman who took satisfaction in discharging her duties well. We had become closer friends than ever, and she invited me to visit her country home.

It was a beautiful place, with a large gray manor house standing on a hill among giant maple trees. Nearby were the cottages of employees and greenhouses filled with lilies, carnations, and snapdragons. In the fields that stretched to the blue foothills of the Berkshires cattle and horses grazed. Mrs. Putnam hugged me as we entered the house, saying, "I've waited so long for this day." In the room upstairs hung with gold satin brocade—after that she always called it "your room"—I told her what her mother had meant by the note she had left among her papers. Surprised and moved, Mrs. Putnam got up and said, "There, child, dress for dinner. We have guests coming." And she quickly left the room.

Sunday morning we attended church, an Episcopal service held in a tiny room over the village drugstore, with the smallest congregation I had ever seen. Later that evening, as Mrs. Putnam and I were talking, I suddenly suggested to her that she build a church. She had so much and she needed something besides business affairs to devote herself to. Thus she began to make gifts to the congregation, and ultimately a new church was built, mostly with her help.

Thereafter we saw each other often and traveled together. My whole family was invited for visits to her home. She and I planned a trip to the Orient in 1937, but we had got only as far as Guam by clipper when we had to turn back because of war in the East.

Early one morning in July 1953 the telephone rang. It was Hannah, who told me that one of her grandnephews, whom she loved dearly, had drowned. She could bear no more; she had lost her faith in God and did not know what to do. I dressed quickly and drove to her home, and at church we took communion together. Once more she became resigned to grief and loss and bore it with courage. She began to devote herself to other people's needs, supporting her church even more; taking care of the sick; sending them food from her farms, dairy, and hothouses; and burying the poor who died with no money. She was active in the Red Cross and made many gifts to the community. She grew steadily in strength and peace of mind and found some consolation for her losses in helping the small family she had left.

She set up a substantial trust for her niece, a voluntary and irrevocable one: at the niece's death the trust would be divided between her two surviving sons. In addition, she created living trusts for each of the boys, adding to them $3,000 each year. These funds could be used not only for education but also for any kind of care the boys needed. When they reached twenty-one, they could claim the entire trusts or allow them to continue.

Even with all her gifts, trusts, and philanthropic activities, Hannah's fortune continued to grow. Together we revised her portfolio, planned the trusts, and had her will drawn. I was named an executor and trustee with the bank. The president authorized this unusual arrangement in writing and I placed a copy of his letter in my safe-deposit box in case I should ever need it. He was particularly pleased at the way I had handled this account: it was a large one and brought a good deal of revenue to the bank through the various services Hannah made use of. Her husband had been a director of the bank and also the son of one of the founders, and she had inherited a good deal of stock. When the bank merged with The Bank of New York and the directors decided to drop the name of The Fifth Avenue Bank, she gave me her proxy to vote as I saw fit, although she herself objected to both the merger and the change of name. She had been guardian of her niece and executor and beneficiary of her mother's and her husband's estates; she had more holdings than ever, and she had created voluntary trusts and provided for additional trusts in her will; she had made use of every facility the bank offered; and finally she placed all her own securities in a custody account.

One thing, however, she would not do, and that was to give power of attorney to anyone. When she went away, she left letters of instructions for the bank; but these were almost always specifically canceled when she returned. In 1955 I got a call from her doctor; he told me that Hannah had suffered a series of strokes and was physically disabled. She wanted me to come to her at once. Her housekeeper and her chauffeur both pleaded with me, and I went. I found her utterly helpless, unable to talk or write or make known her wishes except by nodding her head. Since there was no power of attorney, I did not see how I could possibly manage her affairs, and, sick at heart, I went back to the bank for advice. Suddenly, as if by a miracle, the solution came to me: before taking a trip by dirigible to Europe in 1939, she had left an unusually full and powerful letter of instructions, giving the bank virtually complete charge of her affairs, and this letter had never been canceled. It still stood in the files of the bank and it still had full force.

I asked the president for permission to act under it, and he agreed; then, still amazed, I went back to her and told her that the letter was still in effect. She nodded and smiled and tears came to her eyes; this was what she had been trying to tell me. From then on I was able to assume charge of her affairs. For nine months I spent one day and sometimes two days each week at her house, and gradually I became the lady of the manor in her place. Life went on just as it had before her illness. Calves were born, cattle were sold, crops were harvested, property changed hands, repairs were made to buildings, and all her affairs were kept in order.

I could learn her wishes only by asking her endless questions, which she answered by nodding her head yes or no. One week the doctor summoned me to her home for the third time: Mrs. Putnam was so troubled by something that he feared it might endanger her life. I made a list of over a hundred questions that might bear on what was disturbing her, but she continued shaking her head to indicate no. I assured her that everything was in order. She nodded affirmatively. But I still had not found out what was worrying her, and I left feeling discouraged. As I drove out after my futile visit, I noticed that the grapevines in the hothouses were heavy with fruit. I went back to the house to see if she wanted anything done about them. As soon as I asked her, her face lit up and she smiled and nodded. At last she had made me understand what was weighing on her mind. I found in the storeroom boxes made especially to hold enormous bunches of the grapes and had them sent to all the friends who had been kind to her during her illness.

She died soon afterward, and she is buried beside her husband in the foothills near her estate. Her niece and I had placed on her tombstone the inscription, "His mercy underlies."

Her will was thoughtfully planned, as her later life had been lived, and her family, her employees, her church, her village, and her favorite charities all shared in her estate. For two generations to come, the bank will be administering the trusts she set up for her family's benefit. Through her gifts and trust funds she made a large part of her estate exempt from inheritance taxes.

⚜ ⚜ ⚜

Mrs. Farley was an elderly invalid who came to the bank in a wheel chair pushed by her nurse, Miss Wright, a middle-aged woman who had been her friend and companion for years.

Mrs. Farley told me that Miss Wright had urged her to come in, difficult as it was, because her affairs were not in good order. Her children were all married and far away, and she had no one to look after her but her nurse. After a long conversation, we set about putting her affairs in order. First she placed her securities in a custody account. Nonproductive ones were sold and, since she was very rich, the money was put in tax-free bonds. Some of the profits from large holdings that were sold were canceled by the losses on the sales of the poorer securities. Gradually her portfolio was balanced, her taxes adjusted, and her investments diversified. Then she set up trusts for her children and grandchildren—without loss of income, since she had actually supported them for years anyway. The trusts made the arrangements permanent and secure, just as Miss Kingsley's trusts had done for her mother and her nephews.

Mrs. Farley came in quite often, since she had so many things to arrange, and Miss Wright always came with her. One day she sent the nurse on an errand to Tiffany's and, while she was gone, told me that she intended to leave her a substantial part of her estate, $200,000. But, she said, I was not to tell her and that clause would not be read aloud when her lawyer came in to show her the draft of the will for her approval.

I remember Mrs. Farley's funeral well because as I was following the family in the funeral procession the horn of my car got stuck and I was able to drop out of the line only after what seemed hours of mortification.

After the estate was settled, Miss Wright came to my desk with a check for $200,000. "Can this be me?" she asked in wonder. "I can't believe I'll never have to nurse again. But I've never had any money to manage. Won't you help me the way you helped Mrs. Farley?"

Miss Wright invested the money, following the suggestions we offered her, and her unexpected windfall flourished. Time and time again she has come to the rescue of poorer members of her family

—and of Mrs. Farley's, too, since she never forgot to be grateful for her new-found wealth.

I have at my bedside a little silver clock that bears an affectionate inscription to me from Mrs. Farley. It was the gift Miss Wright bought the day Mrs. Farley sent her to Tiffany's while she discussed the planning of her will with me. And every Easter I receive from Miss Wright an azalea plant, a yearly remembrance of our pleasant association.

⚜ ⚜ ⚜

Mrs. Stillman was not a regular depositor of our bank until she came in one day with a friend who was having trouble balancing her checkbook. We went over it together and quickly straightened it out, and Mrs. Stillman remarked, "I wish I could do that. I've no one to help me with such things."

I suggested that we might work together—I was sure she would learn to handle her affairs very quickly—and the next day she transferred $60,000 from another bank and opened an account with us. It was always a feather in my cap when I got an account from another bank—and it proved helpful to Mrs. Stillman, too. She had felt that no one in her old bank had taken much interest in her affairs. It is a good thing to remember that if you do not get the service you need from your bank, you can always try another, and that if one officer does not seem to understand your problems, another officer in the same bank may prove more helpful.

Mrs. Stillman, who came of a wealthy family, had five brothers, who had always managed her affairs, believing her to be incapable of such work. But she quickly learned to handle her own bank account and to make investments, which she chose well, and her brothers were astounded at her progress.

Married while very young to a famous painter, she was now divorced, but she still had a tremendous interest in modern art, and from her I learned to appreciate more fully that art which had dazzled me on my first trip to Paris. She was one of many cultured women who generously shared with me their knowledge of the arts and helped to make up for the formal education that I had missed. Mrs. Stillman knew such figures as Picasso, Matisse, and Braque personally. She and her husband had entertained them often. I think she liked Picasso's work best; again and again we went to galleries to see his new works and she told me of an evening when he had dined in her home and ruined a beautiful linen tablecloth beyond repair by sketching on it—making the sketch, of course, more valuable to her than the tablecloth had been.

As her husband had become more and more immersed in his work, he had withdrawn from his family and her life had become lonely. Finally she had divorced him, and when we met she lived with her daughter, whom she idolized.

Her daughter Jane was a brilliant and attractive girl who married the man she loved. At the birth of her first son, however, she lost her mind completely. Her young husband took the child and waited patiently for his wife to recover, while Mrs. Stillman took charge of her daughter's care. She spent a fortune on specialists and sanitariums and the girl occasionally showed some improvement. But then she lapsed into a worse state than before. Her mother was devoted and patient, but Jane never recovered her sanity. She was declared incompetent and Mrs. Stillman became her guardian.

In addition to wealth, Mrs. Stillman had a great deal of personal property of value—jewelry and other heirlooms that had come from her family and objects of art that she had acquired. One of them, a sculpture by Brancusi, was famous; she often lent it for exhibition, and people came to her home to see it. She believed it to be a work of art of such value that it ought to go to a museum, and she made a provision for this many years before she died. She gave it to a museum by a deed of gift; then, by agreement with the museum, it was loaned back to her for her lifetime and she was permitted to enjoy it.

She also gave away a great deal of jewelry. "It belongs to young people," she told me. "I had an aunt who clung to everything she owned until she died. When she was old, she wore three rings on every finger, all dirty and uncared for and covered with soap. Why couldn't she have given them to her young nieces and cousins?"

So when her grandson married and had girl children, Mrs. Stillman gave them a piece of jewelry each Christmas. She also made valuable gifts to her nieces. To her grandson and his wife she gave the most valuable of her furniture and paintings.

"As you get older, you need fewer personal possessions," she said, "and I don't want to leave any behind me. I dread the idea of my friends or my family squabbling over them and, anyway, I get more pleasure out of seeing them enjoy them while I'm alive. Every time I go to my grandson's it's like going back to some place I've loved. There are things there I used to have, and it's like seeing old friends."

Under her will Mrs. Stillman created a trust for the care of her daughter; at her daughter's death it will go to the grandson, a banker with a wife and four children, all of whom will benefit from Mrs. Stillman's foresight. She had little enough happiness in her own life, but I know she had great satisfaction from the generosity and foresight she showed for her family.

⚜ ⚜ ⚜

I was surprised one morning to receive a visit from Mr. Follansbee, an English broker I had met some years before at the home of Mrs. Nelson, where he had arrived with his wife for lunch in a Rolls-Royce with two liveried attendants. On that occasion he had shown some scorn and disbelief when I was introduced as a banker —he was of that old school of male financiers who did not think women could understand money—but now, it seemed, he was asking for my help, and I was pleased. His wife and her sister were both depositors of our bank, and both of them were beneficiaries of a trust created by their father, a California lumberman, during his lifetime. The funds were mostly in California real estate that was deteriorating in value, and the income had shrunk. Mr. Follansbee thought that there was a clause in the trust agreement that would make it possible to dissolve the trust and reinvest the funds more profitably.

The California bank that was the trustee happened to be our

correspondent, and as I was going to California on other business I promised to look into the matter. When I got there I saw the trust officer and read the trust agreement; it provided that the trust could be dissolved after both beneficiaries had reached the age of forty if they requested the dissolution in writing. Since both of these ladies were past that age, although they may not have liked admitting it, there was no bar to dissolving the trust. The bank officer took me on an inspection tour of the properties. One was in fairly good condition and producing a reasonable income; the others were terribly run down, almost slums, and it seemed to me that they had no future. The trustee had no power to improve the property or sell it; under the trust agreement it could only act as agent to collect and distribute the income. In this respect the trust agreement was very badly drawn; it made no provision for the possible decline of the investment, which had been a good one at the time. Fortunately, the agreement had a revocation clause which allowed the beneficiaries to dissolve the trust if they wished. On their instructions, the trust was broken and the California bank sold the properties and sent the funds to us. Our bank reinvested them and placed the securities in a custody account.

After Mr. Follansbee's prejudice against women bankers was shattered, he put his own affairs in the hands of our bank and even asked me to keep an eye on them personally.

Having decided that neither of his two sons would make a good executor of his will, he was mainly concerned with providing for his wife, and he named the bank coexecutor with her. At his death we found that among the assets of his estate were a seat on the New York Stock Exchange and a seat on the curb exchange. One of his sons was too young to assume a seat; the other was ineligible because he had been convicted of a misdemeanor. The seats were sold at an all-time high, and the reinvestment of the funds has since carried the widow through many vicissitudes. I worked with her for many years, helping her with her securities, and now, in her eighties, she is five times as wealthy as when her husband died.

Trusts can be used for many purposes. I have heard of people who set up trusts for the vivisection of cats. Others have endowed museums, professorships, scholarships, hospitals, and war orphans through trusts. One of the strangest uses to which I have ever seen a trust put was the rewriting of the Bible.

Mrs. Johnson was the joint beneficiary of a trust fund created by her husband's will for her and her son, and while the boy was a minor she administered it—not wisely, it turned out. When he came of age, her son looked into the matter and found that she had invaded the principal drastically, leaving him much less money than his father had intended. He did not want to put his mother in jail, but once the matter had been called to the attention of the court and Mrs. Johnson was found to have violated the trust, the court had no choice but to sentence her.

For many years Mrs. Johnson had been engaged in writing a new Bible of her own, and it had been placed by installments in her safe-deposit boxes in our bank. When they were finally opened, eighteen boxes were found crammed with manuscripts written in incomprehensible gibberish.

At the time the court looked into her trusteeship it was evident that she was mentally unsound, so instead of sentencing her to prison the judge declared her incompetent and committed her to a sanitarium. Her son continued to spend the principal of the trust fund for her care, and there was nothing left for him.

The trouble with this trust was that the sole trustee was Mrs. Johnson, who had lost her mind and spent the trust fund on rewriting and printing her new Bible. Until her son came of age she had not been accountable for her trusteeship, and then it had been too late to repair the harm she had done by invading the principal. Mr. Johnson would have done better to have made a bank the trustee and placed limitations on the invasion of principal. It is important for anyone who creates a trust to embody in the trust agreement his exact intentions and to see that all the beneficiaries are fully protected.

⚜ ⚜ ⚜

You may recall Mrs. Nelson, of whom I wrote in an earlier chapter. She had had a son, by her first marriage, in whom her husband had taken no interest, and so she had invested her own money to build up an estate to leave to him. Then her husband had persuaded her to change her will in his favor, cutting out her son, and Mrs. Nelson had had to agree.

If she had foreseen her husband's intransigence in this matter, she could have avoided it by creating an irrevocable trust for her son. This is a trust created for a specific purpose, and it may not be revoked or altered. At the time Mrs. Nelson began to invest, the federal laws allowed a tax-free gift of $50,000 (later reduced to $30,000) during one's lifetime and an additional gift of $5,000 each year. If she had used her tax-free bonds for that purpose, her husband need never have known of the trust, since the income from those bonds would not have appeared on their joint income tax return. Neither she nor her husband could ever have touched that money, and her son would have been assured of a share in her wealth. But she had not foreseen her husband's violent objections to her will, and so she had died without leaving any provision for her son.

⚜ ⚜ ⚜

A number of my clients were elderly couples, either childless or with grown children, who managed their affairs jointly and with full understanding and confidence. I recall especially Mr. and Mrs. Fisher, both in their sixties, with grandchildren of whom they were very proud. Each of them had inherited money, and when he retired from a successful career in business they spent much of their time carefully arranging their affairs. Each knew how much the other had—they had arranged their portfolios to complement each other—and they had given each other a power of attorney to use in case of emergency. They had also drawn their wills in favor of each other, and their wills provided for creating a trust for the survivor, which would pass at his or her death to the children and grandchildren. Such a trust is called a marital arrangement; under it one half of the estate of the deceased spouse is exempt from inheritance tax until the death of the other.

Mrs. Fisher died first, and Mr. Fisher received a life interest in her estate (which will eventually pass to their son or to his children). I had lunch with him shortly after her death, and I was impressed by the loving care with which each of them had provided for the other and for the children. We talked over the securities we had bought and the successful investments we had made, as well as our mistakes. His mistakes had never been repeated in her portfolio, and she had always told him of hers so that he could avoid them; by counseling together, they had had twice the fund of experience to draw on that any single investor has. The details of the trust she had created were worked out with great forethought. The arrangement was a classic example of how a testamentary trust can be set up to assure the preservation of the principal for three generations, as well as to provide charitable endowments whose benefits would extend to many generations to come.

⚜ ⚜ ⚜

Other people's trusts may affect your life; it is as important to know the trust instrument by which you live as it is to make a will of your own. Mr. Cartwright came to see me a short time after he had suffered a severe heart attack that had confined him to the hospital for several weeks. His doctor had told him that he might have another—and possibly fatal—attack without warning, and he realized that his affairs were in some disorder. He was the beneficiary of a large trust created by his mother's will; according to its terms, he was to have the income from it for his lifetime, after which it was to pass in equal parts to his four children. He had never saved much money but had spent what he had made freely, along with the trust income. Having never even read the trust agreement until his heart attack had frightened him, he had not realized that if he should die suddenly his wife would be left without a cent. Could anything be done, he asked me, to provide some income for his wife in the event of his death?

I explained to him that the terms of the trust, which the bank administered, could not be changed. But, he wanted to know, couldn't the children agree to waive their interest in it for their mother's lifetime? Three of them were over twenty-one; the fourth was a minor. They were willing, and agreements were drawn whereby the three eldest renounced a third of their interest in the trust in favor of their mother; the fourth child could not make such an agreement until he reached his majority but said he, too, would do so.

If Mr. Cartwright had understood the terms of the trust that provided his income, he undoubtedly would have tried to earn and accumulate enough money to give his wife an independent income. As it was, he could only ask the children voluntarily to waive part of their own rights in it—and it is not at all certain that this kind of solution would work in every case. So if you are the beneficiary of a will or trust agreement, make sure you know its terms and understand what you may expect to receive from it and how it affects your family.

⚜ ⚜ ⚜

A person who creates a trust in his lifetime can have more profit and enjoyment from it than one who waits until his death to distribute his property. Once you are dead, you can enjoy your property no more—and it must always be administered according to the will you have left, which becomes an inflexible instrument of law. Living trusts, on the other hand, offer great advantages for the intelligent use of money.

One of my clients, whom I'll call Mr. Sturges, was a fine artist with a lovely wife and two daughters, of whom he was very proud. He was the only son of very rich parents, but until they died he had had very little money. His family life had not been happy: his mother had lost her mind in her later years and caused him much anxiety, and late in life his father had married a second wife, about whom he cared very little but who had come in for a large share of his father's estate, which had taken six years to settle and had been very troublesome.

Mr. Sturges determined that none of his own family should suffer the feeling of deprivation he had had as a young man, that no possibility of his having inherited his mother's mental instability should prevent him from disposing of his money for his family's maximum benefit. He began to establish trust funds for them while they were still young.

First he created a trust for his wife. Her personal expenses, including clothes, ran to about $3,000 a year, and he gave her a trust fund that would provide that much income. He did not think she should have to ask him if she wanted to make a $25 contribution to her college or pay a little extra for a dress she liked. He liked to see her well dressed and believed she should achieve that quite independently. Their marriage has been an extraordinarily happy one for many reasons—but partly, I'm sure, because he established her personal independence and they gained in mutual respect.

He did the same for each of his daughters as they reached the age of eighteen, so that they learned early to handle their own money, to be independent. It only brought them closer to their father, because they appreciated and responded to his confidence in them.

In each case he made the beneficiary of the trust a cotrustee with our bank, so that his wife and daughters would have control of their own trust funds but, at the same time, have the benefit of the bank's advice. His only condition was that he receive quarterly statements, so that he could see how the funds grew.

His younger daughter married a minister, a fine man but one who was unable to earn a great deal of money; the other daughter married a businessman who has risen rapidly and makes a great deal of money. So Mr. Sturges put an additional $100,000 into his younger daughter's trust, since she needed the money more. There was no reason to tell the other daughter—but her knowing would probably not have made any difference: the girls were brought up to be independent and self-sufficient and they are not prone to envy. Both of the girls work with the bank to increase their funds, which have grown constantly. By the time they make trusts or wills of their own, they will know how to handle their estates. So far, one daughter has taken out $500 of her principal, to cover the expenses of a severe illness, under a clause in the trust agreement that permits the invasion of capital up to $1,500 in any one calendar year. Otherwise the funds are intact.

Mr. Sturges has seven grandchildren, and he has started trust funds for each of them, adding $3,000 yearly for each child under trust agreements which permit the funds to be invested in the bank's common trust. Altogether he has set aside $400,000 for his family, which will not be part of his estate when he dies and will not be subject to inheritance tax; the gift tax, at a far lower rate, has already been paid.

Even so, he is still quite rich. He often came into the bank to discuss his own thriving portfolio with me. Knowing that he was an artist, and that his interest was not primarily in the field of finance, I was surprised at how much he knew about investments, how well he chose them, and how they increased. When I told him so, he laughed and admitted that he'd got his education in investment by watching the quarterly statements of his family's trust funds. He said he was patterning his own portfolio after theirs.

"I'm having the best of it every way," he told me. "I'm glad to have those trusts out of my estate, the way my investments are going up. And, besides, I have the fun of watching the children enjoy them."

None of the things he feared as a young man has happened to him. He profited from his father's experiences. His marriage has been very happy and the members of his family are all close to him; and they idolize him for having been generous in the best of ways—giving them security and the chance to learn how to use their own means and respecting their independence.

As he has made additional trust agreements for his grandchildren, he has, with the help of the bank and his lawyer, who is a friend of the family, added new clauses to meet changing circumstances—for example, giving the bank wider discretion to sell securities and reinvest funds in new industries that are more promising than older ones. The trust agreements that his lawyer draws for him are admirably clear, specific, and comprehensive, and they allow for a good deal of flexibility in investment while, at the same time, safeguarding principal.

This is the advantage of having a bank as cotrustee. Mr. Sturges, having watched these trusts for a number of years, has no misgivings about their future. He has observed that the bank's experts, investing and reinvesting funds, study the whole economic system to discern trends—scientific, technological, and social developments—that may bring forth new investment opportunities. The bank takes its funds out of declining industries and places them in new and growing ones, keeping up with the most advanced fields of economic enterprise. Wisely, Mr. Sturges has not placed limitations on the bank's powers to do this.

Many old-time conservative investors who created trust funds used to stipulate within narrow limits the kinds of bonds and stocks the trustee was permitted to buy—limits often more restrictive than those that the various state laws provide for the protection of funds. A man who had made a great deal of money in western land in the nineteenth century might have wanted his trustees to invest only in real estate. And we have seen what happened to Mrs. Follansbee's trust, which was tied up in California real estate and might have dwindled to nothing if there had been no escape clause. Railroad tycoons have sometimes stipulated that their heirs' trust funds could be invested only in railroad bonds—they could imagine nothing more profitable or secure—but we have seen that railroads in the motor age are no longer good growth companies.

Today a balanced portfolio, or a common trust, comprises stocks in industries that our grandparents could not have imagined; and the common trust of the future will include securities of industries that are still in their infancy. Banks will keep abreast of these developments through constant, careful, and forward-looking research, in order to safeguard their trust funds far into the future.

CHAPTER TEN

SHROUDS DON'T HAVE POCKETS: MAKING YOUR WILL

Is it not lawful for me to do what I will with mine own?

—Matthew 20:15

Some years ago a play opened on Broadway and became a hit, and for some time afterwards many of our depositors, who had not given the matter a thought until then, came in to consult me about planning their wills. As I explained to them the role that the bank could play in the settlement of their estates and sent them off to their attorneys, I reflected a little wryly that a play with a catchy title was accomplishing more than years of counsel on my part.

The play was *You Can't Take It with You*, a statement of an obvious fact that most people find hard to face even though, if they have read the Bible or attended a Christian burial service, they have heard it over and over. St. Paul wrote in I Timothy 6:7, "For we brought nothing into this world, and it is certain we can carry nothing out."

You can't send it on ahead either; whatever you acquire in this world must be left behind when you depart. But you can arrange the way in which it is to be disposed of, and, barring a few limitations which the various states impose on the property of deceased persons, you can do it very much as you wish.

This privilege is yours, however, only if you observe a few basic rules: first, you must make a will that indicates clearly how you want your possessions to be distributed; second, you must have the will drawn properly, preferably by a lawyer, and you must sign it and have it witnessed as the laws of your state prescribe; and third, you must keep it up to date, according to your changing circumstances, so that whenever you die, and however unexpectedly, your will is still effective.

You are the only person who can make your will; other people's wills, though they may affect you in your lifetime, cannot cover the disposition of your property. And the disposition of your own property is all that your will can cover. You cannot dispose of anything you do not own or provide for the distribution of other people's property. Once you are dead, your last will and testament stands, and your estate will be settled according to its terms. It is final and —except in extreme circumstances—unchangeable and irrevocable.

I had many clients who labored diligently to save money, to invest it, to spend it wisely, and who handled all their affairs with the utmost care, yet who shied away from making a will. They were young, they weren't thinking of dying just yet, and they found the thought of facing their demise a little morbid. Or they thought they had so little that it did not really matter what happened to it. If you are over twenty-one, however, and have any possessions, no matter how few or how humble, you ought to make a will. Then you can rest assured that your wishes will be carried out, that your survivors will get what you intend them to have, and that they will not hover like vultures over your unsettled estate.

The most elementary yet comprehensive form of will is so simple that a few minutes with your lawyer will suffice to outline it, and it will cost you very little. Mrs. Todman, my first client, made such a will. It merely stated that she was of sound mind, that the document was her last will and testament, and that she was leaving all her property, both real and personal, to her husband, who was named the sole executor of her estate, to serve without bond. The will was properly drawn by her lawyer and she signed it in the presence of three witnesses, each of whom affixed his signature to it, declaring that he did so in her presence and knew the document to be her last will and testament. (In regard to the form of signing and witnessing a will, different states may make different requirements; naturally your lawyer will know what they are.)

This covered everything. Her only concern was for her husband—she had no children, and her sister, her last living relative, had died. Consequently, she made him sole beneficiary. He was the person whom she trusted most to carry out her wishes, even though he had once come close to being unfaithful to her, and she made him the sole executor—that is, the person who was to carry out her instructions for the disposition of her property. Since he was the beneficiary, she stipulated that he should act without bond. Unless this provision is made, the estate must put up money to obtain a bond from a surety company for two times the value of the estate, covering the executors and protecting the estate and its heirs against any loss that might be incurred by improper handling or dishonesty. The value of the estate is determined at the time of probate, which means proving through the surrogate's court that the will is authentic.

Mrs. Todman's estate amounted to about $30,000; it consisted of a camp in the Adirondacks (this was real property) and some jewelry and a half interest in their alternate checking account (personal property). If Mr. Todman had had to put up a bond for twice the value of the estate, or $60,000, the bonding fee would have been about $300 (or 5 per cent per $1,000) and would have come out of the estate. By stipulating that he could act without bond, Mrs. Todman saved her estate this cost.

State laws grant an executor a fee for his services, usually not less than 2 per cent of the value of the estate, to be paid out of it. This is income to the executor for services rendered, and he must report it on his income tax return. But Mr. Todman could choose to act without fee, thereby saving the income tax on it. He inherited it as a beneficiary anyway, since the estate was under the $60,000 exemption from inheritance tax allowed by the federal government.

This will was completely legal and in perfect order. But there was one serious flaw in it. Since Mrs. Todman and her husband traveled together a good deal, it was conceivable that they might lose their lives simultaneously in a disaster or that he might die before her. If either had happened and she had not made a new will, there would have been no beneficiary and no executor. If there had been a blood relation to claim the estate, he would no doubt have inherited it—but an estate of that size would have been seriously depleted before the necessary legal procedures had been accomplished. If there had been no claimant, the estate would have gone to the state of New York. Thus she should have named an alternate beneficiary and a coexecutor or contingent executor, preferably a bank, to act if Mr. Todman died before her or was unable for any reason to act as executor. Fortunately, nothing went amiss; but she should have provided for an emergency.

Jean Taylor, who had worked as a secretary in the bank before she married Ken Taylor, a broker, frequently asked me to lunch. On one of these occasions she told me, when I met her, that Ken was going to join us.

"You'll think that all we do is pick your brains," she said. "We always have a problem. But this time Ken is rather upset. You know I wanted him to make a will when we bought the house and had to see our lawyer anyway. But he didn't want to. He said we were too young and we didn't have much to leave, but now he's worried." She went on to tell me that an associate of Ken's in his brokerage firm had been killed in an airplane crash a few weeks before. He had left no will, and now his widow, with two small children, was having a desperate financial struggle. The man had left some property and securities, but his widow was having to go through endless legal formalities to get her share of the estate and the guardianship of the children. The expenses were a terrible drain on a small estate, and the widow didn't even think the court would let her handle the money. Ken at last had decided that he'd make a will.

I told her that for the will they must go to a lawyer and said that while they were about it they should both make wills. She wanted to know what the bank could do about an estate. Her boss had been in the investment department, and she had never come into contact with the trust department.

After Ken joined us and we had caught up with news of the

family, we got down to the subject of wills. He wanted to make his short and simple: he would make Jean the beneficiary and executrix without bond. That would do for the time being.

"There's no such thing as a will for the time being," I told him. "Once you're dead, it's forever." I said that they should make their wills so that they would cover every possible contingency; then if they had to make revisions later, there would be that much less to do.

I advised them to make the bank coexecutor of their estates; in that way they could be assured of quick settlement and continued care of their estates no matter what happened. Ken's only concern was to make sure that Jean had full and immediate control of his estate in the event of his death; but Jean had made a list of provisions she wanted to make, to cover personal property and some specific bequests, which Ken thought trivial and sentimental. I did not agree; if you have anything of value and it belongs to you, you alone can provide for its disposition; even if its value is only sentimental, it is nonetheless valuable.

Faced with what he called a feminist conspiracy, Ken yielded on these points, and we sketched out a rough draft of the two wills to be taken to their lawyer.

Their house was in both their names and would automatically pass to the survivor. Ken's insurance was payable to her, so that would not pass under their wills either. Their alternate checking account, too, did not have to be in the wills. But all these would be subject to inheritance tax.

So Ken's will would leave all his other property to her and name her executrix without bond. If she should die before him, then all of his estate would go to their children in equal parts. They had two children, another was expected, and there might be more; so it was important *not* to specify the number of children, or those born after the date of the will might be cut out entirely. His brother and the bank would be contingent coexecutors and cotrustees, his brother to act without fee. And his brother and her sister would be guardians of the children, without bond. (Guardians of property must be bonded, the same as executors, unless the will specifically waives the requirement. Banks, because of their large resources, are not required to be bonded.) The bank would have the power to put his estate into its common trust fund; the cotrustees would have the power to apply the income from the estate to the care of the children and to invade the principal in case of emergency, such as illness or death.

"It seems a lot of will for such a small estate," Ken said skeptically.

"But it might be bigger before we die," Jean said doggedly, jotting down a list of small bequests she wanted to make.

"For heaven's sake, Jean," Ken said when she had written down a number of items, "who cares who gets your father's cuff links or baby shoes or whatever?"

"I care," she said.

"Your will will be twenty pages long and very boring," he said.

"All right, I'll leave everything to you and put it all in a letter," she said.

So it was decided that Jean would write a letter, addressed to Ken, to accompany the will, specifying personal bequests: her engagement ring and the porcelain clock that was a family heirloom would go to their eldest daughter when she reached eighteen; her father's cuff links and the grandfather clock would go to their son John on his graduation from college.

Ken muttered something about his motorboat and decided to write a letter to her to accompany his will, too. (They can always change or add to these letters without remaking the wills.)

Jean's will provided that her personal property—stock, bonds, cash in the savings account—would be left in trust for her children in equal parts, with her husband and the bank as coexecutors and cotrustees, until the children reached twenty-one. In case her husband died before she did, the bank would be sole trustee—with full power to invest the principal in the bank's common fund, apply the income to the care of the children, and invade the principal in case of emergency. As in Ken's will, it was provided that his brother and her sister would be guardians of the children.

What Ken had termed a mortuary luncheon became a spirited

discussion, and by the time we had finished he looked rather smug about having outlined a will that took into account their present situation and would still carry out their wishes even, as he said, if they lived to be ninety. All they had to do was to go to their lawyer and have the wills drawn properly, which would cost about $50 to $75 for both of them. Ken would place his will in Jean's safe-deposit box and she would place her will in his box, so that they would be easily accessible to the survivor in case of death. Then they could put the whole matter out of their minds unless they moved to another state, got divorced, or otherwise changed their legal status.

⚜ ⚜ ⚜

No two wills are the same, and each one has to be drawn with special consideration for the individual's circumstances. Barbara Goodwin, who had only her ailing mother as a dependent, had to make an entirely different kind of will. After they moved to the country house her mother had bought in New Jersey and arranged their finances, Barbara went to the lawyer who had handled the title to the house and made a will of her own.

As the house was in her mother's name (but would pass to Barbara in case of her mother's death), it had no place in Barbara's will. She had first to provide as well as she could for her mother, in case she survived her. She made one personal bequest, leaving some jewelry to the nurse who served her mother so faithfully and had become almost part of the family; it was of little value, but it was the only token of appreciation Barbara could leave. All other personal effects went to her mother outright. The rest of her property—a savings account and some stock—was left in trust for her mother, with her local bank as trustee, with broad investment power, the trustees to apply the income for her mother's care and benefit and to use the whole principal for her mother's welfare if necessary. At her mother's death, one half of the remaining principal would go to her church as a memorial to her mother. The minister was a particular friend, and Barbara thought this was a suitable acknowledgment of his help. The other half would go to her college as an addition to the memorial of her class. She made the bank, rather than her mother, executor of her will, since her mother was too ill and inexperienced to manage money properly.

Since her local bank was a small one, it was willing to accept a small trust. So Barbara's affairs were neatly arranged and in competent hands.

⚜ ⚜ ⚜

Mrs. Kaley was in mourning when she came to see me. Her husband had died recently, and she came to ask advice about her affairs. She had just seen her lawyer, who had asked her for her husband's will, but she had not been able to find one. Mr. Kaley had often talked of drawing one, but apparently he had put it off.

As there was no will, she would receive only her one-third widow's share under New York law. Her daughter, an only child, married to a naval commander stationed overseas, would receive two thirds.

Mrs. Kaley's lawyer first suggested that she apply to the court to be made administratrix of the estate. But then she heard from her daughter, who wanted to be administratrix herself. In this proposal Mrs. Kaley could see the fine hand of her son-in-law, who disliked her. The upshot was that Mrs. Kaley and her daughter were appointed joint administrators. Both of them had to be bonded for twice the amount of the estate, which was around $1,000,000, and before it had even begun to be settled, the bonding fees had drained it considerably. In addition, their respective lawyers represented them and each received a fee.

Mr. Kaley's safe-deposit box was found to contain a life insurance policy for $10,000, payable to Mrs. Kaley, so she had money to live on while the estate was settled. The house was in her name, so it was not part of the estate. When the estate was finally settled and Mrs. Kaley got her share, she sold the house and bought a small co-operative apartment. She was able to live comfortably, but not at all as she had lived when her husband was alive or as he would have wanted her to be situated. Her daughter and her son-in-law, who were independently rich to start with, enjoyed the larger part of the inheritance. How easy it would have been for Mr. Kaley to have named the bank executor and to have left a simple will that would have avoided all that quarreling and expense.

⚜ ⚜ ⚜

Mrs. Webb lived in a home for elderly women because her daughter, Mrs. White, had always hated her and would not ask her to live in her home. Mrs. Webb's daughter seldom went to see her, but her granddaughter Linda was very attached to her and visited her often. Mrs. Webb gave her a lovely ring on her eighteenth birthday but advised her not to tell her mother about it. Linda knew it would be impossible to keep it from her mother, and so she made no attempt to conceal it. Mrs. White was not at all touched by the affection between her mother and her daughter and was somewhat unpleasant about it. Nevertheless, Linda kept on seeing her grandmother, and Mrs. Webb always said that Linda would have everything she possessed when she died. As no one believed she had anything, this was not taken very seriously by the family.

When Mrs. Webb died, the keys to her safe-deposit box were found in her pocketbook; but there was no will or paper of any kind. When the safe-deposit box was opened, five savings account passbooks, totaling $50,000, were discovered—and the interest had not been added for years. Mrs. White was the next of kin and consequently inherited it all—although surely Mrs. Webb had meant it for Linda. But Mrs. White felt entitled to it: she had hated her mother and had put up with her for years, and at least she had this reward.

Her husband, who had been fond of his mother-in-law and would have been glad to have shared his home with her, merely said to his wife, "That money will never do you any good."

Linda said nothing, but she became less and less fond of her mother; and since she had seen her mother's example, it was not surprising that she had similar feelings.

It was surely unfortunate that Mrs. Webb had had a daughter who disliked her; but she not only could have insured Linda's inheritance by making a will but might also have prevented the painful family situation that developed with Linda's increasing estrangement from her mother.

⚜ ⚜ ⚜

Worse than leaving no will is leaving a will that is badly drawn or out of date. A woman whom I knew first socially and later as her counselor learned this from a bitter experience. She was a successful professional woman, a shoe buyer for a large department store, and she made frequent trips to South America to buy leather—snake, alligator, and kid. On one trip she met an attractive gentleman named Fraser on shipboard and they became acquainted. He was an oil executive, highly successful, and separated from his wife, who was at last giving him a divorce. (She had been reluctant to divorce him because she was a Catholic.)

When Mr. Fraser learned that my client was unmarried, he became more attentive, and by the time their ship had docked in Rio they were virtually engaged—pending receipt of his divorce decree. While they were still there, he received a cable from his lawyer saying that the divorce had been granted. They were married the next day.

For the next fourteen years they were extremely happy. He grew richer and she had everything she wanted—a beautiful home, a new Cadillac each year, trips to Europe, jewelry, and clothes. She had retired from her own career and had left everything concerning money to him. Then suddenly he was stricken with a heart attack and taken to the hospital, and in a few days he was dead.

Heartbroken, she came to see me a little after her husband's death. Aside from her grief, she was faced with legal problems that seemed insurmountable.

Mr. Fraser had made a will during his first marriage, a simple one that merely stated that he left everything to his wife. He had never destroyed or revoked that will or made a new one. And now investigation showed that his divorce decree had not actually been signed by the judge until thirty days after the hasty marriage in Rio. Although they had gone through the marriage ceremony in good faith and lived for years as husband and wife, the marriage had been invalid. According to law, the second Mrs. Fraser had been only his common-law wife and all his property belonged to his first wife.

If he had destroyed his will, Mrs. Fraser, under the intestacy laws of the state of New York, would have received a third of his estate, while two thirds would have gone to his son by his first marriage. As it was, she had no claim to any of his property. For the time being, she was permitted by agreement to live in their house, but she could not use the car and she could not even get her own fur coat out of storage, since the storage account was in his name. All she had was a small savings account of her own and $3,000 in cash that he had given to her out of his pocket when he was taken to the hospital. Not even his insurance money was available, since it was payable to his estate.

A good deal of the estate went for legal fees while lawyers searched for a way of getting her some share of his estate. Endless conferences were held. Finally an agreement was reached between the first wife's lawyers and Mrs. Fraser's, and she received a settlement. It was a fairly substantial sum, since Mr. Fraser was a rich man, but it was only a fraction of what he would have wished her to have. He had meant her to have the larger part.

Since she was a good businesswoman, she handled her inheritance well and it increased; but she knew some anxious times before she achieved even a modest security. Now she has got over feeling bitter about it. She is married again and is happy—and her second husband made a new will when they were married.

⚜ ⚜ ⚜

If you change your residence to another state, the chances are that any will you have drawn previously will be affected by it. One of our depositors was Mrs. Tilton, who had inherited one half of her mother's estate. She was married, but she had no children. Her husband was well to do and had no need of her money, so she made a will in New York State, whereby she left all her money to her sister, who lived in Europe. Her sister had children and the money would be useful to her.

The Tiltons moved to California, and after they had lived there a few years Mrs. Tilton died. Mrs. Tilton was a California resident, and under California law one half of your estate must go to a surviving spouse if he claims it. As Mr. Tilton had no great love for his sister-in-law, he claimed one half of the estate, which left far less money than Mrs. Tilton had meant her sister to have when she drew the will in New York. The will should have been redrawn when they moved to California.

⚜ ⚜ ⚜

Mr. and Mrs. Horton were both writers, he a novelist and she a writer of articles for women's magazines. Both were very successful, and they had a beautiful country home and idolized each other.

Mrs. Horton frequently brought in sizable checks from magazine articles and asked advice on investing the money. We came to be close friends, and I enjoyed visiting them. Eventually the time came when Mrs. Horton thought her husband ought to make a will, but she did not want him to leave her any money. She had made a good deal and invested it well, and she could not see why she would need any more. She thought that he should make a will leaving all his money to his three maiden sisters.

Vic Horton could not be bothered with any of this. He had always had plenty of money and had never taken a great deal of trouble about it. According to the laws of his state, if he died without a will, half his estate would go to his widow anyway and the other half would go to his next of kin—in this case his three sisters. Since this was exactly what he intended, why bother to make a will?

I pointed out the dangers of leaving it up to the state. An administrator would have to be appointed by the court, there would be bonds to be obtained, and all kinds of legal fees would diminish the estate.

When at last he gave in and made a will, he decided not to leave anything to his sisters, since they were all quite well off anyway. If he had to make a will at all, he said, it would be for his wife. The bank was named executor, and when he died his estate was settled quickly and with a minimum of expense. As things turned out, it was a good thing he had made such a will.

Eliza Horton was completely undone by grief at his death, and she could not seem to recover. Gradually I realized that she had taken to drinking secretly. She had never drunk before, and she didn't know what it would do to her. She became a hopeless alcoholic and remained one for many years, and now she is old and ill.

She finally sold their country home, and I went there with her nephew to dispose of her personal effects. We went through trunk after trunk of fine clothing that was decayed and moth-eaten; we packed up bound volumes of her articles and her husband's novels and scrapbooks with clippings that told of all the honors they had received for their achievements; we salvaged what we could and sent certain articles to friends; her nephew took the furniture.

Eliza Horton now lives in a hotel suite attended around the clock by trained nurses. All her securities are in the custody of the bank, which pays her bills. The cost of her medical care is enormous, and now and then a security has to be sold to pay bills. The capital gains are offset by the medical deductions from her income tax, but still the principal is dwindling. I am so glad that Vic yielded to my advice and made a will. Even with her own substantial portfolio, she could never have got through these years of illness without the money he left her.

She always wanted her nephew to have a good inheritance. There will be enough to see her through her life—she is in her eighties now—and I hope something at least will be left for the nephew and his two small children.

⚜ ⚜ ⚜

Mrs. Follansbee, the widow of the English broker, had two sons. One was unmarried and an invalid and the other was married and had twin sons. She made a comprehensive will that would allow her to take maximum advantage of tax privileges, by creating trusts, with the bank as sole executor and trustee.

First she requested that she be cremated. She also requested that all inheritance taxes be paid out of the estate, so that the beneficiaries of her will would receive the sums she stipulated free of any tax claims. Her personal effects—clothes and jewelry—were left to her sister. Other specific bequests included $10,000 to her college; $25,000 to Princeton University, of which her husband and sons were graduates; $10,000 to her sister; $10,000 to a fund for research on cancer, from which her mother and father had both died; and $10,000 to the cemetery for perpetual care of the family lot.

She owned real estate valued at about $150,000, which she asked to be sold, since she did not think her sons would be interested in it.

After these bequests and her expenses were taken care of, about $830,000 of her more than $1,000,000 estate remained. Of this, $230,000 went for taxes and legal expenses, leaving $600,000.

This sum she divided into two trusts, one for each son. Her married son would receive the income from a trust of $300,000 for life; at 4 per cent, this would earn $12,000 a year, of which he would receive approximately $10,000 after trustees' commissions and expenses were deducted. At his death his wife would receive the income on one half of this and each of his twin sons would receive $75,000 of the principal outright. When the wife died, the sons would receive another $75,000 outright.

The unmarried son would receive the income of a $300,000 trust fund for his lifetime; at his death the income would pass to his brother for life, and at the brother's death the twin sons would each receive $150,000.

This will, with its testamentary trusts, preserved the principal for Mrs. Follansbee's grandchildren. No one person ever received all the income at any one time, and no one person ever had control of all the principal at one time; it passed, little by little, to the grandchildren over a period of years, to guarantee them the maximum benefit of it. The principal will not be subject to inheritance taxes until the deaths of the two grandchildren. The trusts were irrevocable, and, while the bank was given broad powers of investment, no one had the right to invade the principal during the term of the trusts. Mrs. Follansbee made this will after careful consultations with her lawyer and the bank, and it is a model will of its kind.

Quite in contrast to that will was the will which Mrs. Morse brought to me. Mrs. Morse was a depositor, and she was a partner in a dress shop which kept its business account with us. When she came to see me, she was worried about her husband's health; she had made him executor of her will and she was afraid that he would not be capable of acting, even if he should outlive her. She had a son of seventeen, and she intended that, after a specific bequest of $10,000 to a hospital, the residuary estate should go to him. Her husband was to have the use of their home for his lifetime, after which the home would go to her son. She wanted to know if the bank could be executor of the estate instead of her husband.

The first thing to do when drawing or reviewing a will is to make a careful list of the property you own—the property to which you have a clear title, because you cannot bequeath anything you do not own—and estimate its value. Then you can determine how to divide it among your beneficiaries as you wish.

Mrs. Morse told me that her estate consisted of the following:

Household furnishings and jewelry	$10,000
House and grounds, recently appraised	90,000
Paid-up life insurance policy	10,000
Cash in savings accounts	20,000
Bearer bonds	25,000
Registered U. S. Government bonds	20,000
Half interest in small business (dress shop)	50,000
Land in California, unimproved	15,000
Shares of stock, various companies	15,000
Other stock	60,000
Total	$315,000

When I questioned her about the titles of these various properties and examined the papers she brought me, I found that the house, which she had inherited from her mother, had then been registered in her name and her husband's, with right of survivorship, so that on her death it would pass to him outright. The $20,000 cash in the savings accounts was registered in her name in trust for her son, so that it would go to him at her death. The $10,000 insurance policy was payable to her sister, who would receive the money at her death. The $15,000 registered government savings bonds were registered in her name and payable on her death to five different people. The interest in the dress shop, which brought her income of $8,000 a year, was under a partnership agreement with her cousin, whereby the surviving partner would take the capital of the other. The $15,000 in stocks of various companies was in her name as trustee for her son, according to a trust set up for him under her mother's will. The stocks were the only assets in her estate that were not subject to inheritance tax. The remaining property in the estate would all go for debts, expenses, and inheritance tax. There would be little if anything left for the bequest to the hospital and no residuary estate for her son.

Mrs. Morse's question was this: Could the bank serve as executor? Yes, it *could*, I told her, but there would be very little estate left to administer. Her will had been properly drawn by a lawyer, and there was nothing wrong with it. The trouble lay in the titles to her property. She was trying to bequeath property to which, on her death, her estate would have no title—except for tax purposes.

She wanted first of all to provide for her son. But her house could not pass to both her husband and her son at the same time, her life insurance could not pass to both the sister and her son, her business could not pass to both her partner and her son, her registered bonds could not pass to both her son and five other beneficiaries.

Her mistake had been in not telling her lawyer the true titles of her properties. The will was not faulty; it was merely ineffective.

The only solution would be to change the titles of as many of her properties as she could. First she decided to sell the California real estate; it would, in any case, involve her estate with the laws of another state, which might complicate matters. Then she changed her insurance policy so that the money would be payable to her estate rather than to her sister. She sold her government bonds and reinvested the money in her own name. She also eliminated the bequest to the hospital, much as she regretted doing so. But she could not ask her cousin, who had worked with her for years to build up their business, to terminate their partnership agreement so that her son could inherit her share.

However, she had cleared the titles of at least some of the properties so that they could pass to her son, and she had also left enough liquid assets in her estate to cover inheritance taxes and expenses—always a wise precaution. Since these expenses must be met when they are due, it is sometimes necessary to liquidate property at a great sacrifice in order to meet them.

Mrs. Morse learned that merely making a will did not end her troubles; she also had to make sure that the estate would have title to the property and that there would be sufficient cash for expenses and enough assets to fulfill her intentions toward her beneficiary. The fault was with her estate planning; she had done it piecemeal and never considered it as a whole.

In planning your estate, it is important for you to know the value of your property as well as its title. When Mrs. Murphy died, she left most of her estate to her sister, with whom she had lived for years. They had shared the income from their combined property, and most of it had come from stock that Mrs. Murphy had inherited from her husband. At the time of his death, this had been worth $200 a share. It was not listed on any exchange, and Mrs. Murphy had never tried to sell it; she had received the income from it regularly and had thought no more about it. When she had made her will, she had estimated its value at $200 a share. When her executor (who was her lawyer) had filed the federal estate tax, he, too, had placed its value at $200. But the federal government had claimed that it was worth $1,200 a share.

The lawyer applied to the federal tax court in Washington for a ruling, and a value of $800 per share was finally determined, after the court had taken into consideration such factors as the company's earnings and expenses. The tax on the stock was so high that Mrs. Murphy's sister had to use all of the remainder of the estate to pay it. She was left with far less than she had expected to have and had to reduce her standard of living drastically.

If Mrs. Murphy had realized that this stock had increased so much in value, she could, during her lifetime, have transferred some to her sister, avoiding the devastating inheritance tax to which it became subject, rearranging her estate for her sister's maximum benefit, and leaving sufficient liquid assets to cover taxes and expenses. If a good part of your estate is in securities, you should keep informed on the current values and take them into account when you plan or revise your will.

Other changes in the value of your property may complicate the settling of your will if you do not keep it up to date. Mrs. Freeman purchased 100 shares of stock in her nephew's company and then made a will in which she left the stock to him. He expected to receive all of the stock, but after she made the will the 100 shares became 300 by a change in capitalization—in this case stockholders received an additional two shares of stock for each share they held. The will, however, stated that her nephew was to receive 100 shares. When the will was probated, a legal battle ensued to establish Mrs. Freeman's intentions and her nephew's rights. It would have been much simpler if Mrs. Freeman had revised her will to take the capital change into account.

Another case in which an old will, though still legally valid, was out of date was that of the Misses Springer, maiden ladies who lived in an apartment in a Park Avenue hotel. Like so many elderly women of their generation, they were the last of a wealthy family. Genteel and highly cultivated, they were retiring by nature, and they had lived together since their parents' deaths, self-sufficient and aloof, with few friends and no close relatives.

Abby, the elder sister, was, I knew, frail, and I was not surprised one day to hear her weak voice over the telephone asking me to come to see her. I went at once.

Their apartment was beautifully furnished with family heirlooms of great value: Kermanshah rugs, furniture upholstered in Aubusson tapestry, Tiffany glass, and paintings by Turner and Constable, as well as old family portraits. Each of the two bedrooms had a huge four-poster canopied bed, and in one of them lay Abby, very ill. She was attended by two nuns, one of whom had met me at the apartment door. The other was in the bedroom, and Abby asked her to go out of the room while she talked to me.

"My sister Josephine knows nothing about our affairs," she told me with difficulty. "I've sent her out today because I had to talk to you alone." Then she asked me to go to a desk in the drawing room, find and open a secret compartment, and bring her the contents of it, which included their wills. "Do not let anyone see," she said, but I insisted on having one of the nuns go with me. It was better to have a witness when handling the hidden treasures of a dying person.

I found the ebony desk, inlaid with mother of pearl, and the hidden latch that opened the secret drawer. Inside were a velvet box full of jewelry, the two wills, and $60,000 in New York City 4½ per cent tax-free bonds, with all the coupons intact. They would not mature until 1968. There was also a large packet of letters tied in a blue ribbon.

I immediately called the bank and asked to have the vaults kept open after the usual closing time, as I would be bringing in some valuables to deposit. Then I took the contents of the drawer into Miss Springer. She reached out for the packet of letters.

"I had a sweetheart once," she said. "My sister never knew anything about it. These are his letters. Will you please take them to the fireplace in the drawing room and burn them all? Please do not open any." With the nun as a witness, I took the letters into the other room and burned them one by one. The nun suggested that we read them, but I firmly followed Miss Springer's instructions. Then I went back to her, enumerated the contents of the box, and gave her a receipt for them.

The jewels were fabulous and very valuable: there were two diamond necklaces, two diamond and sapphire bracelets, and rings of sapphire and emerald. None of them had been worn for twenty-five years. How lovely they would have looked on a beautiful young woman, I thought. They had been quite useless to the Misses Springer and would, in fact, be a burden to their estates.

I took the bonds and jewels back to the bank and placed them in the vault. Then I put the wills in the bank's will file. Miss Abby died two days later.

When I got a call from Miss Josephine, I went to see her. We chose a lawyer and she signed an application to the court, with the will annexed, to have the bank made administrator of the estate, using the will as if the bank had been named in it.

The wills had been drawn many years before; the sisters had discussed them one day while they were riding out to Coney Island and then had had a lawyer draw a will for each of them. They had made each other executrix and sole beneficiary, and the wills had been properly drawn and witnessed. Nevertheless, they were out of date. All the witnesses were dead, and the bank had to have their signatures verified by means of affidavits from persons who had known them. And Miss Josephine was too frail physically to act as executor, even if she had been qualified.

Miss Josephine received the entire estate and created a living trust, the principal of which was to pass to various charities on her death. On her instructions the bank had all the ladies' household belongings and jewels sold—something which should have been done years before, since the women had long since ceased to derive any pleasure from them—and they were so valuable that the estate had to pay a huge inheritance tax on them. It would have been so much wiser to have sold them all years before and set up living trusts with the money.

⚜ ⚜ ⚜

There are certain ways to safeguard your will against changing circumstances. One is to use fractions or percentages in arranging the distribution of your estate rather than to leave fixed sums of money.

Mrs. Rosen, a widow who had no children of her own, had many relatives who were close to her, and she drew a careful will in which she remembered them all handsomely. Dearest of all was her niece, to whom she wanted to leave the larger part of her estate. So, after making specific bequests to her brothers and sisters and two sisters-in-law—which totaled $70,000—she left the rest to her niece. (Such a beneficiary is called a residuary legatee.) When she made her will, her estate was estimated at $200,000 after the specific bequests and the expenses were taken care of. But before she died Mrs. Rosen became an invalid, and her medical expenses in her last five years were $10,000 a year, above her normal living expense. Thus the value of her estate decreased. Also, the debts she left were considerable. By the time the estate was settled, her niece received only $20,000, far less than Mrs. Rosen had intended.

She might have provided for a more reasonable balance among the legacies she left by making the bequests in fractions or percentages, by stipulating that her niece receive one third of her estate and the other beneficiaries fractions in proportion to her intentions. Each of them would have received a fairer share. Her will had become out of date because of her illness, and it no longer fulfilled her wishes.

There are many ways in which your intentions regarding your estate may misfire if you do not have competent legal advice to begin with and if you do not review your will periodically and keep it up to date.

⚜ ⚜ ⚜

Mr. Brown made a will that left all his estate to his wife; his mother was living, but, as he had already taken out a large life insurance policy of which she was the beneficiary, she was well taken care of. He died suddenly, and his estate was settled quickly. But there was one point that had not entered his mind: his will provided that all inheritance taxes be paid out of his residuary estate. Thus the tax on his mother's insurance benefit was, in effect, paid for at his wife's expense. Mrs. Brown did not like her mother-in-law very much, and this point was enough to increase her resentment and mar the family relationship. A competent lawyer familiar with estate taxes could have prevented this by putting in the will a stipulation that the insurance would bear its proportionate share of the inheritance tax.

Mrs. Barclay made a will in which she left a substantial bequest to her favorite niece, if living, or, if not, to her niece's heirs. The niece died before Mrs. Barclay did, but the latter did not change her will. The result was that the bequest intended for the niece went to the niece's husband, whom Mrs. Barclay heartily disliked. This could have been avoided if Mrs. Barclay had revised her will or if, in the first place, she had provided that bequests to persons who might predecease her would become part of her residuary estate.

Some people try to make their own wills without the help of a lawyer. If such a "do-it-yourself" will is written *entirely* in the handwriting of the testator, it may be acknowledged as valid by the probate court. If it is not handwritten but is properly executed and signed and witnessed, it may possibly be valid. But there are so many pitfalls in making a will without a lawyer that it is never advisable, no matter how wise the testator may think he is.

Mrs. Raymond's will was so simple that she dispensed with the services of a lawyer and wrote it by hand and had it properly witnessed. Her only living relative was her brother, who was quite well off, and she decided that she would leave him only half her estate. Having suffered from an eye ailment that had nearly cost her her sight, she wanted to leave all her money to aid blind people. Consequently she made a simple will which said, "I leave one half of my property to my brother and the other half to the blind." She had in mind a particular organization for the blind, but she did not put its proper corporate name in her will. When the will was probated and the news got out that a considerable amount of money had been left to the blind, half a dozen organizations and even some blind individuals applied to be beneficiaries of the bequest. As there was no possible way of knowing what organization Mrs. Raymond had intended as beneficiary, and as her records did not disclose who "the blind" were, the court ruled that the second half of her estate was to pass to her brother, as if she had not made a will.

Mrs. Raymond's brother, a depositor in our bank, told me of the ill-fated holograph will when he came in to ask if the bank would be executor of his own will. Being a conscientious man, he included in it a large bequest to an organization for the welfare of the blind, in memory of his sister, taking care to specify the exact legal name of the beneficiary and thus carrying out his sister's intentions.

⚜ ⚜ ⚜

Whenever Miss Hastings came into the bank the tellers always hoped she wouldn't come to their window. She was irritable and cantankerous, and she snapped at everyone. Once I heard her berating our maid Annabel because there was starch in the towels in the ladies' room. The tellers advised me to have nothing to do with her if I could help it.

From her plain appearance and careless dress you would never have imagined that she was quite wealthy. (She was in the Social Register, belonged to the Colony Club, had a pew in St. James's, and lived in a large apartment on Park Avenue.)

I always smiled at her when she passed my desk, hoping she would not stop to speak. One day she did, however.

"I have some stock to be exchanged," she snapped unpleasantly. "Do you think you could do it without making a mistake?"

I said I would try and would pray that I did it properly.

"Don't pray," she said; "just do it."

It was hardly a promising start for one of the closest friendships of my life. But after I had got to know Miss Hastings I found that her outward manner was deceptive; actually she was a kindly and unselfish woman who, though her own life had been full of frustration and disappointment, had never ceased to sacrifice herself for others. Her mother had died when she was a child, and she had been raised by an uncle and aunt. She had had to refuse the proposal of the man she loved in order to take care of them in their old age, and when she had become free she had learned that he had been killed in the war. Her sister had married a man who was nearly penniless but who cared for her faithfully when she became an invalid, and Miss Hastings sent them half her income every month—for which she got little thanks.

In the winter she lived in New York, where she devoted three days a week to translating novels into Braille for the blind; in the summer she stayed at a seaside cottage on Long Island, giving three days a week to voluntary service in the local hospital. She got a great deal of pleasure out of life, in spite of having been thwarted in so many ways. She had a vast knowledge of books, music, and art; she loved the beautiful garden which she kept at her summer place; and she had many good friends.

Some of her income came from a living trust created by her uncle in Boston, and she also had a good many securities of her own. One day, after we had become well acquainted, she brought me her will, by which she planned the disposition of her own property. She had made it herself, she said, or, rather, had simply copied her mother's will, changing the names of beneficiaries according to her own wishes. But she wanted to revise it. She asked me if she could merely insert the changes and copy it over again.

I was glad that we had become friends; if she had been as disagreeable as she had once appeared to be, I would never have wanted to tell her that the will was completely invalid for several reasons. I carefully explained to her that you cannot copy someone else's will, particularly an old one. The state laws regarding wills had changed since her mother's time, and provisions that had applied to property that had belonged by title to her mother would not necessarily apply to her property. And the will had not been properly executed: it had been signed by her and witnessed by two friends, but not in her presence. I suggested that she go to her lawyer, tell him how she wanted to dispose of her property, and have him draw the will properly.

"But I don't want him to know what I'm doing with my money," she said.

I finally persuaded her that she had to tell him everything if she wanted to leave a valid will that would dispose of her property as she intended, and so she agreed. Her sister had died and she had no blood relatives, so she drew a will that left all her fortune in equal parts to ten spinster friends, who were not as well off as she was, and to her brother-in-law (the husband of her sister), who had remarried. She remarked that he didn't really have a claim on her but that, after all, he had been her sister's husband and had cared for her lovingly. She also felt that since he was married again he would need the money more than ever.

We were having lunch one day at my club when Miss Hastings suffered a slight stroke. By the time a doctor arrived, she had recovered sufficiently to walk back to her apartment. She had four more strokes before she improved, but shortly before Christmas she was sitting up and I took her some Christmas envelopes from the bank, into which she placed gifts of money for various friends. When I left she gave me a box to put under my Christmas tree; it contained some things that had belonged to her mother and she wanted me to have them. I still have a string of amber beads that she loved especially.

On Christmas Eve I got a telephone call from her doctor. She had suffered another stroke and wanted to see me. By the time I arrived, she was dead. I accompanied her remains to Boston for burial and then returned to the bank to carry out the instructions in her will, of which the bank was executor.

Hers was one of the most kindly and thoughtful wills I have ever carried out. She provided for genteel ladies of her own class, to whom life had given very little in the way of material comfort, and the income brought them a good deal of happiness in their remaining years.

The wills that are hardest to draw are those of women who are the last survivors of old families; these women have the double responsibility of leaving their money for worth-while purposes and, at the same time, perpetuating the family name in a suitable memorial. I had many such clients—women who were nearly alone in the world or had no very close relatives. They were used to the authority that their means had always given them, but they quite often became incapable of exercising that authority. As representative of the bank, I was assigned the task of keeping their accounts with us and persuading them to allow the bank to act as executor.

As their counselor I was expected to see that they were adequately provided for and that their wills were properly drawn and expressed their wishes. Sometimes it meant a great deal of personal attendance on them, and often I had to manage their households and their personal affairs when they were ill. At one time I had eight elderly ladies in my care.

When I was asked advice about their wills, I had to be very careful about what I said, especially when I was suggesting that they name the bank as executor of their estates. There are four grounds on which a will may be contested: if the person who made it was of unsound mind, if he was subjected to undue influence, if the will was improperly drawn or executed, or if the will was contrary to public policy. I had to be sure that I was not exerting undue influence over clients who sought help.

Miss Linden was an elderly maiden lady who lived in a comfortable hotel suite on the West Side. She always wore beautiful blue dresses that matched her eyes, and her white hair was immaculately groomed. She kept a substantial checking account with us. Most of her income came from a trust created by a friend for the duration of her life. The sole trustee was a judge of excellent reputation, but Miss Linden had no confidence in him; when he died she had the bank apply to be appointed trustee in his place. We found that the securities in the trust fund were of only two companies, one of which was in poor condition, and so we reinvested the money as best we could.

One day I received a call from the manager of the hotel where she lived. She had fallen and broken her hip and required hospital care. I went at once to take charge. After she had been in the hospital a short time, we found an apartment for her (near friends), furnished it, and engaged nurses for her. The bank paid her bills from her account as I approved them, as she had requested in writing.

I was surprised when she asked me one day how she should dispose of her own money in her will; she was so well informed and had such firm opinions on every matter that I had not expected to be consulted. Knowing that she had no relatives and that she was a devout Christian Scientist, I suggested that she leave some money to her church and that she provide scholarships for young people. She did not want to do either: the Mother Church was rich, she said, and young people who wanted education would get it themselves. Instead, she arranged for her money to go outright to five friends who had very little income. They would need it, and she felt she ought to help them as her friend had helped her by creating a trust.

"Why didn't you see that they had some all these years?" I asked.

"I never knew what I'd need, and, besides, I never wanted them to know I had money; they'd have expected it all the time," she said.

⚜ ⚜ ⚜

Miss Wales, who was also unmarried and the last of her line, disposed of her money very differently. She came of a prominent family, and much of the accumulated wealth of generations had passed to her. Her only relatives were descendants of her deceased brother. There was a grandniece in a state mental hospital and a cousin who came to see her once a month, bringing news of the rest of the family. The cousin had a son who was a spendthrift; in fact, all of her brother's share of the family wealth had been squandered.

"I don't want my money to go the way his did," she told me, "and I don't want it wasted. I am not going to leave it all to that worthless family. Will you help me plan a will so that I can put it to good use?"

I tried to leave this request unanswered; it would not be proper for me to tell a client how she should dispose of her money, even though I might recommend the bank as executor. "Please write me a letter as you think my will should be drawn," she insisted.

Eventually she planned a very thoughtful will. All her jewelry—it was beautiful and costly—went to her friends, and she left money to her church and to various charities and made specific bequests to several worthy friends. She did not cut out her brother's relatives; instead, she left each of them a sum of money in trust for life, after which the principal was to pass to two women's colleges to provide scholarships in memory of her parents. Thus she provided for her friends and for her family and, ultimately, for a permanent memorial in the family name that would bring benefits to future generations of young women.

⚜ ⚜ ⚜

Mary Powers, that odd recluse who had first come to see me at the bank late on an eerie winter afternoon, always refused to make a will. In this she behaved entirely in character. The bank got her account—a large part of what she owned, although she withheld much—and it was my duty for twenty-five years to try to keep it in order against every kind of perversity and stubbornness on her part. Once a month I went to her hotel and the clerk announced me by telephone. I went up to her apartment, where she waited at the unbolted door to let me in—after which she shot the bolt in place. Inside was a shambles; dust lay an inch thick and piles of newspapers littered the corners. The air was stale—since the windows were never opened—the curtains were drawn, and the only light came from a tiny bulb in the center of the ceiling. As we worked we laid our papers aside on a sofa whose upholstery was spilling out.

She was preoccupied with trivialities, and I was seldom able to direct her attention to what I knew to be important matters. She hated to cash dividend checks and add to her already large account, so she held them indefinitely; and when she did decide to cash them we had to send them back to see if they were still good. She kept her stocks registered in the broker's name while corporations wrote baskets of letters pleading with her to transfer the shares into her own name. She never completed her income tax return until the day it was due, and then we had to rush to get it into the mail before the deadline. She never surrendered canceled or called stocks or bonds. One corporation pleaded with her for years to get her to cash dividend checks. When she did not, the funds were placed in escrow according to state law and the state started proceedings to claim the money. Newspapers carried the story, much to her indignation. She loathed publicity. On the very last day that she could collect the funds she did so, having put everyone concerned to the maximum inconvenience.

She suffered from eczema, which she tried to conceal by wearing a hat with a veil indoors and keeping the light dim, and she no longer went out at all. One bright spring day I noticed that the lilies of the valley in my garden were blooming and I took her a bunch of them. When I gave them to her, anticipating her pleasure, she threw them on the floor and trampled them.

"Never do such a thing again!" she screamed.

I managed to say "I'm sorry" as she bolted the door in silence.

Then she turned to me and said, "No, I should say *I'm* sorry. Once I picked a bouquet like that for my mother and she punished me. She said I shouldn't give way to silly fancies like that. She said I should never have been born," she added. "She only cared about my brother. Now let's get down to business."

The next time I came the lilies of the valley, dried up, stood in a vase on the mantel.

"See, they are still nice," she said.

She was milder that time, and I brought up again the subject of making a will, since she had no family and, of course, I wanted the bank to be executor. I suggested that she provide for a memorial to her mother—a camp for poor children or college scholarships for deserving young women. She would not hear of a memorial to her mother and she was not interested in poor children.

"What happens if you don't make a will and if you have no blood relatives?" she asked.

I told her that the state of New York would get the money.

"That's a good idea," she said. "The state is always poor."

Another time, when she expressed to me a distaste for the idea of being buried in the ground, I suggested that she erect a family mausoleum. But that came to nothing.

Once I persuaded her to let the president of the bank call on her. Even then she said, "You are good to come. I am in wonderful hands. I do not intend to make a will."

Later he asked me how I could bear such squalor. Couldn't I get the hotel to clean the room?

Miss Powers began to speak of someone she called "Him" and then "a relative of mine." A photograph of a rather handsome man appeared on her worktable and she told me it was "Him." I learned he was a cousin once removed. "I am sure he will claim my estate when I die," she said. When I asked her why she did not make it easier for him by having a will drawn, she said, "No, let him fight for it. Meanwhile he can wonder about it."

The man called "Him" came to see me in July 1940 and told me that his cousin, Miss Powers, was quite ill and wanted me to come to her. I found her in her apartment, but instead of wearing a battered old hat and dress she was sitting up in bed in a clean nightgown—in a clean apartment. She asked me to gather some checks and securities to take to the bank. I found checks dating back to 1922 and thousands of dollars in bonds of the first Liberty Loan.

She died shortly after, and 200 claimants to her estate appeared. The newspapers were full of it—an eccentric recluse worth millions and scores of missing heirs made a good story. I signed the affidavit that enabled attorneys to claim the estate for "Him," her cousin.

I remembered her few moments of kindness, as when I went to see her for the first time after my mother died.

"I am glad to see you," she said. "I did not know if you would ever be able to make it again."

When I told her that I had to try not to give in to my grief, that my mother would scold me when we met again, she said, "You don't believe all that tommyrot, do you?"

I hope that I gave her some solace of mind and heart; she needed friendship and sympathy so much.

Her will was the subject of long legal proceedings, during which much of the estate was dissipated in lawyer's fees, fees to the public administrator representing unknown heirs, court costs, and bond requirements. The cousin applied to be made administrator (a person who handles the settlement of an estate when there is no will), and more of the money went for his expenses. When an estate is administered by a person who is not familiar with it, there is inevitably much waste. But in the end the cousin got a substantial amount. When he thanked me for having been of help to him and hinted that I deserved some reward, I suggested that he place markers over the graves of Miss Powers, her mother, and her brother.

They are buried, strangely enough, not far from my parents' graves in Woodlawn Cemetery, and when I go there I stop at three tombstones and wonder if any of those people who worked so relentlessly to accumulate money ever had any pleasure from it. And I can't help thinking how much happier Miss Powers' last days might have been if she had planned a few worth-while charities and had had some satisfaction from disposing of the money that had brought her nothing but anxiety and loneliness all her life.

Not many of us have $5,000,000 to leave and no close relative to leave it to, but I cite Miss Powers' case as a good example of what happens to a person's money when she dies without a will. Everyone concerned is subjected to extraordinary inconvenience. A great many lawyers and other functionaries collect fees, which is nice for them, but their employment is quite futile and unproductive and it uses up money for which there are better purposes. The machinery of the law moves relentlessly and impersonally. In the end someone gets what is left of the money, but only after a struggle that is without pleasure and without merit. Or else the funds simply disappear into the state treasury.

⚜ ⚜ ⚜

Mrs. Wilks—that was her real name—always arrived at the bank in a big Pierce-Arrow limousine, went into the ladies' department, and then went to the vault, where she spent hours clipping coupons from bonds. Shortly after the death of her husband she came to me with a question, and from that time on all her business at the bank went through my hands.

She was tall, angular, and rather stern in appearance, and she wore thick-lensed, steel-rimmed glasses. She was always dressed in black, with a large hat and a feather boa, and she usually wore carpet slippers—not from carelessness or eccentricity, but simply because her feet hurt.

Many very rich women acquire a reputation for being eccentric. Sylvia Wilks had a very good claim to that description because she was, in her time, probably the richest woman in the world. The enormous balance she carried with us was only one of her many bank accounts, and she had vast interests of every kind—securities, real estate, and personal property. She lived in a huge apartment on Fifth Avenue and also had a large estate in Greenwich, which she had inherited from her late husband. But most of her wealth had come to her from her mother, who was Hetty Green, famous as "the Witch of Wall Street."

Hetty Green and Mrs. Powers, mother of the strange recluse whose affairs I tried to keep in order, had been friends, but I do not believe that the girls ever knew each other well, and probably neither one suspected that I was the friend of both. In many ways their childhoods in New Jersey had been similar—unhappy and deprived. Hetty Green had been a miser, and as a young girl Sylvia had had to cook, clean, and sew for her multimillionaire mother, who had been too stingy to hire servants. Miss Powers, too, had never known any affection or consideration from her mother, who had also been devoted to accumulating money. But they had grown up to be very different kinds of persons. Miss Powers was timid and shut herself away from people; Mrs. Wilks was bold, authoritative, and afraid of no one. Because of her forbidding appearance and independent manner, it was thought that she simply did not like people and gave all her devotion to her pets. This was far from the truth; Mrs. Wilks had been happily married and had known a brilliant social life, and I knew, from her generous gifts to friends, that she was a very warmhearted woman.

She had married, with her mother's blessing, Matthew Wilks, member of a wealthy old New York family, who had signed a prenuptial agreement relinquishing any claim to the vast fortune that Sylvia would inherit. He had had enough money of his own and had married for love, and Hetty Green had approved of him and had left him a small legacy in her will.

Mrs. Wilks's brother, who was deceased, had also shared the tremendous fortune, and Mrs. Wilks was involved in some litigation with her brother's widow, who did not see eye to eye with her on the disposition of the Green inheritance. When the judge of the court that heard the case asked her who her attorney was, Mrs. Wilks replied imperiously, "I am my own attorney, your honor. Who else could have my interest better at heart, be more familiar with my situation, or keep his fees more equitable?" She had her way.

When the first war loans were offered for subscription in 1917, each officer in the bank was assigned certain accounts and Mrs. Wilks's came to me. She was not easy to approach, and I was apprehensive when I first asked her to subscribe. To my astonishment, she subscribed at once to $1,000,000 worth of bonds, saying, with a wink, "I guess that will show the men the stuff we girls are made of."

My quota was instantly oversubscribed many times.

When the next loan was announced, she came in without my asking her and increased her subscription. By this time I was a little concerned at the way her balances in the bank dwindled whenever she subscribed to the bonds.

"Does this make you unhappy?" she said. I admitted that I felt a certain panic at the way her balances were decreasing. "Don't worry," she told me kindly; "I'll give you a check on another bank." And she did, for an amount even higher than she had pledged. She took to heart the verse in Matthew 6 that says, "When thou doest alms let not thy left hand know what thy right hand doeth."

One day when she was sitting at my desk a prominent attorney came in, bringing a client who had recently become a widow, to discuss her affairs. Mrs. Wilks had been at my desk for some time, telling me how she had sat up all night with a sick kitten. (She was noted for her devotion to cats.) The attorney and his client listened in on the conversation impatiently and my secretary told him that it would take a few minutes more.

"Would he like my chair?" Mrs. Wilks said loudly.

I explained that he had an appointment, but she continued. I had to hear how the kitten had got through the night, she said. And she went on for ten minutes more. Then she got up and I accompanied her to the door.

When I returned to my desk, the attorney said stiffly, "Miss Armbruster, I'm not accustomed to being kept waiting for an appointment, and especially by a hag like that."

"That 'hag,'" I told him, "is Mrs. Wilks."

He flew toward the door, hoping to get another glimpse of her, then came back saying, "If I'd known, I'd have waited hours just to look at her!"

Mrs. Wilks's charity was not all for cats. She and I planned several large trusts for certain needy friends of hers who were old and ill. The trusts were to be completely anonymous—the beneficiaries were never to know that the money came from her—and her other banks were not to know of the trusts. She created them with the government bonds she had purchased through me. She also made countless smaller gifts, always anonymously, taking no credit for them. She loved animals, and she made appropriate gifts and bequests to societies that cared for them.

When she died, after having given away enormous sums of money, her estate was valued at over $90,000,000. All of it went to charity, as she had no living blood relations to make any claims against it, and the benefits of her generosity will be felt for years to come.

I have in my garden a snow-white North Carolina rhododendron that she gave me as a token of friendship, and each time I look at it I think of how kindly she disposed of the fortune that had been so heartlessly acquired.

⚜ ⚜ ⚜

One of the most important considerations to bear in mind when you draw a will or revise it is the executor. He is the agent charged with carrying out the wishes you have expressed in your will and he has a great responsibility. He must be a person of integrity and sound business judgment, a person in whom you have absolute confidence, and one whom you can trust to bear in mind your family's needs and treat them with sympathy and understanding. He must have a knowledge of every form of property of which your estate consists—securities, real estate, and any special kinds of personal property which will come under his care. For example, a man who has spent a great deal on collecting paintings will want as executor someone who understands their value. If you leave a business, then your executor must be capable of taking charge of its management. After your will has been probated, the assets of the estate must be collected and a value placed upon them. The debts and taxes must be paid and claims must be examined and settled; everything you leave must be administered and cared for until it passes into the possession of your heirs or trustees.

An executor's task is complicated. At the very outset he must take ten steps to safeguard the estate. They are these:

1. See that burial instructions are carried out.
2. Have mail directed to executor.
3. Locate witnesses to will.
4. Locate heirs.
5. Be sure that there is insurance covering all property.
6. Be sure home is locked.
7. If there is real estate, discontinue water, gas, electricity, and telephone.
8. Gather all valuables together and place in estate safe-deposit box.
9. Arrange for appraisal of real estate, securities, and other properties.
10. Determine cash requirements and arrange for liquidation of assets to meet them.

You should also be sure to choose an executor who will be physically and mentally capable of carrying out the responsibilities and one on whom they will not impose an unfair burden.

Few individuals have the ideal qualifications of a good executor; hence, many people name coexecutors. In any case, naming more than one executor is a wise precaution, in the event that one should die or become disabled before your estate is settled.

A corporate executor—a bank or trust company—has all the qualifications necessary to carry out the terms of your will. It never dies, gets sick, or goes away; it has the experience and the facilities to assume full responsibility for all your affairs; and it does not require a bond. A corporate executor, on the face of it, may seem too impersonal to treat your family with understanding, but, actually, a good trust officer is as experienced in dealing with human needs as with handling and preserving property. The fee for a corporate executor is no more than that to which an individual executor is entitled, and it is fixed by law. The fee varies in different states, but, as an example, the legal fee in New York is 4 per cent on the first $10,000 of an estate's value, 2½ per cent on the next $290,000, and 2 per cent above $300,000.

The ideal arrangement—one that affords you maximum protection and security—is that of making the most trusted, experienced, and fair-minded member of your family coexecutor with the bank. The individual executor may waive his fee if he wishes, and generally a member of your family or a close friend will do so. The bank takes care of routine matters and handles actual transactions; your individual coexecutor, who knows your wishes and your family needs, advises and brings to bear whatever special knowledge and skill may be useful in settling your estate to the best interests of your beneficiaries and has equal authority with the bank. Of all possible arrangements, this seems to me the one that gives you the greatest assurance that the terms of your last will and testament will be carried out according to your intentions.

CHAPTER ELEVEN

WOMEN AND MONEY

For wisdom is a defense, and money is a defense, but the excellency of knowledge is that wisdom giveth life to them that have it.
Ecclesiastes 7:12

On a cold February day in 1951 I walked out of The Fifth Avenue Bank building with Roberta Hunter, my secretary, both of us stiff as ramrods and trying not to show our emotion. We had agreed not to look back; if we had, I am sure we would have broken down and cried. The bank had been merged since 1948 with The Bank of New York, and the old building was being abandoned to the wreckers and we were moving into temporary quarters until a new building was erected on the site. For more than seventy-five years the bank had been a landmark on the avenue; it was world-famous because of its historic association with the growth of New York and the transformation of Fifth Avenue from an elegant residential street to a great business thoroughfare. That day we had received 5,000 visitors, who had come to say farewell, as to an old friend.

The merger with The Bank of New York had been a sad occasion for us old employees, although the identity of The Fifth Avenue Bank of New York had been preserved as the name of the chief uptown branch. The "Gold Room," at whose entrance I had sat for twenty-five years, was to be reproduced in the ladies' wing of the new building. But the physical disappearance of our old home gave our hearts a wrench.

That night I went to the opera with a friend, Kay Brown, who observed that she had never seen me so downcast and uneasy. I told her that nothing since my mother's death in 1941 had affected me so much as the razing of our building. I even overheard a man sitting next to her say, "They're tearing down the old Fifth Avenue Bank. I just can't believe it." Everyone who knew the bank and the avenue had that personal feeling for it.

After the opera, Kay jokingly asked if I wanted to drive up Fifth Avenue to see if the building was still there, and I suddenly decided I did. As we approached I saw the entire vault of the bank, hoisted in the air on ropes, being moved out onto the avenue, protected by a cordon of police. We parked her car and went over to a policeman and asked him to let us pass through the line.

He refused, looking askance at my evening dress and opera glasses.

"It's all right," I said. "I'm an officer of the bank, and I'm going through."

"Hey," the policeman yelled to a sergeant, "I got a crackpot here says she's an officer of the bank and wants in."

At that moment one of the men from the vault department who was supervising the operation saw me and called, "Hello, Miss Armbruster; come on in."

The policeman looked at me, pushed his hat back, and scratched his head. "Well, can you beat that," he muttered, and we crossed the cordon and joined the vault boys. We sat in the hole where the vault had been, drinking coffee, until four in the morning, while the huge vault containing millions and millions of dollars in money and securities was moved to the new quarters.

This was one of the moments in my career that I shall always remember. There were others equally memorable. My appointment as assistant cashier will always be a high point, because for a woman banker it was a nearly impossible achievement at that time. I shared my happiness with my parents and with my dear friend Mrs. Lewis, who on that occasion urged me to buy a home of my own for my parents. And it was due to her insistence that I acquired my present home in Bronxville.

Twelve years after that, in January 1945, Mr. Hetzler again called me to his office—to tell me I was an assistant vice-president. "Mr. Frissell would be proud of you," he said as he shook my hand. "It's a good thing you got that rose on your desk," Mr. Foley said as he congratulated me.

My home life had changed by that time. My parents were both dead and my three brothers were all away in service with the Air Corps. John, now a major, was married and stationed in Hawaii as a finance officer. Raymond, also a major, was stationed at the Pentagon. Christian was a cadet and had just been graduated with honors from the Radio Mechanic School at Truax Field. Marion, my only sister, a graduate of Mount Holyoke with a Doctor of Science degree from Bryn Mawr, was living with me and commuting daily to Kearney, New Jersey, where she was the only woman research member of the U. S. Steel Research Laboratory. She was not coming home that evening, and it would be some time before I could tell my good news to the boys.

I was feeling a slight pang of loneliness in spite of my success when, as if by a miracle, my brother Raymond suddenly appeared at my desk. He had just flown up from Washington on an assignment, which later fully materialized when he went to Europe as a member of the U. S. Strategic Bombing Survey appointed by the President. He bought me an orchid and we had an extravagant dinner at Le Pavillon to celebrate my promotion. It became a gala evening.

Another occasion I will never forget was the merger of The Fifth Avenue Bank with The Bank of New York in May 1948. For me and for most of our older employees it was a difficult moment; we had such a strong attachment to our old bank. The morning of the public announcement I felt depressed. Then the wife of the former president of The Bank of New York—and present chairman of the board of the merged banks—came in and brought me a corsage of gardenias. Smiling very sweetly, she said, "I know it's a trying day for you. I came in especially to see you and to wish 'our' bank success." I was immediately reassured and I started the tasks of the day.

The last of my appointments came in 1952 when the president,

Mr. Simmonds, telephoned me to say that the board of trustees had made me a full vice-president. The lady who happened to be sitting at my desk at the time wept with me. We had planned to go to lunch together at Schrafft's, but instead we went to the Algonquin.

"Now you're a celebrity," she said. "That's the place they go."

Always at those times—and often since my retirement in 1959—I looked back and reflected on the long way that women have come since 1784, when The Bank of New York was founded, and on the even greater advances they have made since 1917, when I went to work in the bank to replace a man who had been called to the Army.

In the years since then I have devoted nearly all my time and energy to helping women save and, especially, manage money, and I have seen lives saved and ruined by money. Some people—men and women—dedicated themselves solely to the accumulation of wealth, denying themselves the pleasures it can bring and overlooking every opportunity to put it to good use. Mrs. Greer, the beautiful show girl who married into New York society, invested the $40,000 in gold pieces that she had hoarded in her safe-deposit box and became so shrewd a businesswoman that she increased it to over a quarter of a million dollars in about twenty years. With gifts from her husband, she was worth almost half a million when she died. But her obsession with money and social position overrode every other concern. She was hardly an innocent girl when she married Mr. Greer, and she harbored all her life a secret that brought her intense anxiety and unhappiness and broke into a sordid scandal after her death. She had an illegitimate son whom she would not acknowledge once she became a rich society woman. She had abandoned him while he was still young. Quite deliberately she had cut him out of her will and provided that all her money should go to Harvard University—a very worthy provision in itself, but hardly an excuse for neglecting the child who was the victim of her own folly and social ambition. Later the will was contested by a man who believed he might be her son but who could not prove it. The identity of her real son was established only after he had died an alcoholic in the public ward of a Boston hospital. How different his life might have been if Mrs. Greer had cared for him in his childhood, and how much happier her own life would have been if she had fulfilled her duty as a mother and a human being and used her wealth to give the boy his rightful start in life.

I saw much of her: she was a constant visitor to the bank, driven there by her compulsion to make more and more money, and she often descended unannounced on our home, where, because of her loneliness, she enjoyed the company of my family, especially my father. When he died she sent to his funeral a cross of lilies ten feet high. A beautiful and commanding woman, and a fascinating one, she had achieved her worldly ambition—riches and high social position—but at a terrible cost. I was her confidante, and she exacted from me the promise that she be buried in her wedding dress. I took it with me to the little room in St. Thomas's on Fifth Avenue where she lay in her coffin. An undertaker's assistant advised me gently to go away and not try the impossible. But a promise was a promise, and I kept it. Mrs. Greer had had a tiny, narrow waist when she was married, but in her later years she had developed considerable girth. I took a pair of scissors, slit the dress down the back, and laid it over her, grieved at her death and her useless life, yet relieved that my last pledge to her was fulfilled. At that moment the organ boomed out and I had the uncanny feeling that it was the voice of God. Why am I here? I wondered. I should be back at the bank helping women who have real problems instead of standing here among the organ pipes paying my last respects to this woman who did so much damage and created so little happiness for herself and others.

Poor Miss Powers, too, never enjoyed money or used it to help anyone else. But hers was quite a different case; her childhood had been blighted by an indifferent, miserly mother who had disliked her, and although there had been a streak of warmth and affection in her, the cruelty she had known had nearly extinguished it. She was not an unworthy person—merely an unfortunate one—and she might have been much happier if she had been poor. Mrs. Wilks, however, of a similar background and of the same generation, had made a good life for herself, however remote and strange it might have seemed to the world, and she created immense benefits with her wealth. Mrs. Putnam, having early in womanhood suffered far more human loss than anyone should have to bear, had changed from a headstrong and rebellious girl into a serene woman of admirable faith and wisdom. She lived well and enjoyed the pleasures of money, but without ostentation and extravagance. Rather, she regarded the wealth she had inherited as a responsibility and herself as a trustee with a sacred obligation. The later years of her life she spent almost entirely in using her wealth to help people—all her living relatives, her friends, her servants, her church, and her community—and in planning her estate well so that it would continue for years after her death to bring help to those who needed it. She brought to her task the warmth and sympathy that is a woman's special gift to life.

These women were wealthy and could well afford to be generous; but I have also known many poor women who shared their small incomes generously with others and who planned lovingly for the disposition of their meager estates. I like to think of Mrs. Gay, who came to me after the death of her husband to ask my help in arranging her small holdings to provide her with an adequate income. She had idolized her husband, who, it seems, had been rather a saintly man, and had been so devoted to him that I wondered how she would bear her loss, with no children or other relatives to comfort her. Yet she found a vocation and lived out her life very happily, even though she lived alone in a small uptown hotel. She was a talented musician and she made a new life for herself by teaching choir boys Gregorian chants; and in her will she provided a small trust to perpetuate the teaching of the music that had brought her so much solace. I attended her funeral mass, and as I listened to the choir boys and watched their faces as they sang for the teacher they had loved I reflected that Mrs. Gay, with so little in the world, had used it to create great spiritual wealth in her own life and in many lives to come.

Two men, besides my father, had a tremendous influence on my career: Mr. Frissell and Mr. Foley. Mr. Frissell was a gentle man and a visionary, and he had the foresight to create a whole new means of taking care of women's accounts because he recognized the handicaps under which women of his generation labored in dealing with money matters. Mr. Foley was gruff, outspoken, sometimes harsh in manner, and he always expected me to do the impossible, but he was, in a different way, as generous and warm-hearted as Mr. Frissell.

After Mr. Foley retired, I saw him often. A bachelor, he lived alone with a woman servant to look after him. His apartment was full of books, which he loved, and of flowers, for which he had a fondness that no one would have suspected in such a brusque, hearty man. I often asked him to our home for dinner, and he sometimes invited me to dine with him. His needs were few: all he ever spent money on were books and stickpins, of which he had quite a collection—his one concession to vanity.

One day he told me that in making his will he had named me as executrix, instead of the bank, since he did not have enough for the bank to be bothered with. I thought little of this at the time, but I imagined, since Mr. Foley was an excellent banker and had held an important job for many years, that he would have a fairly large estate and that, since he had no close relatives, having left his family behind him in Ireland many years before, he would leave everything to his favorite charities. At his death I took charge of his affairs, according to his instructions, and bought a single lot in Woodlawn Cemetery not far from our family lot. There he lies—he who loved growing things so much—in the shelter of a beautiful tree. I like to think it was the kind of spot he'd have chosen himself.

What astonished me when I settled his affairs was that there was no residuary estate after his expenses had been paid—nothing. No wonder he had not wanted the bank to know what he had; it was hardly a good recommendation for a banker! How could a man of Mr. Foley's quiet habits have disposed of the money he must have accumulated? Then I remembered how, again and again, he had given money to people who needed it. One woman who had had a minor job in the bank had lost her husband suddenly and had not had the money to bury him. Mr. Foley had dug down in his pocket and given it to her: he had not lent it or exacted an accounting; he had simply given it. Another time the wife of a young man in the bank had had a serious and costly operation. Mr. Foley had given him the money to pay his bills. For years he had taught us all the high importance of saving money, investing it, caring for it—and all the time he had constantly been emptying his own pockets to help people in need. It is not quite what I expected of a banker, but it is a wonderful way to use money when you know there will be no relatives to leave it to. Every time I hear of the proverbial tight-fisted, skinflint banker, the memory of Mr. Foley warms me.

⚜ ⚜ ⚜

In the last forty years I have watched the status of women in society and business change and have had the privilege of taking part in that transformation. I always loved to study the history of early New York and the women who lived there, and I learned much about it from some of my clients who were descended from them.

There were many women of considerable means in the old New York whose first families were largely Dutch settlers. One of my first clients was Mrs. van Inten, a very old lady of Dutch ancestry whose great-grandfather had been a diamond merchant who traveled back and forth between New York and Antwerp trading in jewels. Once she showed me a lovely brooch, a turquoise set in gold and encircled with diamonds, that she was putting into her safe-deposit box: her ancestor had brought it back from Europe to give to his wife on their twenty-fifth wedding anniversary. It was to go to Mrs. van Inten's daughter on her twenty-first birthday: she would be the fifth generation to own it.

Other women who came to the bank were of English or French descent; their great-grandmothers, too, had played a part in building New York. One told me that her great-grandmother's home had been the headquarters of Revolutionary officers and that that lady had given a whole year's income to the public treasury of the new United States of America. Another woman's ancestor had held off a British officer by talking brightly to him while a group of rebel soldiers had hidden under the very staircase where she stood. Dozens of times I visited the homes of those women and saw the priceless heirlooms that had come down from their Revolutionary ancestors and heard a grandfather clock that still chimed as it had 200 years before, when New York was only a colonial mercantile port.

These early American women had substantial property, some of it in their own right. More often than not they outlived their husbands, and then the responsibility of disposing of the wealth fell on them. But they had little authority over it. In an old account book of the bank I found only sixteen women's names, and these only after 1848, when it became legal for women to have their own bank accounts. Usually a household account was in a man's name with an instruction, such as "My wife Ann may sign." Even with the handicaps of ignorance and legal restraint, these women preserved their wealth and distributed it wisely, and they were responsible for many of the museums, schools, charitable institutions, scholarships, churches, parks, and monuments which New Yorkers enjoy to this day.

When I first went to work in the bank in 1917, there were still very few women in business. They had gained a small foothold early in the century, but outstanding businesswomen were still exceptional and, indeed, thought to be freaks. The idea that women have only domestic functions dies hard, and we are still struggling against inherited ignorance and prejudice in this field. For generations rich women made their influence felt and poor ones were cruelly exploited at hard labor. The professional woman came into her own only after the First World War. Now she stands at the top in every field of enterprise and her place in our economic system and in public affairs is now so firmly established that it can never again be questioned.

The American woman of today owns 79 per cent of the nation's wealth; she spends 80 per cent of the family's budget—on clothing and food and home necessities; she is the beneficiary of 80 per cent of all trust funds and the greatest beneficiary of insurance policies. She also owns well over half of the outstanding shares of stock in corporations and is co-owner of half a million small businesses. Of the nation's savings accounts, she owns 65 per cent. She accounts for the earnings of a third of the gainfully employed workers in the country, with about $45,000,000,000 a year in wages.

Women are officers and directors of large corporations; they are stockbrokers, bankers, economists, business consultants, engineers; they are prominent as lawyers, judges, doctors, educators, publishers, editors, writers, public-relations experts. Naturally enough, the modern woman excels in those fields that have always been related to women's particular interests—design, fashion, decoration, and the domestic arts, all of which have become big business. And, as always, she has a strong voice in religious, charitable, and philanthropic affairs—including inspiring and guiding the good works of many of our great men philanthropists. And in my own profession of banking, where forty years ago women were very few and then employed only in menial tasks, women are now top executives, bank officers, counselors, public-relations advisers, economic researchers. Of the more than half a million bank employees in the United States, 360,000 are women and 180,000 men. And of these women, over 10,000 have reached executive status in a very brief span of time. In a business where automation—in the form of business machines that handle vast numbers of checks and perform accounting tasks that formerly consumed countless hours of labor—is an increasing factor, this change does not mean that women will be displaced by machines; rather, it offers the opportunity for women to move out of routine jobs into tasks that require the use of their full capacities as human beings and, specifically, as women.

For women, in having proved themselves the peers of men in every kind of endeavor, except possibly warfare, need not lose their unique attributes. Nor in an eagerness to share all of men's tasks and privileges should they lose sight of their singular responsibility to remain women and to confer on every enterprise they undertake the singular grace of womanhood.

The Indian poet Tagore said many years ago: "At the present stage of history, civilization is almost exclusively masculine, a civilization of power, in which woman has been thrust aside in the shade. Therefore it has lost its balance and is moving by hopping from war to war, its motive forces are the forces of destruction, and its ceremonies are carried through by an appalling number of human sacrifices. This one-sided civilization is crashing along a series of catastrophes at a tremendous speed because of its one-sidedness. And at last the time has arrived when woman must step in and impart her life rhythm to the reckless movement of power."

He also wrote: "Wherever there is something which is concretely personal and human, there is woman's world. The personal world where every individual finds his worth as an individual, [and] therefore his value is not the market-value, but the value of love; that is to say the value God in His infinite mercy has set upon all creatures. . . . This personal world has been the gift of God to woman. She can extend her radiance of love beyond its boundaries on all sides . . . she is born in the center of her own true world, the world of human relationships."

In our time, as our economy expands, the world grows more impersonal. Machines take over the functions of human beings, and we are in danger of losing sight of our humanity in the growing dehumanization of the processes by which we run our society. It is precisely here that women can best fulfill their function of bringing the human and the personal touch into every field of enterprise ruled by men. In banking I tried to grasp the special, individual need of every client who came to me for help. I did so first because I was interested in the clients; then, through experience, I learned that it was the only way in which, as a bank counselor, I could really help them. I have observed that the most successful businesswomen bring a human sympathy to bear on the problems of their professions; and this is even more true of women in public affairs. In the United Nations, it is women who uphold human rights against the drive of power politics; in government, it is women who bring domestic good sense into the managing of public business, who soften the harsh impersonal processes of administration with humane understanding.

By entering into the larger world of business and public affairs, women do not renounce their traditional roles of mother and homemaker. They have risen above the old conflict between a business career and the claims of marriage. Close at hand I have observed young women who worked with me in the bank, particularly my three secretaries, all of them fine businesswomen and good bankers. Two of them left to be married, and although their husbands are successful and they do not have to work they have come back into business in part-time jobs. They do not find that they neglect their homes and families. The qualities that make them good wives and mothers are invaluable to them in the business world, and what they have learned in business helps them to run their homes more efficiently and to escape the drudgery of full-time housekeeping. They and their families enjoy spending the money which, as women in banking, they learned to save and invest. Their professional lives enhance their domestic lives.

For my part, I have never regretted my decision to devote all my life to banking. I feel, as the psalmist said, "The lines are fallen unto me in pleasant places." I did not marry and have a family of my own largely because I already had a family of brothers and a sister to care for. And I had the pleasure of making my parents' last years a great deal happier than they would have been without material advantages, and of watching my brothers and my sister acquire good educations and rise high in their professions.

John and Raymond are successful in fields allied to my own interests; Marion, until she gave up her work to become the mother of twins, was one of the finest research chemists in her field; Christian is a lawyer, active, as all my family has been, in civic affairs and a New York State Assemblyman. As for myself, although my status is "retired," I am still busy with commitments made years ago to old friends. I have estates to settle, guardianships to fulfill, trusteeships, and many other duties; and I still take great satisfaction in giving counsel, when they ask me, to women who were my clients and to their daughters and even their granddaughters. I am proud of these young women, as I was of their mothers and grandmothers. All of them have proved beyond the need of repetition that women can excel in all those fields that were formerly reserved to men. But what is more important is that they must enter these fields and bring into a larger sphere the qualities of sympathy and understanding that men are apt to neglect in their effort to build and increase our material society and without which our civilization will be an empty achievement. The place where every woman can start, whether she contemplates a full-time professional career or not, is in that last citadel of masculine power, the management of money. Whether she has a large fortune or a small one, a woman can and should learn to manage it, to control it, and to spend it wisely. It is her surest way of safeguarding the spiritual heritage of which she is the trustee.

QUESTIONS AND ANSWERS

These are the questions that women asked me most frequently. When the answers can be given briefly, they are given here. When they require a fuller explanation, the reader is referred to the pages of the text which illustrate them.

WHAT IS A CERTIFIED CHECK? A depositor's check that has been presented to the bank for certification. The bank stamps it "certified" and withdraws funds from the depositor's account and puts them in a special account. The bank becomes responsible for the check's payment.

WHAT IS A STOP PAYMENT ORDER? See p. 42.

WHAT IS THE FILLING OF A CHECK? See p. 41.

WHAT IS AN OVERDRAFT? See p. 42.

WHY WILL A BANK SOMETIMES PAY AN OVERDRAFT? See p. 42.

WHAT IS A SERVICE CHARGE? See p. 89, and 116.

WHAT IS A COUPON? See p. 102, 140.

WHAT IS A DIVIDEND? See p. 144.

WHAT IS A LETTER OF CREDIT? See p. 76.

WHAT DO I DO IF I LOSE A BOND? Notify your bank and ask it to place a stop payment order with the paying agent.

WHAT SHOULD I DO IF I LOSE A STOCK CERTIFICATE? Notify the transfer agent to stop payment. See p. 116.

WHAT IS A TRAVELER'S CHECK? See p. 75.

MAY I TAKE A LOAN WITH MY BANK? See p. 62, 69.

WHAT IS PURCHASING STOCK ON MARGIN? See p. 121.

WHAT DOES "PLACE AN ORDER" MEAN? See p. 116, 118.

WILL MY BANK BUY STOCK ON MARGIN FOR ME? See p. 123.

WHAT IS SHORT SELLING? See p. 122.

WHAT IS THE MONTHLY STATEMENT THAT THE BANK SENDS ME? See p. 41.

IS THE SAFE-DEPOSIT COMPANY PART OF THE BANK? See p. 50.

WHAT IS A "FORGED SIGNATURE?" See p. 42.

CAN I BUY STOCK THROUGH MY BANK OR MUST I GO TO A BROKER? See p. 116.

SHOULD I BUY STOCK AT A PRICE OR AT THE MARKET VALUE? See p. 118.

WHAT DOES "BID AND ASKED" MEAN IN THE PURCHASE OF STOCK? See p. 118.

WHAT IS AN ODD LOT? DOES IT COST MORE THAN A ROUND LOT? See p. 119.

WHAT IS "TRADING"? DO BANKS ADVISE IT? See p. 120.

AM I TAXED BY THE GOVERNMENT ON CAPITAL GAINS ON STOCK? See p. 121.

HOW DO I KNOW WHAT STOCK TO BUY? See p. 124, 125.

WHERE CAN I FIND OUT WHAT MY SHARES OF STOCK ARE SELLING FOR? See p. 137.

WHAT IS A PORTFOLIO? See p. 139.

WHY DO ANNUITIES USUALLY PAY A HIGHER RATE OF INTEREST THAN OTHER SECURITIES? See p. 138.

WHAT DOES A "POINT" MEAN IN THE QUOTATION OF A STOCK PRICE? See p. 137, 138.

MUST SAVINGS ACCOUNT INTEREST BE REPORTED ON MY INCOME TAX? See p. 48, 139.

WHAT IS AMORTIZATION? See p. 100.

SHOULD I INVEST THE AMORTIZATION PAYMENTS ON A MORTGAGE I HOLD? See p. 100.

ARE COUPONS GOOD AT ANY TIME? See p. 140.

IF I LOSE MY COUPONS, ARE THEY VALID FOR THE PERSON WHO FINDS THEM? See p. 140.

HOW DO I KNOW WHEN A BOND IS CALLED? See p. 140.

IS THE INTEREST ON ALL BONDS PAID BY COUPON? See p. 141.

WHAT IS A CONVERTIBLE BOND? SHOULD I CONVERT IT? See p. 142.

WHAT ARE SOME TYPES OF PREFERRED STOCK? See p. 143.

WHEN DO I RECEIVE DIVIDENDS? WHAT DOES PASSING A DIVIDEND MEAN? WHAT IS "EX-DIVIDEND?" See p. 144.

SHOULD I READ THE ANNUAL REPORTS OF COMPANIES I HAVE INVESTED IN? See p. 146.

HOW CAN I VOTE MY STOCK? See p. 147.

WHAT IS A DEBENTURE? See p. 103.

WHEN IS THE BEST TIME FOR INVESTING? See p. 151.

WHY DO I NEED A LAWYER WHEN I BUY A HOUSE? WHY CAN'T THE BANK HANDLE EVERYTHING FOR ME? See p. 155.

MUST I DRAW A WILL? See p. 196.

DOES MY HUSBAND'S WILL COVER ME? See p. 196.

CAN I WRITE MY OWN WILL OR SHOULD I HAVE A LAWYER? See p. 216.

TO WHOM SHOULD I GIVE A POWER OF ATTORNEY? See p. 40.

SHOULD A HOUSE HAVE A MORTGAGE OR SHOULD I PAY FOR IT ALL OUTRIGHT? See p. 67.

MUST MY WILL BE SIGNED BY ME IN THE PRESENCE OF WITNESSES? See p. 196, 197.

IF ANY OF MY PROPERTY IS ALTERNATE WITH MY HUSBAND, IS MY SHARE TAXABLE IN MY ESTATE? See p. 199.

HOW CAN I ARRANGE IN MY WILL FOR THE CARE OF MY MOTHER, WHO IS AN INVALID? See p. 201.

IF I OWN ONE HALF THE HOUSE IN WHICH WE LIVE, CAN I LEAVE IT TO MY CHILDREN? See p. 210.

SHOULD I HAVE THE BANK AS MY EXECUTOR? See p. 230.

IS IT ALL RIGHT TO PUT MY WILL IN MY SAFE-DEPOSIT BOX? See p. 52.

WHAT ARE FEDERAL AND STATE INHERITANCE TAXES? See p. 174, 176.

SHOULD I LEAVE MONEY TO MY COLLEGE? See pp. 105, 201.

WHAT ARE THE DISADVANTAGES OF BUYING AN UNLISTED STOCK? See p. 137.

WHAT IS A REFUND ANNUITY? See p. 145.

INDEX